Gómez Manrique, Statesman and Poet
The Practice of Poetry in Fifteenth-Century Spain

LEGENDA

LEGENDA is the Modern Humanities Research Association's book imprint for new research in the Humanities. Founded in 1995 by Malcolm Bowie and others within the University of Oxford, Legenda has always been a collaborative publishing enterprise, directly governed by scholars. The Modern Humanities Research Association (MHRA) joined this collaboration in 1998, became half-owner in 2004, in partnership with Maney Publishing and then Routledge, and has since 2016 been sole owner. Titles range from medieval texts to contemporary cinema and form a widely comparative view of the modern humanities, including works on Arabic, Catalan, English, French, German, Greek, Italian, Portuguese, Russian, Spanish, and Yiddish literature. Editorial boards and committees of more than 60 leading academic specialists work in collaboration with bodies such as the Society for French Studies, the British Comparative Literature Association and the Association of Hispanists of Great Britain & Ireland.

The MHRA encourages and promotes advanced study and research in the field of the modern humanities, especially modern European languages and literature, including English, and also cinema. It aims to break down the barriers between scholars working in different disciplines and to maintain the unity of humanistic scholarship. The Association fulfils this purpose through the publication of journals, bibliographies, monographs, critical editions, and the MHRA Style Guide, and by making grants in support of research. Membership is open to all who work in the Humanities, whether independent or in a University post, and the participation of younger colleagues entering the field is especially welcomed.

ALSO PUBLISHED BY THE ASSOCIATION

Critical Texts
Tudor and Stuart Translations • New Translations • European Translations
MHRA Library of Medieval Welsh Literature

MHRA Bibliographies
Publications of the Modern Humanities Research Association

The Annual Bibliography of English Language & Literature
Austrian Studies
Modern Language Review
Portuguese Studies
The Slavonic and East European Review
Working Papers in the Humanities
The Yearbook of English Studies

www.mhra.org.uk
www.legendabooks.com

STUDIES IN HISPANIC AND LUSOPHONE CULTURES

Studies in Hispanic and Lusophone Cultures are selected and edited by the Association of Hispanists of Great Britain & Ireland. The series seeks to publish the best new research in all areas of the literature, thought, history, culture, film, and languages of Spain, Spanish America, and the Portuguese-speaking world.

The Association of Hispanists of Great Britain & Ireland is a professional association which represents a very diverse discipline, in terms of both geographical coverage and objects of study. Its website showcases new work by members, and publicises jobs, conferences and grants in the field.

Editorial Committee
Chair: Professor Trevor Dadson (Queen Mary, University of London)
Professor Catherine Davies (University of Nottingham)
Professor Andrew Ginger (University of Bristol)
Professor Hilary Owen (University of Manchester)
Professor Christopher Perriam (University of Manchester)
Professor Alison Sinclair (Clare College, Cambridge)
Professor Philip Swanson (University of Sheffield)

Managing Editor
Dr Graham Nelson
41 Wellington Square, Oxford OX1 2JF, UK

www.legendabooks.com/series/shlc

STUDIES IN HISPANIC AND LUSOPHONE CULTURES

1. *Unamuno's Theory of the Novel*, by C. A. Longhurst
2. *Pessoa's Geometry of the Abyss: Modernity and the* Book of Disquiet, by Paulo de Medeiros
3. *Artifice and Invention in the Spanish Golden Age*, edited by Stephen Boyd and Terence O'Reilly
4. *The Latin American Short Story at its Limits: Fragmentation, Hybridity and Intermediality*, by Lucy Bell
5. *Spanish New York Narratives 1898–1936: Modernisation, Otherness and Nation*, by David Miranda-Barreiro
6. *The Art of Ana Clavel: Ghosts, Urinals, Dolls, Shadows and Outlaw Desires*, by Jane Elizabeth Lavery
7. *Alejo Carpentier and the Musical Text*, by Katia Chornik
8. *Britain, Spain and the Treaty of Utrecht 1713-2013*, edited by Trevor J. Dadson and J. H. Elliott
9. *Books and Periodicals in Brazil 1768-1930: A Transatlantic Perspective*, edited by Ana Cláudia Suriani da Silva and Sandra Guardini Vasconcelos
10. *Lisbon Revisited: Urban Masculinities in Twentieth-Century Portuguese Fiction*, by Rhian Atkin
11. *Urban Space, Identity and Postmodernity in 1980s Spain: Rethinking the Movida*, by Maite Usoz de la Fuente
12. *Santería, Vodou and Resistance in Caribbean Literature: Daughters of the Spirits*, by Paul Humphrey
13. *Reprojecting the City: Urban Space and Dissident Sexualities in Recent Latin American Cinema*, by Benedict Hoff
14. *Rethinking Juan Rulfo's Creative World: Prose, Photography, Film*, edited by Dylan Brennan and Nuala Finnegan
15. *The Last Days of Humanism: A Reappraisal of Quevedo's Thought*, by Alfonso Rey
16. *Catalan Narrative 1875-2015*, edited by Jordi Larios and Montserrat Lunati
17. *Islamic Culture in Spain to 1614: Essays and Studies*, by L. P. Harvey
18. *Film Festivals: Cinema and Cultural Exchange*, by Mar Diestro-Dópido
19. *St Teresa of Avila: Her Writings and Life*, edited by Terence O'Reilly, Colin Thompson and Lesley Twomey
20. *(Un)veiling Bodies: A Trajectory of Chilean Post-Dictatorship Documentary*, by Elizabeth Ramírez Soto

Gómez Manrique, Statesman and Poet

The Practice of Poetry in Fifteenth-Century Spain

GISÈLE EARLE

LEGENDA

Studies in Hispanic and Lusophone Cultures 31
Modern Humanities Research Association
2018

*Published by Legenda
an imprint of the Modern Humanities Research Association
Salisbury House, Station Road, Cambridge CB1 2LA*

ISBN 978-1-781885-81-9 (HB)
ISBN 978-1-78188-582-6 (PB)

First published 2018

All rights reserved. No part of this publication may be reproduced or disseminated or transmitted in any form or by any means, electronic, mechanical, photocopying, recording or otherwise, or stored in any retrieval system, or otherwise used in any manner whatsoever without written permission of the copyright owner, except in accordance with the provisions of the Copyright, Designs and Patents Act 1988, or under the terms of a licence permitting restricted copying issued in the UK by the Copyright Licensing Agency Ltd, Saffron House, 6–10 Kirby Street, London EC1N 8TS, England, or in the USA by the Copyright Clearance Center, 222 Rosewood Drive, Danvers MA 01923. Application for the written permission of the copyright owner to reproduce any part of this publication must be made by email to legenda@mhra.org.uk.

Disclaimer: Statements of fact and opinion contained in this book are those of the author and not of the editors or the Modern Humanities Research Association. The publisher makes no representation, express or implied, in respect of the accuracy of the material in this book and cannot accept any legal responsibility or liability for any errors or omissions that may be made.

Trademark notice: Product or corporate names may be trademarks or registered trademarks, and are used only for identification and explanation without intent to infringe.

© Modern Humanities Research Association 2018

Copy-Editor: Richard Correll

CONTENTS

	Acknowledgements	ix
	Introduction: The Historical and Social Background	1
1	Learning the Craft: Courtly Love Poetry and Related Writings (*c.* 1430–*c.* 1455)	11
2	Two Elegies for Knights (*c.* 1458–*c.* 1460)	32
3	Gómez Manrique's Continuation of Juan de Mena's *Debate de la Razón contra la Voluntad*	49
4	Cut and Thrust: *Preguntas y Respuestas* (*c.* 1458–*c.* 1470)	61
5	Matters of State (*c.* 1463–1473)	95
6	Family Consolatory and Devotional Writing	132
	Conclusion	153
	Bibliography	160
	Index	167

For my family and especially for Tom

ACKNOWLEDGEMENTS

This book is based on the doctoral thesis that I wrote following my retirement after many years of teaching Spanish and French in a variety of secondary schools. I came to academic research late in life and I am extremely grateful to the department of Spanish, Portuguese and Latin American Studies of King's College London for admitting me as a mature student. I should first thank Professor Julian Weiss who suggested that I should opt for a unit on fifteenth-century Spanish literature that he taught in conjunction with Professor Robert Archer on the MA course in Hispanic Studies. It was during that time that my interest in the literature of fifteenth-century Castile was aroused to the extent that I decided to return to King's to work on a doctorate. Robert was my supervisor and I owe him a huge debt of gratitude for his wise and tactful guidance during the time that I took to complete my thesis and for offering me valuable advice on preparing this book.

Converting the thesis into a book has been a slow process, but I have received encouragement from various people along the way, particularly those attending the seminars of the Medieval Hispanic Research Seminar at Queen Mary, University of London. I should like to mention in particular Dr Jane Whetnall, Professor Dorothy Severin and Professor Jeremy Lawrance, who all offered helpful advice and suggestions. I should like to thank the Taylorian Library, Oxford, for the excellent service that was always provided. Looking many years further back, I should like to express my gratitude to the Modern Languages and Classics departments of North London Collegiate School, particularly to Gillian Finlay, who taught me Spanish and introduced me to Jorge Manrique's famous *Coplas*.

I should also mention the warm welcome that I received from the Franciscan community of nuns at the Real Monasterio de Nuestra Señora de la Consolación de Calabazanos. When I attended a performance of Gómez Manrique's nativity play, *La Representación del Nacimiento de Nuestro Señor*, Sor Ana María arranged for me to stay in the convent guest-house which is normally closed in December. It was a truly memorable experience to see the play performed in the convent's chapel where Gómez Manrique is buried and to meet some of the actors afterwards.

Finally I thank my family for their encouragement while I worked on this project, especially my husband Tom, who was always there to give me wise advice.

G.E., Oxford, December 2017

INTRODUCTION

The Historical and Social Background

> La ynmensa turbaçión
> d'este reyno castellano
> faze pesada mi mano
> y torpe mi desçriçión;
> que las oras y candelas
> que se gastauan leyendo,
> agora gasto poniendo
> rondas, escuchas y velas.
> (Gómez Manrique 2003: 233–34, ll. 1–8)

These lines tell us much about Gómez Manrique: his deep-seated unease in the face of the political turmoil of Castile, his dedication to performing his military duties and how this commitment prevented him from pursuing his interest in literature and learning. Literary interests, however, took second place in Manrique's life, as the turbulence of the fifteenth-century Iberian Peninsula meant that he had to put his military training into practice from an early age. It was probably with his brother Rodrigo that he first experienced serious combat at the siege of Huéscar when the city was captured from the Muslims in 1434. Fernando del Pulgar tells us that Rodrigo's determination against all the odds not to abandon the siege resulted in victory and that, 'Ganada aquella cibdad, dexado en ella por capitán a un su hermano llamado Gómes Manrrique, ganó otras fortalezas en la comarca' (Pulgar 1971: 50–51). Fighting the Muslims was not the only conflict in which the Manrique family was involved: they were bitterly opposed to Juan II's favourite, Álvaro de Luna and with the infantes de Aragón, participated in campaigns to weaken his power, one result of which was the imprisonment of Manrique's father, Pedro, in 1437. The fickleness of fifteenth-century nobles with regard to their political allegiances is indicated by the fact that after Pedro regained his freedom, the Manriques and Enrique de Aragón were present in Valladolid in 1440 to welcome Blanca of Navarre on her forthcoming marriage to the future Enrique IV of Castile (Carrillo de Huete 1946: 344). Manrique, however, continued to fight in Enrique de Aragón's army until the latter's death in 1445 from wounds received at the first battle of Olmedo. The struggles against Luna continued until the *condestable*'s execution in 1453, but on the death of Juan II the following year the Manriques and their followers decided to support the new king, Enrique IV. Manrique was appointed *corregidor* of Salamanca that same year, a post that he retained for three years and which no doubt prepared him for later administrative roles he would hold.

His whole background and family origins had set him on this course from the start. He was born around 1412 in Amusco in the province of Palencia, the fourth son of Pedro Manrique and Doña Leonor de Castilla. His ancestry could hardly have been more aristocratic as his father was descended from the house of Lara and his mother was the granddaughter of Enrique II of Castile. The family motto, 'Non venimos de reyes | sino los reyes de nos', gives an idea of how the family regarded themselves. His upbringing was typical for a man of his class and time in that his military training began at an early age. He makes this clear when responding to a request for a compilation of his poetry from Rodrigo Pimentel, the conde de Benavente, with an implied denigration of his own literary abilities, saying that his skill in arms was superior because it was 'mamado en la leche' (Gómez Manrique 2003: 97). He continues with a tribute to his deceased elder brother, Rodrigo Manrique, who schooled him in this art and later became Master of Santiago.

Manrique was privileged in another important way, since he was born into an extremely cultivated milieu where it was perfectly normal to have literary interests. His paternal grandmother was Juana de Mendoza, known as 'la rica hembra' who was descended from Pedro López de Ayala, author of *Rimado de palacio* among other works, and the Guzmán family who counted the poet, historian and author of *Generaciones y semblanzas*, Fernán Pérez de Guzmán, among their members. His wife, another Juana de Mendoza, was the daughter of Diego Hurtado de Mendoza and Teresa de Guzmán, so he was doubly related to the Guzmán and the Mendoza families and refers to the marqués de Santillana as his uncle. Few details of his early life have come down to us, but he expresses gratitude to Santillana for the encouragement he received from him in his literary endeavours in a letter to the marqués's son, Pedro (364–65). In the introduction to his edition of Manrique's works Francisco Vidal González suggests that in his youth Manrique may well have accompanied his mother, Leonor de Castilla, to the Aragonese court where she had been companion to Catherine of Lancaster and later became *camarera mayor* to the queen, María, wife of Alfonso V (16). It was perhaps there that Manrique knew Santillana, who spent his formative years at the Aragonese court. Manrique's wife, Juana, also had literary interests: she was a friend of the nun, Teresa de Cartagena, daughter of Pedro de Cartagena and niece of Alonso de Cartagena. The rubric to her *Admiraçión operum Dey* tells us that it was written 'a petiçión e ruego de la Señora Doña Juana de Mendoça, muger del Señor Gomes Manrique' (Cartagena 1967: 111).

A further important source of influence on his work was the household of Alfonso Carrillo, the Archbishop of Toledo, whose service he entered as commander of his private army some time after the death of the marqués de Santillana, in 1458. Carrillo figures in Pulgar's *Claros varones de Castilla* where his principal aim is described as 'fazer grandes cosas e tener grand estado por aver fama e grand renonbre' (Pulgar 1971: 62). This was a productive period in his literary career when he produced a number of his more serious poems, combining the roles of soldier and poet. A number of scholars and writers were made welcome in Carrillo's entourage, not all of whom shared Manrique's aristocratic background. Some of them wrote responses to Manrique's verses, namely Pero Guillén de Segovia, Juan Álvarez Gato, Rodrigo Cota and Pero Díaz de Toledo amongst others. Meanwhile, there was increasing dissatisfaction with Enrique's style of government and he soon lost favour with a large section of the nobility. In 1465 a group of nobles including the poet and Carrillo took matters into their own hands and dethroned an effigy of Enrique in Ávila, proceeding to crown Enrique's young half-brother, the infante Alfonso as king (Palencia 1998–99: II, 307–08). Alfonso gained in popularity and frequent fighting broke out between the two rival camps.

After Alfonso's premature death in 1468 the question of who should succeed Enrique became a pressing one. The choice was between Isabel and the infanta Juana, believed by many to be the daughter of one of Enrique's favourites, Beltrán de la Cueva, rather than the king's daughter, and known to many as Juana la Beltraneja. Both Manrique and Carrillo strongly supported Isabel's claim to the throne and eventually they witnessed Enrique confirm Isabel as his successor at Toros de Guisando in September 1468. Their next task was to outwit other contenders for Isabel's hand and to arrange her marriage to Fernando of Aragon, an event they achieved with considerable stealth in 1469 in Valladolid. Although Enrique revoked his support for Isabel, Manrique worked constantly to promote the cause of Isabel and Fernando by negotiating with those who were hesitant in their support of the couple. Manrique's military career lasted at least until 1474 when, leading Carrillo's army, he triumphed at the siege of Canales (Gómez Manrique 1885–86: II, 308–14). When Enrique died in December 1474 Isabel was immediately crowned in the absence of Fernando. Carrillo, who had hoped to be rewarded with a post in the new government, saw his plans frustrated and retired to Alcalá de Henares, transferring his allegiance to Afonso V of Portugal who had designs on the Castilian throne. Manrique was then free to be appointed *corregidor* of Toledo in 1477, a post that he retained until his death in 1490 and presented him with a number of challenges since Toledo was a city that had suffered greatly in the anti-Semitic riots of 1449 and would see further serious upheavals during his tenure of office.

It was during this turbulent period that Manrique wrote much of his poetic work. Although fifteenth-century Iberia was racked with political unrest and internecine strife amongst the powerful nobility, it was also a time when verse very much dominated as a literary form, as Brian Dutton's seven-volume compilation, *El cancionero del siglo XV, c. 1360–1520*, attests (Dutton 1990–91). This may have been partly due to a perception that verse was a superior form to prose, as the marqués de Santillana declared in his *Proemio e carta* to the *condestable* of Portugal: 'me esfuerzo a dezir el metro ser antes en tiempo e de mayor perfecçión que la soluta prosa' (Santillana 2003: 645). It was also doubtless because verse was a form of composition accessible to a great many men who possessed the basic skills for it, but among whom levels of poetic talent varied enormously. Few fifteenth-century poets stand out alongside the influential marqués himself or the towering figure of Juan de Mena, but they are, with rare exceptions, competent versifiers who were able to use poetry for their particular ends and to do so in the relative certainty that their contemporaries would take the trouble to read or listen to their compositions. Every man with a basic training in classical rhetoric, an acquaintance with a few metres and stanza-forms, and the standard poetic genres could turn out verses, and in some social contexts was expected to do so.

Writing for aspiring poets at the end of the fourteenth century in one of the other great traditions of the Peninsula, Luis de Averçó translated, in his *Torcimany*, a large part of an earlier Provençal poetic manual, the *Flors del gay saber*, into Catalan, believing that by following certain rules anyone could write acceptable verses and thereby derive benefit:

> La primera cosa es que aprima l'enteniment, la segona cosa es que adoba la subtilesa, e la terça cosa es que entriqua l'enginy, en tant que per aquesta sciencia, pot hom dictar altament en sentencia, plana en scriptura e fina en art, per las quals cosas se seguex vertadera intelhigencia dels dictatz, axí en sentencia com en scriptura, com en art (Averçó 1956: 14).

> [The first benefit of the practice of poetry is to focus the mind, the second to develop subtlety of expression, and the third to sharpen your wit, because by means of this art of poetry you may write in a way that is noble in content, clear in expression and artistically skilful. From this it follows that your poems will be properly understood for their meaning, and properly appreciated for their expression and style.]

A similar happy belief that you did not have to be born a poet to write, but could make yourself one if you chose, must surely have been held in Castile. There were good reasons for taking the trouble to learn the tricks of the trade: verse was an accessible way of making your voice heard, together with your ideas and viewpoint when the occasion required it.

The importance of Manrique's work lies in the fact that he was not a Juan de Mena or an Ausiàs March, but a distinguished example of that great mass of versifiers who wrote ceaselessly in all kinds of social and political contexts during the troubled central decades of the fifteenth century. Despite pursuing an active career as a soldier and statesman he found the time to produce a large body of verse on a very wide range of topics and believed firmly, unlike some of his class, that it was possible to combine an interest in both arms and letters. He supports this view in the above-quoted letter to the Rodrigo Pimentel, scorning 'algunos haraganes [que] digan ser cosa sobrada el leer y saber a los caualleros, commo si la cauallería fuera a perpetua rudeza condepnada' (Gómez Manrique 2003: 98–99). In another letter written as a preface to his elegy for his mentor, the marqués de Santillana, he tells his cousin, Pedro González de Mendoza, that the marqués was 'el primero de senblante prosapia e grandeza que en nuestros tyenpos congregó la çiençia con la cauallerýa e la lóriga con la toga' (363). Later, when addressing the infante Fernando as a future monarch in the *Regimiento de prínçipes*, he encourages him to read widely in order to be able to govern prudently (635).

Manrique's work perhaps takes us closer than that of more famous practitioners to the basic function of verse for people of his class and time. He lived and wrote close to those holding the reins of power throughout his long life, and addressed in his poems people of enormous political influence as well as a wide range of others from lower social strata. For few writers of the period can such an overwhelming case be made for studying his work in the context of the social, economic and political background in which it was produced in order to gain an insight into the preoccupations of the nobility in fifteenth-century Iberia and an understanding of the problems they faced.

Unlike the work of his more famous nephew, Jorge Manrique, that of Gómez Manrique was largely neglected until two manuscripts were found in Madrid within a short space of time in the 1880s: the beautifully illuminated one prepared for Rodrigo Pimentel was discovered in the Palacio Real by Zarco del Valle and the second in the Biblioteca Nacional by Antonio Paz y Melia. Paz y Melia recognized the importance of the historical context of Manrique's literary production and went on to produce a complete edition of the poet's work in two volumes in 1885–86, the first substantial scholarly work on Manrique that we have. He opens his introduction by highlighting the poet's use of the modesty topos and quoting from the final lines of his letter to Pimentel which accompanies his collected poems. Having granted Pimentel's request, the poet writes, 'Suplico que [...] quiera mandar tener este libro cerrado en su cámara' (Gómez Manrique 1885–86: I, viii), an appeal that seems to have been heeded since it was only found four hundred years later. He makes no attempt to analyse any of the poems, but, using the historians Palencia, Salazar and Zurita as his sources, he records in his introduction a number of military campaigns in which Manrique participated and his many attempts to secure peace during the numerous upheavals that arose during his lifetime. The appendix to this edition contains some useful material, notably an account by Pero Guillén de Segovia of the siege and capture of Canales in 1474 in which Manrique distinguished himself when leader of Archbishop Carrillo's private army (Gómez Manrique 1885–86: II, 308–14). A letter to Manrique from Isabel I, urging him to leave his post in Toledo and go to the court at Valladolid to comfort his sick wife, is reproduced, as is his will. Of particular interest is the inventory of his library that lists the books he possessed (316–17; 320–26; 332–34).

With a few exceptions there is little further work on Manrique until Kenneth Scholberg's *Introducción a la poesía de Gómez Manrique* in 1984, a slim volume of which more than half is devoted to style and metrics. This is a valuable study of the techniques the poet used, but it is disappointing that scant attention is paid to the content of the poems and little attempt is made to place the work in the historical context in which it was written.

A major step towards our understanding of Manrique is the edition of Francisco Vidal González of 2003 which amplifies the political and historical context of his writings. In the introduction to his edition of Manrique's complete works Vidal begins by reminding us of the internecine strife amongst the nobility and monarchy that characterized fifteenth-century Castile and into which the poet was born. He gives a full biography of the poet, the early part of which he admits has to be based on supposition, adding details of significant members of his extended family and stressing their ancient lineage and royal connections. He also makes a connection between events in the poet's life and the content of many of his works, thus helping us to date some of the poems.

Apart from Scholberg's monograph and Vidal's introduction to his edition there are a number of articles on individual poems by Manrique, notably on the elegy for Garcilaso de la Vega. The political context is very much the focus of Carl Attlee's two articles, one on the afore-mentioned elegy and another on the poem to Arias Dávila, while the *Esclamaçión e querella de la gouernaçión* is the subject of a recent and valuable essay by Nicholas Round. The nativity play, *La Representaçión del nasçimiento de Nuestro Señor*, has been discussed by Stanislav Zimic, Harry Sieber, Alan Deyermond, and more recently Nicasio Salvador Miguel, all of whom approach the work in different ways. I shall refer to these publications as I write about the poems in turn.

Building on this work, in this study I try to map, as far as possible, the development of Manrique's writing throughout his productive life. Initially I attempted to isolate subject areas within his work, such as moral, political and didactic poems, and poems in which certain issues are raised in the tradition of debate poetry, together with some reflections upon his attitude towards women. This is the procedure followed by Kenneth Scholberg who separates the poems into six categories in his monograph of 1984, and by Vidal who divides the poems into ten different categories in his edition. I soon found, however, that it was unhelpful to classify Manrique's work into discrete categories of genre or theme in this way because it distorts the way we read the poems, which deserve to be understood for what they actually do as poems and impedes our ability to trace how Manrique's writing evolved over his lifetime.

The difficulties entailed by imposing generic rubrics is reflected in the way that Scholberg places the *Esclamaçión e querella de la gouernaçión*, the *Regimiento de prínçipes* and the *Coplas para Arias Dávila* in a section devoted to 'las obras didáctico-políticas' (Scholberg 1984: 30–37), whereas Vidal includes the first two of the afore-mentioned poems in a section of political poetry and the third in another of moral poems. The *coplas* addressed to Arias Dávila are indeed strongly moral in tone, reflecting on the transient nature of worldly goods and honours, but Manrique's motivation for writing this poem was, as Atlee (2007) argues, almost certainly political in part due to the resentment that he felt towards a man perceived by many to be corrupt and to have become a favourite of Enrique IV. The problem of classification arises again with the debate poems which are all very different in tone and content. Those addressed to Juan de Valladolid, for instance, are mocking and confrontational whereas others, such as the exchange of ideas on the subject of nobility among Manrique, Francisco de Noya, Rodrigo Cota and Guillén de Segovia, manifest a more dispassionate attempt to discuss issues of wider interest and concern to contemporaries.

Since few of Manrique's significant poems can be classed as belonging solely to one of the various categories identified by Scholberg or Vidal González, I have decided to consider his work in a broadly chronological framework, as far as this is possible. This approach still enables us to appreciate the multi-faceted nature of Manrique's interests, while at the same time allowing us to trace the development of his use of verse throughout his career. Thus the necessity of labelling his poems as 'political' or 'moral' disappears and it is possible to have a more comprehensive overview of his work that can be seen in relation to the shifting political situation in which he lived and which reflected many of the issues that preoccupied him. Many of these issues are related to the fact that he was deeply involved in the Castilian political scene, but he also wrote a considerable amount of verse to members of his family, especially to the female members, and in what is believed to be his final poem, the *consolatoria* to his wife, we glimpse something of his true feelings concerning the tragedy that has befallen them.

This book is the result of approaching Manrique's work from two very different but complementary angles. Firstly, I have analysed all his poems, selecting the more representative and interesting of them to include in the final version of the book. My aim in doing this was to establish what it was, at the level of the text, that motivated the composition of the text artistically. I have often found that Manrique's use of rhetorical techniques and figurative language, especially metaphor and simile, can provide clues to his aims, artistic or otherwise, and I have endeavoured to give this aspect of his work the space it deserves. This also allows us to see how his poetic techniques developed over his productive life. My second angle of approach has been to explore as extensively as possible how his work relates to the contemporary background in which he was writing.

We can learn much about the people Manrique addresses in his work and his intentions in so doing, from chronicles such as the *Memorial de diversas hazañas* by Diego Valera, Alfonso Palencia's *Gesta hispaniensia ex annalibus suorum dierum*, translated into Spanish by Brian Tate and Jeremy Lawrance, the *Crónica anónima de Enrique IV de Castilla*, and Enríquez del Castillo's *Crónica de Enrique IV*, as well as from historical studies that draw on these and other sources. I refer to these at several points. Apart from helping us to date some of the poems, the chronicles also tell us much about the society in which Manrique lived and the same is true of the verse and prose works of some of his contemporaries who treat similar subjects. One example of this is Manrique's poem to Diego Arias Dávila whose unpopularity led him to become the butt of several satirical poems such as the *Coplas de la Panadera* and the *Coplas del Provincial*. Similarly, when considering the advice given to the infanta Isabel in his *Regimiento de príncipes*, much can be gleaned about some contemporary attitudes towards women from Martín de Córdoba's *Jardín de nobles doncellas*, just as it can from Pere Torroella's *Maldezir de las mugeres*. Since he frequently engaged in verse dialogue with other poets, I have studied some of the poems alongside those of other writers of the same period, thus throwing into relief his own contributions. The way in which Manrique's work relates to all this is much more meaningful if, as I explain above, we try to establish some kind of working chronological framework for his own output. The distribution of the chapters of this book follows this framework.

My first chapter is devoted mainly to his courtly love poetry, as it is likely that much of this was written when he was a young man during the reign of Juan II of Castile. This phase of his writing reflected the desire of young men of his class to conform to the image of the courtier who was able to combine the dual roles of a knight on the battlefield and that of a composer of lyric poetry. This must have been a period in which Manrique was cutting his poetic teeth and I therefore examine some of the rules of rhetoric to which any aspiring poet needed to adhere. I also study his engagement with the polemics about the nature of woman that was set in motion in courtly circles by Torroella's *Maldezir de mugeres* to which Manrique wrote a spirited reply.

The second chapter consists of two elegies for knights, both of which can be dated to the late 1450s. The *Defunsión del noble cauallero Garci Laso de la Vega* is an elegy for Garcilaso, whose family was related to the Manriques, and who died during a skirmish against the Muslims in 1458 in which Manrique, his brother Rodrigo and Enrique IV participated. Enrique was ever reluctant to engage in large-scale campaigns against the Muslims and attracted criticism on account of his liking for many aspects of Muslim culture and customs. Manrique portrays the Muslims as revelling in and laughing at the young man's death, although he does not go as far as Palencia who reports that the king took pleasure in witnessing Garcilaso's final agony (Palencia, 1998–99: I, 184). The poem contains a hint of its author's disapproval of Enrique IV's decision not to pass on the *encomienda* that Garcilaso had enjoyed to his young son. It is in this poem that we first find a fusion of Christian and Stoic sentiments with which much of Manrique's poetry is subsequently imbued. The *Planto* for the marqués de Santillana, who also died in 1458, was probably written two years later, but is a much longer work in the form of an allegory. Its final stanzas reflect not only the poet's sadness at the demise of a man he much admired, but also his foreboding with regard to the future of Castile's governance.

Juan de Mena died in 1456 leaving his *Coplas de los siete pecados* unfinished, having only written on four of the seven deadly sins. Manrique was one of three poets who took it upon themselves to finish this work, the others being Pero Guillén de Segovia and Jerónimo de Olivares, probably in the late 1450s or the following decade. Chapter 3 discusses how Manrique chose to compose his continuation which reveals his considerable knowledge of biblical texts as well as his interest in moral issues.

My fourth chapter considers verses that Manrique exchanged with other poets or prominent members of society. As a member of Archbishop Carrillo's household in Toledo, Manrique came into close contact with men not all of whom were born into such aristocratic families as his and who have been dubbed the 'Carrillo circle' by critics such as Moreno Hernández (1985). He exchanged verses with Juan Álvarez Gato, Juan de Valladolid, Pero Guillén de Segovia, Rodrigo Cota, Juan de Mazuela and Francisco de Noya, all of whom were members of this circle, thought to be formed soon after the death of the marqués de Santillana in 1458 (Moreno Hernández 1985: 18). All except Noya were almost certainly practising Christians of Jewish descent, known as *conversos* or New Christians. Their verse dialogues were not like the *preguntas y respuestas* of earlier decades when poets or troubadours often sought to score points off each other, but instead are mostly thoughtful, collaborative exchanges on subjects such as the difficulty of composing verse and the issue of what constituted true nobility. On the other hand, his exchanges with Juan de Valladolid are of a very different nature: he heaps scorn and ridicule on him, accusing him of poor poetic style, mocking his humble origins and singling him out among his *converso* correspondents for his Jewish blood. The Carrillo circle probably lasted until 1470, as after that date relations between Carrillo and Isabel and Fernando became strained, with Manrique supporting the infantes rather than the Archbishop. Exchanges with other poets are more difficult to date, such as that with Pedro de Mendoza.

The focus of Chapter 5 is on the works that reflect the political turmoil of the central decades of the fifteenth century. Although the poem bearing the rubric *De Gómez Manrique quando se trataua la paz entre los señores reyes de Castilla e de Aragón e se desabinieron* (Gómez Manrique 2003: 619–21) contains no references to any specific incidents, Manrique expresses desire for peace and unity between the two kingdoms, believing that both would be stronger if united in the face of their enemies. This is significant because the Manrique family had not always remained loyal to the Castilian Crown and during Juan II's reign was closely allied with the infantes de Aragón. In spite of this change of heart, their support and that of many nobles for Enrique IV was short-lived. One reason for this was his promotion of men deemed unsuitable to hold public office as well as financial problems experienced in the kingdom. Manrique saw fit to address a letter and long poem to Enrique's *contador*, Diego Arias Dávila. While the letter is strongly moral in tone, it cannot be denied that Manrique also reveals his objections to a man like Arias holding a position of such importance in the kingdom. His growing impatience with the situation erupted with the *Esclamaçión e querella de la gouernaçión*, which expresses anger and frustration at the poor government of Castile, is markedly different in tone from the rest of his output, and elicited several responses, notably from Pero Díaz de Toledo. At some point between 1469, when Isabel and Fernando were married, and 1474, when Isabel succeeded to the Castilian throne, Manrique composed his *Regimiento de príncipes*. In this poem, which is accompanied by a letter, he sets out his advice on good government to the couple; it is worthy of mention that only fourteen of the seventy-nine stanzas of this poem are addressed to Isabel, no doubt because he did not foresee how important a role Isabel would play.

In my sixth and final chapter, devoted to work dedicated to family members, I discuss the only poem that we can say with any certainty Manrique wrote during the reign of the Catholic Monarchs, the *consolatoria* that he started to compose for his wife, Juana de Mendoza, in 1481 after two of their adult children had died the previous year. This was not his first consolatory piece, since some twenty-five years before he had written one for his sister. Deviating from my intention of a chronological framework, I consider them together as they both lie outside the shifting political context in which most of the work can be set. This is obviously true of the nativity play, *La Representaçión del nasçimiento de Nuestro Señor*, composed for one of the poet's sisters, a nun at the convent of Calabazanos. It is a sign of the critical distortion that has afflicted studies of Gómez Manrique's *oeuvre* that this work has probably drawn more attention from scholars than any other work of the poet.

There are, of course, inevitable problems in treating Manrique's work within this kind of loose chronological framework. While the courtly love poetry studied in Chapter 1, for instance, is almost certainly the product of Manrique's youth, it is also in the context of this poetry that we need to consider his response to Torroella's *Maldezir de las mugeres*, a poem impossible to date, but in all likelihood written some years after the main body of his love poetry. Another problem is the dating of his debate poems: while some of these clearly belong to his years in the household of Alfonso Carrillo, which began in the late 1450s and lasted until roughly 1470, other verse exchanges with people outside the circle are difficult to date. Nevertheless, I think that the advantages of this kind of broad chronological approach outweigh the drawbacks when we wish to consider all Manrique's extant work as a coherent whole, produced over a long life spent in a shifting political, social and personal context.

★ ★ ★ ★ ★

For this study I have used Vidal González's 2003 edition which follows the text, but not the disposition, of the manuscript prepared for the Conde de Benavente (MP3) some time after 1476 and which contains nearly all the poet's major works. An important exception is the *consolatoria* for Juana de Mendoza, composed after 1480, for which Vidal González gives the text of MN24, as he does for several other dialogues. I also refer to two prose works not found in either manuscript: the *Carta de buena nota*, attributed to Manrique and edited by Pedro Cátedra (2001), and the correspondence between the *protonotario* Juan de Lucena and Manrique, edited by Manuel Carrión (1978). Occasionally I refer to verses by other poets that are not readily available in a modern edition and quote from Dutton's compilation.

Translations from Virgil's *Georgics* are by H. Rushton Fairclough, from Seneca's *Moral Essays* by John W. Basore, and from Seneca's *Letters from a Stoic* by Robin Campbell. Robert Archer translated the passage from *Torcimany* on page 4. The other translations are my own.

CHAPTER 1

Learning the Craft: Courtly Love Poetry and Related Writings (*c.* 1430–*c.* 1455)

Introduction

Gómez Manrique's writings include a large number of texts of different kinds that are centred on the composition of love poetry, no doubt because, as a fifteenth-century aristocrat, he was influenced by the prevailing atmosphere at court, where the production of poetry flourished, and the ability to compose verses was a hallmark of the ideal courtier. Having been born around 1412, he might well have been acquainted when still a young man, if not with the actual words, at least with the sentiments expressed by Juan Alfonso de Baena in the prologue to his *Cancionero* which appeared around 1430. Baena writes about the various diversions in which princes and noblemen engage, such as games of dice and chess, as well as the very physical activities of jousting and hunting which bring pleasure, but also test a man's courage and prepare his body for 'los grandes menesteres de las guerras e conquistas e batallas e lides e peleas' (Baena 1996: 13). He asserts, however, that for kings and noblemen the greatest pleasure is not to be derived from these very physical pursuits but from 'leyendo e oyendo e entendiendo los libros e otras escripturas de los notables e grandes fechos passados' (13–14). Poetry is singled out as the highest form of literary art to which only a few can aspire, since a poet needs to be well read in several languages as well as 'noble fydalgo e cortes e mesurado e gentil e graçioso e polido e donoso' (14). These qualities, in Baena's opinion, are enhanced in the nobleman when he presents himself as a lover, although it is sufficient to feign love for a woman for the purpose of writing:

> e que siempre se preçie e se finja de ser enamorado; porque es opynion de muchos sabyos, que todo omme que sea enamorado, conuiene a saber, que ame a quien deue e como deue e donde deue, afirman e disen qu'el tal de todas buenas dotrinas es doctado. (15)

The suggestion by Baena that it was sufficient to create the literary fiction of being in love suggests that poetic activity involved a certain amount of role-playing which was a rite of passage into adult courtly society. Manrique was a relative and a great admirer of the marqués de Santillana who expressed similar opinions on the subject of poetic composition in his famous *Carta e Prohemio* to Don Pedro, condestable de Portugal. Having been asked by Don Pedro to send him a collection of his poetry, Santillana is rather dismissive of most of his own output, saying that writing poetry was something he did in his youth and that it was on a par 'con el vestir, con el justar, con el dançar, e con otros tales cortesanos ejerçiçios' (Santillana 2003: 642). He concurs with Baena, however, in believing that poetic talent is only to be found in 'los animos gentiles, claros ingenios e elevados spiritus' (643). Such 'exercises', when poetry was often recited in a public place, enabled the young nobleman to make an impression of himself on his audience and thereby gain prestige amongst his peers.

As Roger Boase comments, 'The centre of patronage and justice was the royal court. [...] Here the composition of love poetry was a sign of good breeding, a means of contending for favours and one of the most popular forms of entertainment' (Boase 1978: 152–53). The poet Fernando de Ludueña is aware of this when he writes about love in his *Dotrinal de gentileza*. To play the role of a lover is a game or 'deporte' and should be the ambition of all aspiring courtiers:

> porque tan dulçe cognorte
> y tan penado deporte
> que Vençe Todo sauer
> justamente deue ser
> de la gentileza norte.
> (ID1895, Dutton 1990–91: II, 400, ll. 690–94)

There was much vying for favours at court and to succeed it was necessary to cultivate an image of gentility, something that no doubt would have been encouraged by Juan II who appreciated poetry and was on the throne when Manrique was a young man.

Some insight into the literary activities at court can be found in Fernán Pérez de Guzmán's portrayal of Juan II in his *Generaciones y semblanzas*. Although he had a very low opinion of the king where his political virtues and ability to govern were concerned, he speaks in generous terms of his cultural attributes. The king, he says, enjoyed listening to the speech of other men who were 'avisados e graciosos' (Pérez de Guzmán 1965: 39), taking notice of what they said, and he had received a classical education that enabled him to speak and understand Latin. Regarding poetry, Pérez de Guzmán tells us that the king 'oía muy de grado los dizires rimados e conoçía los viçios dellos, avía gran plazer en oír palabras alegres e bien apuntadas, e aun él mesmo las sabía bien dizir' (39). This quotation makes us aware of two important facts, one being that at this time poetry at court was often recited aloud rather than being circulated in written form, the other that Juan II, and probably many around him, were so well trained in the rules of rhetoric of the *gaya ciencia* that they were able to spot the 'viçios' or defects in a poem's composition.

We cannot be sure exactly when Manrique composed his love poetry, but it might be safe to assume that most of this part of his output of some thirty poems was produced when he was a young man, mindful of the above-quoted words of his model, the marqués de Santillana, when referring to his own poetry. Also, when he was composing his love poetry, Don Gómez may well have been influenced by the above-mentioned Ludueña with whom he exchanged verses and who later became *maestresala* to Isabel la Católica. Victoria Burrus draws attention to Ludueña's poem of over thirteen hundred lines entitled *Dotrinal de gentileza* in which he gives advice on various aspects of how a courtier should conduct himself (Burrus 1998: 117–18, 122–23). On the subject of love he states that the role of the courtly lover is very much the province of the younger man when he writes:

> El Galan a de tener
> o primero tal hedad
> que de treinta y seis no pase.
> (ID1895, Dutton 1990–91: II, ll. 35–37)

Indeed he makes fun of the idea of an elderly lover when he says,

> pues aquestas y otras tales
> Gentilezas espeçiales
> Que los amores guarnezen
> ni a los Viejos pertenesçen
> ni las consienten sus males. (ll. 723–27)

While there is no reason why some of the *cançiones* should not have been written at later periods of his life, it seems safe to assume that most of them are from early on in his production.

The Importance of Rhetorical Training

That Juan II was able to pass judgement on a poem in the way mentioned above reflects the fact that an essential part of an aristocrat's education in the Middle Ages consisted of a grounding not only in Latin but also in the arts of rhetoric and poetics. Medieval compilers of textbooks on rhetoric that guided students through these rules were highly influenced by classical writers such as Cicero. In the treatise on public speaking, *Ad Herennium*, attributed to Cicero in the past, the anonymous author writes about *inventio*, *dispositio*, *elocutio*, *memoria* and *pronuntiatio*, topics that remained the basis of the teaching of rhetoric in the Middle Ages. Although Cicero was almost certainly writing with political speech-making in mind, what he had to say was still relevant to fifteenth-century writers of poetry since their compositions were frequently received orally at court and they were keen to impress their audiences. On the reasonable assumption, then, that it was in the court that Manrique cut his poetic teeth, we can approach his love poems specifically for what they tell us about what he learned as a composer of verses; the topic of the poems as such would have been of very minor importance in comparison.

How did people such as Juan II develop an understanding of what was good poetry? In his book on literary theory in fifteenth-century Castile, Julian Weiss considers the much-debated question of whether a poet was born or made, referring to exchanges between Villasandino and certain contemporaries, concluding that 'the consensus was that poetry was a gift from God, implanted in the poet at birth. Talent alone, however, was not enough; it was necessary to refine one's skills through constant practice and imitation of great writers' (Weiss 1990: 27). Weiss explains that poetic composition was not taught as a separate subject, but the poet Enrique de Villena in his *Arte de trovar*, written some time between 1427 and 1433 (56),[1] shows concern that many people, in attempting to compose verse, only saw fit to heed the rules of metrics due to 'mengua de la sçiençia', with the consequence that 'no es fecha diferençia entre los claros ingenios, e los obscuros' (Villena 1993: 43–44). In fact he reproaches the marqués de Santillana on this score: 'no podéis transfundir en los oydores de vuestras obras, las esçelentes inuençiones que natura ministra a la serenidat de vuestro ingenio, con aquella propiedat que fueron conçebidas' (45).

These views of Villena, who also wrote in Catalan, may well have their source in the writing of the Catalan Lluís d'Averçó, who around the turn of the fifteenth century produced a manual of rules for aspiring poets, the *Torcimany*. Much of the material in the *Torcimany* on the subject of the pitfalls to be avoided when writing poetry appears in the earlier Occitan manual, the *Flors del Gay Saber*, attributed to Guilhem Molinier. Molinier was closely connected to the Consistori del Gai Saber, established in Toulouse in 1323 as an academy for the revival and promotion of poetry in the tradition of the troubadour lyric. Averçó and Jaume March, with the support of Joan I of Aragon, founded a similar establishment in Barcelona in 1393, the Consistori de la Gaya Ciençia, and it is significant that Juan II of Castile's first wife was María, princess of Aragon, suggesting that there was a considerable Aragonese cultural influence in the Castilian court apart from Santillana's even more important contribution. Although *Torcimany* and the *Flors* refer to a different metric system and to other types of stanza, not found in Castilian poetry, *Torcimany* is the only known and detailed manual in an Iberian language written specifically for poets and was almost certainly known to Santillana and those who frequented the royal court.

The poetic defects themselves are subdivided into two main types: content, and style and metrics. In a section of *Torcimany* the first group, 'en sentensa' (Averçó 1956: I, 113–32), is broken down into seventeen *vicis*. The majority of these are general faults that should always be avoided, such as self-contradiction, ambiguity, verbosity and excessive praise of people. A *vici* worthy of note is that of *dezonestat* (122) which in this context means the opposite of respectable and decent and is particularly relevant to love poetry: it must not include any improper requests made by the man to his lady. Also on the subject of love poetry, it is interesting to note that there is a comment to the effect that the reason for writing it is so that the woman addressed might be more disposed to marry the man who serenaded her. This is not a tradition that was carried into fifteenth-century Castile, where the expression of courtly love never implied a desire to marry the woman addressed.

The section on the *vicis* that are 'fora sentensa', referring to all matters of style and metrics, includes fourteen faults to be avoided concerning choice of vocabulary and word order. The *vicis* of rhyme and syllable count are obviously different in Catalan, but the principle remains the same in Castilian.

---

[1] Weiss quotes Elvira de Aguirre, *Die 'Arte de trovar' von Enrique de Villena* (Cologne, 1968) regarding the date of composition of this work.

I mention these rules of rhetoric in order to emphasize the parameters within which poets such as Manrique had to work and the constraints that they must have felt when attempting to express themselves in verse, always conscious of the *viçios* that their audience could well be quick to spot. Obviously, for this study, the ways in which Manrique strove to avoid such faults while developing the basic rhetorical elements of *inventio*, *dispositio* and *elocutio* are particularly relevant. *Inventio* was about finding the best means to express what the poet wished to say; *dispositio* was how he arranged this material; the *elocutio* was the style he used to complete his work. Since his love poetry, like that of his contemporaries, dwelt for the most part on similar themes such as the sadness of experiencing unrequited love, the pain of separation and parting from the beloved, and the fear of rejection, *inventio* was of paramount importance to show that he had found a different way of expressing these sentiments in the competitive atmosphere of the court. *Dispositio* was more relevant in the longer poems and the use of a number of different figures of speech meant that *elocutio* could also contribute to his acquiring a more individual style of poetry, although many of the metaphors used by Manrique were commonly used by poets who were his contemporaries. In studying this part of Manrique's work I have chosen to separate the *canciones* from the *decires* since the latter are for the most part longer and can be classified according to their thematic content, unlike the *canciones*. Both *canciones* and *decires*, however, are primarily of interest because of the rhetorical devices used and because they almost certainly reflect the efforts of Manrique at an early stage of his poetic career, when he was forging his skills as a poet, and before he went on to use these same skills when treating other subjects of a more serious nature than courtly love.

The *cançiones*

Fifteen of Manrique's love poems merely bear the title *canción* and are of either twelve or twenty lines in length, always beginning with a quatrain followed by one or two stanzas of eight lines. These shorter poems, perhaps intended to be set to music, are necessarily limited as far as the development of *inventio* is concerned and this is particularly true of the twelve-line poems in which repetition in the form of an *estribillo* at the end of each stanza limits still further the poet's scope for developing the subject matter in an ingenious way. Therefore, while considering the *canciones*, I focus on the stylistic features of these poems.

There are many examples of the use of the *estribillo* where either the final line or lines of the first verse are repeated at the end of the second and third verses. Sometimes the wording of the refrain is changed slightly or only part of the line is repeated, but the intention is to remind the listener or reader of the thought that the poet wishes to convey. One example of the *estribillo* is found in the *canción* 'El que arde en biua llama' (Gómez Manrique 2003: 120–21) which is not directed to any woman in particular, but expresses the poet's conviction that when suffering from unrequited love it is impossible to feel for others in a similar predicament. In the opening quatrain he uses metaphors that are often found in the context of courtly love, one of which is to liken passion to a flame, as in the first line quoted above.

The combination of his lack of success and his continuing devotion to her results in him feeling as if he has been condemned. In the first half of the second stanza the poet refers to himself suffering 'tan afortunadas penas' (l. 6), this oxymoron implying that such suffering is fortunate because it suggests that the poet is capable of noble feelings. The final couplet, 'no puede, según es fama | sentir la pasión agena', emphasizes the poet's message, repeating almost exactly the final two lines of the first quatrain.

Another stylistic feature found in the love poetry and in a number of Manrique's other poems is the use of the *pie quebrado*, a line of four syllables, which, by breaking the rhythm of the octosyllabic poem, gives greater force to the words it contains. In 'Dexadme mirar a quien' (123–24) for example, the *pie quebrado* occurs in the second and fourth lines of the first stanza when the poet declares that he wishes to gaze upon the object of his affections in spite of the fact that she does not reciprocate his feelings for her. These two short lines 'me faze mal' and 'nin comunal' stress the idea of his lack of hope which is echoed in the final four lines:

> que morir a mi conuién,
> si no me val
> la que nin me faze bien
> nin comunal.

A number of rhetorical devices are to be found in these *cançiones*, their function being to add subtlety and acuity, or 'agudeza' to the sentiments expressed. In his book on the rhetoric of *cancionero* love poetry, Juan Casas Rigall considers that 'la agudeza constituye un vehículo para desvelar realidades inefables, como la hermosura de la dama en la tradición cancioneril' (Casas Rigall 1995: 14). One rhetorical figure often used by Manrique to heighten the effect of his writing is antithesis, the placing of words of strongly contrasted meaning in parallel. An example of this is to be found in the twelve-line 'Esperança de venir' (Gómez Manrique 2003: 125), and is appropriate here since the poem expresses the idea that the joy of being reunited with the beloved outweighs the pain of departing from her later:

> Esperança de venir
> alegre, si Dios quisiere,
> causa que no desespere
> con el dolor del partir. (ll. 1–4)

The first four lines contain three examples of simple antithesis, 'esperança' being contrasted with the verb 'desesperar', alegre' with 'dolor' and 'venir' with 'partir'. In the second stanza the same technique is used, with 'la gozosa venida' contrasted with 'el pesar de la partida' (ll. 6, 8) and the last two lines of the first verse are repeated at the end of the second as an *estribillo*.

Anaphora, the repetition of a word or words in successive lines for added emphasis, is found in a *canción* the first three lines of which read:

> Con la beldad me prendistes,
> con la graçia me robastes,
> con la bondad me feristes,
> (127–28)

Similarly, anaphora occurs in another *cançión*, 'Vuestros ojos me prendieron' (128), where the poet recalls when his eyes first caught sight of the lady he is addressing: 'Viéronvos tanto fermosa, | viéronvos tanto polida' (ll. 5–6).

An example of anadiplosis, the repetition of a word at the end of a line at the start of the next, occurs in 'Si los fines ni miré' (Gómez Manrique 2003: 123). In this piece the poet is admitting that he has brought his sorrows upon himself: 'pues los yo, triste, los busqué' (l. 4). By repeating 'Busqué' at the start of the following line he emphasizes the fact that he is blaming himself.

Antanaclasis, defined by Casas Rigall as the use of a word with more than one meaning, occurs in the *cançión* 'Señoras que muncho amo' (122) with its use of the word 'amo', giving this poem a playful and humorous tone. In the first line the poet admits to a love of women, using the verb 'amar' and then appeals to the ladies of the court to find him 'algún amo' (l. 4), as he is unattached or 'esento' (l. 2). It soon becomes clear in the second verse, despite the masculine ending of the word 'amo', that he is seeking a woman to love as he swears to remain true to one who will love him. The masculine form 'amo' has a long tradition behind it going back to the troubadour *midons*, but here it also effectively maintains the rhyme scheme, while its occurrence as the last word of each stanza insists on the idea of the subservience required of the noble lover who seeks to court a woman. In the third stanza, when he admits to the foolishness of his desire to engage in behaviour typical of a younger man, he uses a stock metaphor to express the loss of freedom that will ensue: 'queriendo mi libertad | poner en fuerte cadena' (ll. 15–16).

Metaphors do not figure greatly in the *cançiones*: those used by Manrique in these poems are generally of the stock variety just quoted, where the lover views falling in love as a loss of freedom or imprisonment, where the woman is the gaoler. The notion of capture and loss of freedom occurs again in 'Con la beldad me prendistes' (127–28) where the poet declares, 'De la prisión no reçelo | que de mi grado será' (ll. 5–6). These lines demonstrate a certain linguistic symmetry here as the word 'prisión', with its shared etymology, looks back to 'prendistes' in the first line and 'grado' refers to 'graçia in the second. Similarly, 'robo' looks back to and extends the significance of the line 'con la graçia me robastes' (l. 2) and likewise, the 'golpe' (l. 9) alludes to the verb 'feristes' in the third line of the first verse.

In another *cançión*, 'Con la belleza prendés' (127), Manrique refines and develops his use of metaphor in a poem where the relationship between man and woman is seen in terms of a battle with the latter achieving a conquest, a much-used trope in medieval poetry. Again the verb 'prender' occurs in the introductory quatrain that tells us that the woman captivates all the men she looks at and this verb is also associated with the idea of taking prisoner, something that follows a defeat in battle. The pain of love is expressed by the image of the man being wounded by her catapult or 'fonda de fermosura' (l. 8). The metaphor is developed in the second stanza where the battle is seen as involving the siege of a city with the lady in question aiming at those besieging her from the city's walls and able to captivate all her opponents with her weapon. The battle imagery is further extended by the allusion to the 'arnés' of armour worn by the men which affords them no protection against their attacker (ll. 9–10).

Although virtually all Manrique's love poetry treats the well-worn themes of unrequited love and the pain of rejection or separation from the beloved, there is an exception to this in the *canção* 'Si no me vençe pasión' (130–31). Here there is a departure from the traditional courtly topics; instead he sings the praises of the lady, not just on the grounds of her physical attractions but also on account of her virtuous character, so much so that in loving her he feels that there is no conflict between reason and his inclination:

> [...] vuestros valores
> son inmensos ciertamente;
> tanto que dan ocasión,
> fablando con vos verdad
> a no poder la razón
> contrastar la voluntad. (ll. 15–20)

The awareness of a conflict between 'razón' and 'voluntad' arises often in the writings of fifteenth-century Castilians, but more often in works that are written with didactic intentions, such as Juan de Mena's *Debate de la Razón contra la Voluntat*, which Manrique completed after Mena's death, rather than in love poetry that was written for entertainment at court. Francisco Vidal González suggests that this poem is in fact addressed to the poet's wife, Juana Mendoza, since in the third and final stanza he says, 'No vos loo por amores, | que la ley no lo consiente' (131n; ll. 13–14), an allusion to the conventions of the courtly code which dictated that love poems should not be addressed to a spouse. We know that Juana regretted that she received no poems from her husband as a young woman, because Manrique refers to this in the letter that he wrote to accompany the *consolatoria* that he composed for her many years later after the death of two of their adult children. One of the factors that led him to write that poem was this memory: 'tu merçed [...] en la moçedat me solía dezir, estando en nuestros plazeres, que por qué de quantas trobas que hazía no enderesçaua a ella alguna' (452). In this poem, therefore, Manrique's adherence to the rules here is in stark contrast with the rest of his love poetry which concentrates on the conventional sufferings of love. Instead, by praising Fortune for endowing this lady with the attributes of a sympathetic and virtuous character, he conveys a sense of serenity and contentment.

Finally, in this section on the *canções* Francisco Vidal González includes in his edition a *Canção ajena*, 'Donzella desconoçida', considered to be anonymous (ID1880, Dutton 1990–91: II, 238, 501), which Manrique has expanded reworked with a gloss (Gómez Manrique 2003: 174–76). The original poem is a lament on the part of a man who, rather than writing of eternal devotion to the woman despite her indifference, composes a denunciation of her, hoping that she will always be 'desamada y mal querida' (174, l. 8), an unusual sentiment in the context of Castilian courtly love poetry. Manrique expands this poem to twice its length by inserting two lines of his own before each couplet of the original and thereby adding a greater emphasis to the feelings expressed. To this end, for example, he introduces the first stanza by saying that his experience has led him to lose all hope and refers to the poem as a 'grida' (l. 14) or cry of despair, and as a prelude to the first use of the *estribillo*, 'de mí fueste bien querida, | yo desamado de ti', he declares, 'De la ora en que te vi, | la qual nunca se me olvida' (ll. 17–20). Similarly, when the original poet wishes that the woman might suffer as well, saying, 'Porque más sin dubda creas | la mi pena dolorida', Manrique introduces these lines with 'Véate yo perseguida | del dolor que me guerreas' (ll. 21–24). By using the verbs 'perseguir' and 'guerrear', associated with conflict, he emphasizes the intensity of feeling on the part of the rejected lover whose verses he glosses. Thus he softens the bluntness of the original poem and renders it more in keeping with the 'cortesía' traditionally expected of this genre.

The *decires*

I have made no attempt to classify the *cançiones* other than by the use of rhetorical devices by which Manrique sought to underline the main effect he intended. Nor have I analysed any of them in detail, because their content is not very diverse and their brevity means that scope for developing *inventio* is limited and inventiveness of ideas was not the point. The *decires*, however, are for the most part considerably longer and, although they focus on the same themes of unrequited love, Manrique is able to present them with a much greater variety of *inventio* and I have, therefore, endeavoured to classify these poems into sub-groups according to the way the theme is approached. They include poems which appear in the manuscripts with various other rubrics, but for present purposes are here treated as *decires*. A common feature is the use of hyperbole to emphasize the feelings that the poet claims to experience.

Poems of Praise

Praise of the poet's lady is the overriding theme found in the poem *Quexas e conparaçiones*, 'Donzella, diez mill enojos' (158–60). Here Manrique takes a measured and thoughtful attitude towards the sufferings of the rejected lover with none of the hyperbole found in some of his other love poetry and there is a certain irony in the way he chooses to express himself. Although he sets out to praise his lady, he does so by focusing on all the negative aspects of falling in love. He structures the poem so that the first line of each of the six stanzas refers to an aspect of the sorrow he experiences on failing to win the lady's affections, working through the emotions commonly felt by lovers, speaking of 'enojos', 'amarguras', 'ansyas', querellas', 'pasyones' and 'desdenes'. She is all the more praiseworthy, however, because her attributes, 'graçia y fermosura' (l. 4) and 'donayre' (l. 10), are such that his negative emotions fade when he finds himself in her presence. To describe how his mood becomes positive when he sees her, each stanza contains a clause introduced by the word 'commo', sometimes used hypothetically, as in the second half of the first verse:

> avnque no quedo guarido
> de mis penas,
> commo sy fuesen ajenas
> las oluido.

The sixth stanza also contains a hypothesis when he declares, that on seeing the woman, it is 'commo sy grandes bienes | reçibiese' (ll. 43–44). In the other verses 'commo' introduces a short simile, such as in the third verse, where his 'ansyas secretas' are chased away on seeing her 'bien commo las cueruas prietas | perseguidas del neblí' (ll. 19–20), and in the fourth where his 'justas querellas [...] fuyen commo las estrellas | ante los rayos febales' (ll. 25, 27–28), both figures are drawn from the natural world.

Use is made of the *pie quebrado* in the sixth and eighth lines of each verse, the interruption of the rhythm drawing attention to certain key words which he is seeking to emphasize. A good example of this occurs in the second verse when he speaks of the way the bitterness he feels vanishes in her presence:

> e quanto me days dolor
> e cuydado,
> en vos ver, es transformado
> en amor.

The rhyme scheme enhances the impact that the poem makes on the reader or listener: in the first quatrain of the initial stanza, for example, the 'enojos' experienced by the poet on account of the woman's 'desmesura' are dispelled by the sight of her 'ojos' and her 'fermosura'. The rhyme of 'dolor' and 'amor' in the second stanza (ll. 13, 16) emphasize the pain of love effectively. The wording of the *fyn*, with its *pie quebrado*, draws on the traditional metaphor of love sickness:

> No vos plega más dexarme
> Padeçer
> pues sola tenéys poder
> de sanarme. (ll. 49–52)

Despite the effect that the woman's presence has on him, he is not 'guarido' (l. 5). Similarly, in stanza V he tells her that however much he looks at her, 'no sanáys' (l. 40) while in the final lines of stanza VI he implores her, 'pues queredme guareçer | o matarme' (ll. 47–48). Herein lies the modest *inventio* in the subject matter of this poem: the poet sees himself as a sick man who can only be cured by his lady reciprocating the feelings that he shows for her and the vocabulary is chosen to sustain this idea.

Praise of the woman is also the theme of *Loor a vna dama*, 'Quanto á que sé mirar' (137–38), a poem of five nine-line stanzas. Here there is no appeal to the woman to respond to the poet's feelings, but he sets the lady apart from all others, not only on account of her physical beauty, described in the first verse, but also because of her prudence and wisdom or 'cordura' (l. 18), in the second. The central idea, that beauty and prudence together are never to be found in other women, is expressed in the third verse through antithesis:

> Estas dos contrariedades
> que siempre son enemigas,
> fermosura e bondades,
> quiero, mi bien, que sepades
> ser en vos grandes amigas. (ll. 19–23)

He uses antithesis again in the fourth verse where, rather than lamenting that his feelings are not reciprocated, he sees something positive, 'Si d'esto mal me viniere, | dolo por bien empleado' (ll. 28–29), taking comfort from the idea that he has fallen captive to such a paragon of beauty and prudence. The use of the *pie quebrado* in the seventh and ninth lines of each verse, integrated into the rhyme scheme of the final four lines, adds emphasis to the thought expressed. For example, in the final four lines of the first verse the rhyming words 'contienda' and 'enmienda' strengthen the idea of the woman's perfection, whilst 'vna' and 'ninguna' stress her uniqueness:

> en el mundo solo vna
> sin contienda,
> más perfeta sin enmienda
> que ninguna.

The poem ends on a playful note when the poet, having exalted the lady he admires to such a degree, realizes that in so doing he may cause offence to other women, and asks them to forgive him: 'perdónenme las casadas | e donzellas' (ll. 44–45).

The Imagery of the Cárcel de Amor

The other poem, also entitled *Requerimiento*, 'Largos tienpos he gastado' (155–58) treats the subject matter in more detail in eight ten-line stanzas. In the first the poet explains that he has been suffering in silence for fear of offending the woman and he uses the effect of the rhyming *pie quebrado* of 'padeciendo' and 'encubriendo' in the second and fifth lines to stress this. The rhyme scheme of the final four lines of this stanza also emphasizes the poet's sentiments:

> que, commo la byua flama
> es de natura que quema,
> bien asý el que bien ama
> es neçesario que tema.

In the second stanza the *pie quebrado* again stresses the conflict between the love of the poet and his fear of rejection with the rhyme of the second and fourth lines, 'amador' and 'el temor', and this is reinforced with the antithesis of 'amiga' and 'enemiga' in the antepenultimate and final lines of this stanza. The topos of the *cárcel de amor* is introduced in the third stanza when the poet makes a comparison between himself, as the lover on the point of declaring his passion, with the criminal who confesses to a crime after being subjected to torture. The rhyme of 'malhechor' and 'dolor' (ll. 2, 5) are appropriate in the context, as are 'tarde' and 'cobarde' (ll. 27, 29) to denote the poet's hesitance in declaring his love. In the fourth stanza the poet begs the woman to cast her eyes over 'este blanco papel' (l. 33), a line which suggests to us that this poem was probably not composed to be recited aloud, and he continues by telling her that her beauty has been responsible for 'tornar en seruidora | mi voluntat libertada' (ll. 39–40). This is another example of antithesis since the 'voluntat' that has been freed refers to his ability finally to address the woman, but this has made him her servant which implies the loss of his freedom. Another allusion to this situation is found at the end of the sixth stanza when the poet uses an oxymoron in two consecutive lines: 'e voluntaria presyón | o cárçel de libertados' (ll. 59–60). A similar figure of speech is used at the end of the seventh stanza when he describes himself as 'esforçado tan judío | e de libre catyuado' (ll. 69–70).

Parting and Separation from the Beloved

While several of Manrique's love poems dwell on the pain of separation from a woman, '¡O sy naçido no fuera' (168–70) sets out to recall the benefits and pleasure that he derived from this past relationship. Vidal González surmises that this piece was written for the poet's wife, Juana de Mendoza, partly because the woman is addressed as 'vuestra merced' in the same way that Juana is addressed in the *consolatoria* (168n).[2] Whether or not this poem was written for the poet's wife, its tone and content suggest a far greater emotional intimacy between man and woman than in any other of Manrique's love poems. In the introductory verse he expresses his present sadness, wishing either that he had never been born or that he could have died when he knew that he was still loved. The first two lines echo those of Job when he curses the day he was born: 'Why died I not from the womb? Why did I not give up the ghost when I came out of the belly?' (Job 3. 11). He then compares this state of affairs with the time when, he tells the lady, 'vuestra merçed sentía | mis angustias y tormentos' (ll. 6–7), thus revealing the closeness they had once shared. The poet proceeds to reflect in the following four verses on the different aspects of their relationship that brought him comfort. Each of these four verses begins with 'quando' as the poet takes stock of the past and this word is repeated constantly as he adds to the list of memories. An example of the healing power of the relationship is demonstrated when he declares:

> Quando mis tribulaçiones
> con vuestras consolaçiones
> y mis llagas se curauan
> con muy süaues blanduras. (ll. 13–17)

He also recalls that their partings were only out of necessity, 'de pura fuerça forçadas' (l. 22) and gives the impression of being at peace with the world and surrounded by friends whilst the opposite could be said of his enemies:

> quando con vientos contrarios
> ciauan mis aduersarios,
> yo bogaua con los buenos. (ll. 38–40)

With the departure of the woman, all this was reversed and he is prompted to see death as preferable to his present state. The *fin* begins with a series of lamenting exclamations and it ends on a dark note with the suggestion that he would take his own life if it were not against God's law.

Advice to Other Lovers

A poem bearing the rubric *A vnos galanes*, 'Quien el fuego mucho atiza' (170–72), differs from the others discussed so far in that, as its title suggests, it is not addressed

---

2   In fact she is addressed as 'tu merced' in the *consolatoria* and its accompanying letter.

to a woman. It is immediately noticeable that the language is more conversational and reminiscent of the style of many of Manrique's *preguntas y respuestas*, with the first stanza opening with two proverbial sayings, the first being 'Quien el fuego mucho atiza | a las vezes lo mató' and the second, 'nunca moho la cubrió | a la piedra mouediza'. The poet ponders on the question of whether there are advantages in switching one's affections from one woman to another and expresses a view on loyalty that contradicts the advice offered in the *Carta de amores*. The first of the four stanzas ends with an appeal to the 'galanes' who have not remained steadfast in their devotion to one woman:

> dezidme sy os va mejor
> en tener más alegría
> o menos pena. (ll. 8–10)

In the second stanza he reflects on the adage 'God helps those who help themselves'[3] and yet observes that in his experience not one of those who has acted upon this has benefited from such a move. In fact, he declares in the third stanza that these 'galanes' are worse off and he now sees them as marginalized when he compares them to what they were in their former situation:

> que yo muy bien vos dexé
> avezindados de juro
> al mercadal;
> agora, quando torné,
> fállouos çerca del muro,
> en el raual. (ll. 25–30)

Thus he suggests that their behaviour has excluded them from courtly society whose ethos demanded loyalty and devotion. The use of the *pie quebrado* in this stanza is particularly effective, with its stress on the contrast between the 'mercadal' the young men formerly frequented and the 'raual' which is where they now belong. The *fin* of this poem exhorts all loyal lovers not to lose heart and reproaches the others for the hastiness of their actions. Here Manrique again uses a colloquial saying to make his point in the final three lines of the poem:

> pues vos pueden conparar
> que fuestes en la tardança
> agua en çesta.

A *Carta de buena nota* Attributed to Gómez Manrique

The ethics of courtly love reached out beyond verse composition; having just discussed the subject of giving advice to lovers in two poems, it is fitting to mention an article by Carmen Parrilla in which she draws attention to two previously unpublished prose letters included in a manuscript in the Biblioteca Colombina in

---

3   Although Manrique asserts that these people think they are 'ayudados de Dios' (ll. 11–12) there appears to be no biblical support for this and the adage quoted above is more likely to derive from Aesop's fables.

Seville (Parrilla García 1986: 341–50). One of these letters is certainly anonymous, bearing the rubric *Carta de buena nota*, and requests advice from the addressee on how to react after his lady has lost interest in him, and the other letter is a reply, attributed in the manuscript to Gómez Manrique. A close examination of the manuscript by the writer of this article leads her to doubt whether the reply is really by Gómez Manrique because his name is written in different handwriting from the rest of the heading (342). This is not a strong argument, nor is her assertion that it is hard to reconcile the *respuesta* with the style of the author who wrote the *Regimiento de príncipes*, considering that Manrique wrote a large amount of love poetry like the compositions we have been considering, in addition to his other poems of a more serious and reflective nature. While I do not contend that the *carta* and its *respuesta* necessarily belong to the same period as the *canciones* and *decires* discussed in this chapter, they reflect the concerns of the period and the way in which the concept of *gentileza* pervaded the cultural landscape.

The anonymous writer of the *carta* uses a series of metaphors at the beginning of his letter, the first being a comparison between the addressee and a falcon as he assumes that the poet, when in love, has been in a similar situation.[4] Just as a falcon that flies readily towards a decoy is deceived by what it finds, so the poet is lured by the charms of a woman only to be disappointed. The second paragraph uses the familiar metaphor of the 'prison of love' where the writer speaks of the 'cadenas' in which 'este deus' holds him, explaining that in his previous experiences of this 'prison' he had felt less closely confined. This time, however, he needs help and believes that the poet has the key to unlock his prison cell. The third paragraph contains another much-used metaphor, that of the 'fire of passion', which in the writer's case has been extinguished, as he observes: 'vino un agua tan sin tienpo que mató su propósito' (77). He refers to the metaphorical prison again in the final paragraph of his letter when he appeals for help in either winning his lady or forgetting her because, if he does not achieve one of these objectives, 'no avrá otra prisión en que haga presa sinon la muerte' (78). The allusion to 'este amor deus' (77) at the start of the second paragraph implies that the obsession with love has taken the place of religion.

The reply to this letter, attributed to Manrique in the manuscript, shows that the writer was well aware of the ironic tone of the letter he has received. Furthermore, he dislikes its anonymity, protesting that it mocks him: 'me pesa porque queréis conoçerme para burlar y no queréis que os conozca para loaros' (78). He does, however, acknowledge that his present state means that 'todas las pieças de mis defendimientos [el amor] ha desbaratado y desguarneçido' (79). The advice meted out in the reply reflects both the attitude of the courtly lover and that of the misogynist, since the writer first suggests that his correspondent should never cease to serve the lady. In the same sentence, however, he suggests ignoring the woman 'porque las mugeres, mientra más las olvidan, más se acuerdan' (79). The next piece of advice is to appear happy and be seen laughing in the woman's presence and, if

---

4   Quotations from these two letters are taken from *Tratados de amor en el entorno de Celestina*, ed. by Pedro M. Cátedra (Madrid: Sociedad Estatal España Nuevo Milenio, 2001), 75–80.

that has no effect, to speak to her with 'palabras ásperas' (79). He should tell her that he will never return if this does not move her or even, as a last resort which is not really recommended, threaten to vilify her publicly. If he wishes to forget the woman he may seek solace in religion and, if this should fail, occupy himself with other cares. Finally, in advice that clearly derives from Ovid, he suggests imagining the woman as ugly: 'Figuralda fea [...] no menos suzia que rota y trasquilada' (80). In the final paragraph the ironic tone of the reply returns, when he declares, with a rather backhanded compliment, that he would like to meet his correspondent to judge whether his grief is as great as his discretion.

Torroella's *Maldezir de las mugeres* and Gómez Manrique's Response

If there is doubt concerning the authorship of the reply discussed in the last paragraph, it may seem to be supported by the fact that some of the advice it gives about women has parallels with the attitudes found in the infamous, misogynistic poem of Pere Torroella, 'Quien bien amando persigue', known as the *Maldezir de mujeres*, or sometimes as the *Coplas de las calidades de las donas*. Written at some point before 1458, it exists in seventeen fifteenth- and sixteenth-century manuscripts (Archer 2001: 267) and was immensely influential. The work elicited a response from a number of poets, some of whom concurred with Torroella, but Manrique composed a spirited defence of the female sex in which he replies to eleven of Torroella's thirteen verses, using an identical rhyme scheme (Gómez Manrique 2003: 191–202).

In his poem of thirteen stanzas, to use the version given in Archer's edition of Torroella's work (Torroella 2004: 202–20), the Catalan poet launches into a diatribe against the female sex. The initial verse reflects the feelings expressed in much courtly love poetry, since Torroella complains that any man who seeks to court a woman sets out upon a path of self-destruction because women evade the men who court them. They are contrary in pursuing men who are not interested in them and the last lines introduce a note of the cynicism that is to follow when Torroella states that women are 'por sola tema regidas' (l. 8). The use of word the 'tema' may be intentionally ambiguous as it can mean 'fear' or 'obsession'. In his response to the first verse Manrique says that those who write about women in this way are guilty of malice since many women are born ignorant of wrongdoing, 'naçidas | ynorantes malefiçios' (Gómez Manrique 2003: 192, ll. 14–15), and it is in their nature to hate it: 'porque de su condiçión | las maldades aborreçen' (ll. 86–87). Those women who err, however, should not be made to accept the shortcomings of men. Torroella's second verse claims that women are ruled by what they fancy and their apparent honesty is but an excuse for rejecting a man's advances. To this Manrique retorts that Torroella's remarks on female dishonesty are founded on 'manojos | de raýzes de maldad' (ll. 31–32) by a man who 'olvidó de cortesía' (l. 33) and he continues by saying that men are more dishonest. Torroella's third stanza likens women to three animal species: 'lobas' because she-wolves were traditionally believed to choose the worst male to mate with; 'anguilas' because eels are slippery to catch; 'erizones' because porcupines have a prickly exterior that discourages physical contact. Women have no appreciation of the finer human qualities in their admirers and are only interested in what they can gain from them. To this Manrique replies that women show considerable fortitude in resisting men's advances (ll. 50–54). In the fourth verse Torroella addresses other lovers, warning them that women express in public sentiments that are contrary to what they say in private, but Manrique refers again to the courage of many women who have faced death in order to preserve their virtue (ll. 70–72). In his fifth stanza Torroella declares that women bask in the praise they receive for their apparent honesty, but will yield to any man who offers them what they demand. This elicits another accusation of spite from Manrique who claims that Torroella fails to appreciate the 'discrecion' possessed by many women (l. 88). Torroella then alleges that some women may be elusive due to a physical defect they wish to conceal, but Manrique does not really respond to this, and instead asserts that it is always the man who makes the first move in any amorous advance and that even 'la más mala tiene | vergüeña de requestar' (ll. 105–06). In addition he reminds his adversary that all men are born of women, a standard argument based on honouring one's mother.

These first six stanzas of Torroella's poem could all have been written by a rejected suitor, since they are mainly concerned with female behaviour in courtship, but after this Torroella's criticisms subsequently take on a more general character. The seventh verse accuses all women of being dishonest, duplicitous, inconstant and contrary, of forgetting absent admirers, and wishing to attract others instead. In reply to this Manrique objects that it is unreasonable to take such an extreme view and he cannot accept that such a judgement should be made on all women: 'no consiento | que ayan un apellido' (ll. 122–23). Manrique chooses not to respond to Torroella's eighth verse that claims that women take criticism badly, love flattery and always choose what is forbidden rather than what is considered appropriate for them.[5] Torroella continues by arguing that because women are aware of the power exercised over them by men they resort to using cosmetics and behaving deceitfully with the intention of exerting their own power over them. They are also mendacious and given to weeping or laughing for no reason. Manrique contests this stoutly with a reminder of the unblemished nature of many women, 'muy más claras que vedrío' (l. 137) and cites the example of Lucretia. In stanza X Torroella claims that women seek only pleasure and profit, that it is only out of fear that they are kept from wrongdoing, the one thing that makes it possible for men to live with them. Manrique declares that such criticism will not harm the good reputation of virtuous women and goes as far as to say that it is through the bad influence of men that women err:

> Que si nuestra desauida
> maluestad no interuiniese,
> esta fe tengo creýda:
> no ser ninguna naçida
> que de lo tal presumiese. (ll. 158–62)

5   This stanza does not appear in the ms. MP3 and Vidal González includes it as a footnote in his edition.

In the eleventh stanza Torroella's attitude softens a little when he refers to the Aristotelian definition of woman as being an imperfect man, 'un animal [...] procreado en el defecto | del buen calor natural' (Torroella 2004: 213, ll. 91, 93–94), a theory propounded by the ancient Greek writer, Galen. Women's failings, therefore, are natural and they are not to be blamed for their shortcomings. Manrique chooses to ignore this verse because, as Archer comments, 'Torroellla cita esta concepción de la mujer, aceptada casi de manera universal' (Archer 2011a: 254), but it would have weakened his defence. Subsequently, Torroella seems to backtrack in the following stanza where he says that what reason women possess guides many of them towards behaving virtuously.[6] This leads him to make a patronizing comment in his twelfth verse to the effect that this is all the more praiseworthy considering the defects that they possess naturally. These two stanzas prepare us for the palinode of the final verse when he declares that his lady is one of the few who deserve such praise: 'vós sois la que desfaséis | lo que contienen mis versos' (Torroella 2004: 261, ll. 113–14). Manrique's reaction to these final stanzas is to declare that Torroella is very much mistaken in his claims, expressing the opinion that women have the strength to rule the world, and finally reminding him that they are of God's creation.

Torroella's poem has to be seen as something of a marker in Castilian literature of the fifteenth century, as not only was it 'uno de los más exitosos de toda la tradición cancioneril: aparece en nada menos que diecisiete manuscritos copiados entre la década de 1460 y 1541' (Archer 2011a: 247), but it provoked a considerable response from contemporary writers. Although there is a long tradition of misogynous discourse, for example by Ovid and Boccaccio, and in Castilian prose literature by Martínez de Toledo,[7] women had never before been portrayed in this way in Castilian verse (256). Indeed, they were always revered, and speaking ill of them was decried, as the *Flors del gay saber* explicitly states, 'quar degun temps lunhs bos trobadors que sia estatz lials amayres. no sentendec. en avol amor. ni en dezonest dezerier' [for no good troubadour, having been a faithful lover, has resorted to any lecherous or dishonourable behaviour] (Gatien-Arnoult 1841–43: V, 360).

The fact that Torroella was from the Empordà and wrote nearly half of his work in Catalan is significant since there had been a tradition since the late twelfth century in Provençal literature of invective against women, originating with Bernart de Ventadorn. He and his followers developed the *mala cansó* in which, initially, individual women were denounced for the suffering they had caused the poet, but in some cases this led to generalized misogyny. Occasionally a misogynous *mala cobla* might even be inserted into a love poem, something Bernat himself famously did, and this *cobla* was included in Matfre Ermengaud's *Breviari d'Amor*, a work whose cultural influence was still felt in the nearby kingdom of Aragon in the fourteenth and fifteenth centuries and led to the development of the Catalan *maldit* (Archer 2011a: 260–61). Some of these poems were directed at one woman in

---

6   In some manuscripts l. 104 reads 'así la parte mejor' or 'así la parte meyor', both of which seem to make better sense in the context than 'la parte mayor'.
7   A copy of Martínez's *Corbacho* is listed in the inventory of Manrique's library (Gómez Manrique 1885–86: II, 333).

particular, but others were denunciations of women in general. Thus it is reasonable to assume that, had Torroella written his *Maldezir* in Catalan, he would have been following a tradition that was firmly established in Catalan literary culture and would not have made a great impact. To express these views in Castilian was an act of cultural transference that shocked because 'tanto la difamación de las mujeres en general como el vituperio de una dama en particular eran géneros poéticos prácticamente desconocidos en la lírica de cancionero castellano' (256). Moreover, Torroella's palinode in the final stanza did not succeed in dispelling the negative tone of his work.

Archer claims that Manrique's primary concern in writing this reply to Torroella was not so much to defend women as to decry the lack of *cortesía* that it expressed: 'la intención principal de Manrique no es defender a las mujeres. De hecho, la mayoría de sus palabras van dirigidas contra los maldizientes, y sobre todo contra Torroella' (281). He quotes Manrique as saying that Torroella 'olvidó la cortesía' (281) and, to support this opinion, it could be added that the reply contains a number of accusations against Torroella of malice, such as in the first stanza when he says that anyone who criticizes women 'de la verdad refuye | e con maliçia consigue' (Gómez Manrique 2003: 192, ll. 12–13), and again in line 83 when he opines that the poem is founded on 'maliçia'. The *coplas* are 'llenas de maldezir' (l. 103) and the verb 'maldezir' occurs again later in the poem when he asserts that to write in this way is foolish since the defamer only defames himself, 'maldezir es desvarío' (l. 138), referring to Torroella's work as 'vuestra disfamación' (l. 154). In this way Manrique shows himself to be offended by the content of this poem, but he obviously enjoyed the cut and thrust of debate with other writers and courtiers, as the number of *preguntas* and *respuestas* in which he participated bears witness, and by engaging in this debate he was earning himself a certain prestige in court and literary circles.

In commenting on Manrique's response to Torroella, Archer overlooks the fact that it contains a number of criticisms of men in an effort to set the balance straight between the sexes. In the first stanza of his reply Manrique sets the tone of his defence when he warns against being too judgemental towards women who have erred from the strait and narrow, suggesting that men might do well to consider their own weaknesses:

> e las qu'en ellos [malefiçios] caýdas
> non deuen ser retraýdas
> acatando nuestros viçios. (ll. 16–18)

Vidal González suggests that this is an allusion to John's gospel (192n), referring to the story of the woman who, caught in the act of adultery, is saved from the Pharisees' judgement that she should be stoned to death when Jesus challenges any man who is free of sin to cast the first stone. Manrique clearly sees an element of hypocrisy and self-righteousness in the stance adopted by Torroella and seeks to counter this in his response by mentioning some of the shortcomings of men. On the subject of dishonesty he declares 'de la desonestidad | nosotros somos la guía' (ll. 35–36), and on men's moral weakness, that women resist men's advances resolutely, 'vençiendo nuestra flaqueza | con vna tal fortaleza' (ll. 53–54). In another verse he states that in comparison with many upright women, 'nuestras obras son prietas' (l. 139) and elsewhere he makes a reference to 'nuestra dasauida | maluestad' (ll. 159–60). He thinks it is unjust that all women should be subject to this blanket criticism, since those who have erred have copied male models:

> no consiento
> que ayan un apellido
> las buenas, que son sin cuento
> e las que an con mal tiento
> nuestros consejos seguido. (ll. 122–26)

In this reply to Torroella, Manrique is surely going beyond the mere defence of courtliness in poetry. Had this been his sole intent he need not have responded point for point to Torroella, but instead could have written something more akin to the *respuesta* of Suero de Ribera, which does little more than focus on the concept of courtliness and how it is the preserve of those of noble birth. In his *Respuesta en defensión de las donas* (ID0199, Dutton 1990–91: II, 7–8; Pérez Priego (ed.) 1990: 142–44) Suero states in the first stanza that it is demeaning for a man to write ill of women, as this is due to 'sobra de maliçia' (l. 7). In the second stanza he suggests that to write as Torroella has done flaws an 'hombre de buen linage' (l. 11) who would be better advised to write 'usando de cortesía' (l. 16). He begins the third stanza of his poem by commenting that it is natural for those of lowly birth to express themselves without discretion, but 'los fidalgos han de ser | defensa de las mugeres' (ll. 23–24). Insistence on a gentlemanly stance in these matters is repeated in the following verse which opens with, 'En boca de gentil hombre | mal está la villanía' (ll. 25–26) and ends with the declaration that men are the first to make advances to members of the opposite sex. Because of this fact, he advises in the fifth verse that female indiscretions are best ignored: 'callar es gentileza' (l. 36). The *fin* of the poem contains an appeal to all men to refute any criticism they may hear of the opposite sex.

It is also worth mentioning that in his *Dotrinal de gentileza* Manrique's friend, Fernando de Ludueña, also defended the behaviour of women at court from the type of criticism that Torroella was making. He maintains that it is a part of court life for a woman to participate in the game of courtly love-making, and to condemn her for so doing 'nunca fue tan gran error' (ID1895, Dutton 1990–91: II, 394–406). He remarks further that some people will automatically think the worst of the woman:

> y la ley lo determina
> quel de condiçión maligna
> sienpre piensa lo peor. (ll. 1114–16)

To posit the argument that Manrique's reply to Torroella reveals an incipient pro-feminine stance would obviously be a wild exaggeration, but it is significant that he chose to participate in this debate about the demerits and virtues of the female sex and sought to offer a more just and balanced view of women that went further than a debate about *cortesía*. Torroella's criticisms are obviously a series of generalizations and sweeping statements which many readers of the time found untenable. Manrique came from a social class in which women, although not expected to play a dominant role in society, were nevertheless often well educated. We know that it was at the request of his wife, Juana de Mendoza, that he composed a religious poem which bears the rubric *Los cuchillos de dolor de Nuestra Señora puestos en metro por Gómez Manrique a ynistançia de doña Juana de Mendoça, su muger*. Juana was a friend of Teresa de Cartagena, the nun who wrote the *Arboleda de los enfermos* and subsequently defended her right to engage in such an activity in her treatise *Admiraçión operum Dey*. The only existing manuscript copy of this second work has a heading that states that it was written 'a petición e ruego de la Señora Doña Juana de Mendoça, muger del Señor Gomes Manrique' (Cartagena 1967: 111). Manrique was certainly aware of Teresa's efforts and may well have read the *Arboleda de los enfermos*, since in the introduction to her defence Teresa writes to Juana, 'me dizen [...] que el ya dicho bolumen de papeles borrados aya venido a la notiçia del señor Gómez Manrique e vuestra' (114). Although these are only snippets of information, they suggest that Manrique was sympathetic to Teresa's literary endeavours and more generally to female interest in both literary and spiritual matters. Together with his response to Torroella they support the view that he realized that women's lives could embrace more serious preoccupations than the author of the *Maldezir de las mugeres* would have us believe.

As Julian Weiss remarks, 'The debate over women in fifteenth-century Castile was not exclusively about the female sex', but 'is inextricably linked with a range of other ideologies that structure social castes and classes, notions of race, morality and medicine' (Weiss 2002: 242). By engaging in the debate about women Manrique appears as a player in what scholars in recent years have referred to as the drama of 'male anxiety' which was experienced by those in power and close to the Crown in the fifteenth century when certain figures did not fit the conventional role-models expected of them. The weakness of Juan II as a monarch is well documented and during his minority his mother, Catherine of Lancaster, acted as co-regent with Fernando de Antequera, who was also King of Aragon from 1412–16. Pérez de Guzmán's description of her suggests that she did not conform to the traditional stereotype of a woman when he remarks, 'En el talle e meneo del cuerpo tanto parecía onbre como muger' (Pérez de Guzmán 1965: 9). Juan II's son, Enrique IV, was also an extremely weak king who attracted accusations of effeminacy from his enemies who began to wage 'political battles on the ideological terrain of sexuality and gender' (Weiss 2002: 240), fearing that the strength of male dominance in the social hierarchy was threatened. It is significant that the twenty years of Enrique's reign were eventful ones in the life of Manrique. We cannot date his reply to Torroella, but if it was written after the death of the *infante* Alfonso in the summer of 1468 this 'male anxiety' would have been heightened, since the only two serious contenders for the Crown of Castile were Isabel and her rival, Juana, whose legitimacy as the daughter of Enrique IV was in question. Until now I have omitted a point made by Manrique in his reply to Torroella when he says that women's attributes are such that 'podrían en derredor | el mundo todo regir'

Eduardo Camacho Guizado, inasmuch as it contains the four elements traditionally included: the presentation of the event with the announcement of the death, the expression of sorrow and lamentation, the panegyric, and the consolation (Camacho Guizado 1969: 21). A striking feature of this poem is that it contains a substantial amount of narrative that enhances the announcement of the death. This was sometimes a feature of the *planctus*, as Robert Archer remarks apropos of the works of Ausiàs March: 'pot introduir-se una alusió al llinatge noble del difunt, abans de passar a la descripció del país o les persones que es lliuren al dol' (Archer 1996: 51). [An allusion to the noble lineage of the deceased may be introduced before the description of the place or the grief-stricken]. Sieber observes that the structure of the poem does not fully conform to that of the medieval *planctus*, commenting justifiably: 'it could be argued that some stanzas fulfil thematic functions belonging to other categories' (Sieber 1989: 281).

The announcement of the death occupies the first ten stanzas. We know that Manrique had a long military career, but this is the only known poem in which he describes a battle. Although he did not witness the death of Garcilaso, he is the narrator of the event, recalling his experience to portray the scene with vivid description. Not only do the cries and laments of the Spaniards fill the air, together with the clashing of weapons, but the triumph of the Muslims, or 'perros paganos' (Gómez Manrique 2003: 350, l. 29), adds to the general cacophony: 'así los llorantes e los que reýan | con bozes discordes el campo atronauan' (ll. 15–16). The chaos of defeat is highlighted again in line 20 with the use of 'desacordado'; and the sense of grief heightened by the use of the verb 'llorar' or 'llorante' four times, 'gemidos' twice and other words such as 'sospiros', 'lágrimas' and 'plañían'. He stresses the fear of the routed Spaniards as they are defeated: 'Allí era el llanto con el miedo mezclado' (l. 17) and the deep impression the event has left on the survivors:

> avía rüydo, e tan espantoso,
> que ninguno era tan poco medroso
> que non estuuiese asaz demudado. (ll. 22–24)

Stanza IV ends with the observation that the 'lança temida' of the Muslims has wrought death and injury on many Castilian soldiers.

It is not until stanza V that the narrator learns of the death of Garcilaso and there follows praise of him spoken by an anonymous informant. The dead man's skill as a warrior and his bravery and selflessness in the face of danger are emphasized: he died because he had refused to wear a 'bauera' (l. 47) since it restricted his movements and, like Achilles, he sustained a fatal injury to the only unprotected part of his body. Such were his valour and fearlessness and his many triumphs in battle that he is compared favourably with heroes of classical antiquity such as Hector and Achilles:

> que non le fue más el fijo mayor
> del buen rey troyano nin su matador,
> por muncho que Omero lo pinte famoso. (ll. 54–56)

Manrique attributes these qualities to the dead man's lineage, reminding us of his ancestor of the same name who, with his brother in a previous campaign, crossed the river Salado at great risk to himself (352n). We are also told that where Garcilaso met his death was the place where he was knighted by the poet's brother, Rodrigo Manrique, whom he dubs 'el segundo Çid' (l. 71). Tribute is paid to the fact that he died defending the values of the Order of Santiago by fighting the Muslims, and his noble lineage is stressed again as he had proved himself a worthy nephew 'del noble Marqués [de Santillana], señor de Buytrago' (l. 80).

The second section, the main expression of grief, begins at stanza XI where Manrique returns to the use of the first-person narrative, intensifying his demonstration of personal sorrow at the sight of the dead man's body. Giving the impression of having been close to Garcilaso, he refers to him as 'aquel muerto que yo tanto amé, | que non más que a mí yo mesmo quería' (ll. 85–86) and his thoughts turn to the dead man's mother. There is much weeping and lamenting on the part of the poet and his companions whose feelings are compared with those of the Trojans on the death of Hector. This is hardly a true analogy since the Castilians were allowed to give Garcilaso a proper burial, whereas the Greeks initially refused to return Hector's body to his father, Priam; instead Achilles gloated over his victory and dragged Hector's body around the walls of Troy for all to see, pulled behind his chariot. Manrique may have been mindful of this when earlier he comments on the reactions of the Muslims: 'los moros quedaron | tañiendo añafiles, arbuérueras dando' (ll. 91–92). Stanzas (XIII–XV) describe Garcilaso's funeral and the outpouring of grief on the part of all those present: 'allí fue llorado de los más onrrados | de toda la corte con gran sentimiento' (ll. 107–08). A tearful messenger is despatched to Seville to deliver the news of the death to the deceased's family.

The focus of this section on grief shifts at the start of stanza XVI and is seen in the context of Garcilaso's immediate family. The anxiety his mother has suffered on account of her son's exploits has left its mark on her physically: 'que todo su rostro estaua gastado | con las auenidas del muncho llorar' (ll. 125–26), but there is no doubt about her moral courage in the face of adversity, as her heart is 'más fuerte que roca' (l. 136). Although she is 'temerosa' at the sight of the messenger, she is also stoically resigned: 'non muncho turbada' (l. 137). It is noticeable how direct she is in the way she addresses him:

> ¿A qué vienes?
> Dímelo ya. ¿Por qué te detienes
> e fazes estar a mí tan penada?
> Dímelo ya; no pienses que nada
> me puede fazer más triste sin duda
> que lo é seýdo después de biuda. (ll. 138–43)

Her directness is in stark contrast with the messenger's discomfort and the difficulty he has in bringing himself to announce the news of Garcilaso's death. He is 'no poco turbado' (l. 128) on his arrival and when he starts to speak it is with 'vna boz gruesa del muncho llorar' (l. 145), his narration punctuated with 'su gran sospirar' (l. 148). In choosing to have the news of this death delivered by a messenger the poet is using a technique much used in the tragedies of Seneca, some of whose works were part of his library (Gómez Manrique 1885–86: II, 333).

To prepare his audience for the bad news he must announce, the messenger begins his speech by reminding Garcilaso's mother of her noble family's long history of Stoic fortitude when confronted by misfortune. In stanza XX he alludes to the 'valles y llanos' (Gómez Manrique 2003: l. 154) which are safe from the ravages of war and disaster, unlike the buildings that are placed on 'las cuestas e altos collados' (l. 156). He continues with the observation that the poor have no understanding of such disasters and do not fear 'los golpes que da la fortuna | a los que sostienen los altos estados' (ll. 159–60). It takes the messenger four stanzas finally to deliver the news of Garcilaso's death, something seen as a defect by Alan Deyermond because his reflections 'aplazan la respuesta que demanda la madre, prolongando así su angustiada incertidumbre' (Deyermond 1987: 104). If, however, Manrique was influenced by Seneca, he would have recalled how the messenger always delivers a long speech to announce an event of great importance. Furthermore, the messenger's circumlocution serves to emphasize his own challenged fortitude in the face of tragedy, and his apprehension at the thought of bearing such bad news. The length of his speech prepares Garcilaso's mother emotionally to receive the blow that he is about to deliver.

The third part of the poem, the panegyric, commences in stanza XXII when the messenger launches into a eulogy of the dead man, saying how he was loved by all who knew him and feared by all his adversaries, that his valour was outstanding and that he died serving God and having made his final confession. The messenger has no doubt that his soul will be saved and offers consolation to the mother by declaring that the death should not be mourned, as her son did not die in vain but, 'ganando por sienpre la çeleste gloria, | dexando de sí perpetua memoria' (Gómez Manrique 2003: ll. 194–95). Having finished his speech the messenger, despite his brave words intended as consolation, is described as drained of energy and grief-stricken himself:

> Así concluyendo el reportador
> a quien yua ya esfuerço menguando,
> de lágrimas biuas sus pechos regando. (ll. 201–03)

The poet observes the irony of the fact that it is the messenger rather than the mother who is in need of consolation and this anticipates the role the mother will play after the death has been announced.

As a preface to the final, consolatory section of the poem the following four stanzas, XXVII–XXX, add to the narrative element of this work as they describe the scene immediately after the news has been broken. Manrique compares the hysterical weeping and tearing out of hair, initiated by the sister of the dead man and copied by the other women present except for the mother, with that of the Roman women who, on hearing the news of the battle of Canna, uttered 'palabras a Dios desplazientes' (l. 229). The mother, however, is depicted in a very different light, torn between her feelings of sadness and the need to behave wisely, but she is able to overcome her emotions and beg the others present to cease their lamentations:

> desque con seso la furia vençía
> del entrañable dolor maternal,

> a ellas poniendo delante su mal,
> que no llanteasen rogando dezía. (ll. 237–40)

The final stanzas, XXXI–XXXVII, contain the consolatory fourth section of this poem, the response of Garcilaso's mother which acknowledges the irony of the situation: it falls to her to do the consoling when it is she who ought to be receiving consolation. The demonstrations of grief around her only make her own more intense and she declares that it would be more reasonable for her to behave as the other women are doing. She quotes Aristotle on the subject of repeated misfortunes: one consequence is that it makes the survivors 'al fin no sentirlos con tanta pasión' (l. 252). The fact that Manrique saw fit to portray a woman of his class with knowledge of Aristotle is significant. Moreover, his portrayal of her as a woman of great fortitude reminds us of his comments in response to Torroella in defence of the female sex, in particular his reference to Lucrecia (198–99, ll. 140–42).

The reaction of Garcilaso's mother to the news is an expression of Christian doctrine combined with the influence of Stoic thought when she reminds those around her that the world we live in is only a temporary dwelling like a 'mesón' (360, l. 256). We are all travellers on a journey on this earth:

> en el qual vedes que todos posamos
> como caminantes por una pasada,
> non lo teniendo por propia morada. (ll. 257–59)

Referring to this world as a vale of tears that we should not regret leaving, she asks:

> ¿por qué nos quexamos
> en espeçial según lo pasamos
> en aqueste valle de lágrimas lleno
> a do ningún día nin vn rato bueno
> sin muchos malos auer esperamos? (ll. 260–64)

Here her words seem to echo those of Seneca in his consolatory epistle *Ad Marciam*, when he urges her not to weep for her son, reminding her that 'New ills will press on before you have done with the old' (Seneca 2006: II, 32–33).[1] Although the mother shows her humanity and feels sadness on the death of her son, she shows resignation and acceptance of God's will, quoting the famous words of Job 1. 21: 'Dominus dedit y Él lo tiró' [The Lord gave and the Lord hath taken away] (Gómez Manrique 2003: l. 271). This quotation is also in harmony with the Stoic belief in destiny: 'No man dies too soon, because he lives only as long as he was destined to live' (Seneca 2006: II, 74–75).[2]

In the final stanza of four lines Manrique expresses the anguish he experienced on writing this poem and likens his feelings to those of the Trojan women on seeing Priam's reaction to Hector's death. There are other references to the Trojan War in this poem: one of these compares Garcilaso's military strength with that of Hector and Achilles (ll. 53–56). The feelings of the Spaniards at Garcilaso's death

---

1 'urgebunt nova incommoda, priusquam veteribus satis feceris'.
2 'nemo nimis cito moritur, quia victurus diutius quam vixit non fuit'.

are compared to the Trojans' after Hector's death (ll. 89–90), all of which suggests that Manrique wished to demonstrate his acquaintance with Greek literature. Some of this he no doubt gleaned from the copy of *La destruyción de Troya* which was included in the inventory of his library (Gómez Manrique 1885–86: II, 332). This account of the Trojan War, however, is incomplete and breaks off with the arrival of the Greek fleet at Troy and a bloody encounter on the shore beneath the city walls (de Colonna 1970: 166–67). Also in his library was 'Un libro de Metamorfoseos' (Gómez Manrique 1885–86: II, 334), presumably Ovid's *Metamorphoses*, books XII and XIII of which would have provided him with part of the story of the conflict. He might also have read Juan de Mena's translation into Spanish of the Iliad which ends with the burial of Hector. The description of the lamentations of the Trojan women before the funeral pyre recalls similar scenes of grief at the death of Garcilaso: 'E ya estavan aý en derredor las madres troyanas rompiendo con delicadas manos los cabellos fermosos y rasgando e firiendo sus pechos' (Mena 1996: 221).

The *Defunsión* has attracted attention from a number of scholars and with very different reactions. Augusto Cortina considered it 'de lo más hinchado y antipoético que produjo el autor', continuing with a reference to 'las plúmbeas estrofas de arte mayor', and invites the reader to analyse some examples of what he calls 'vulgarísima prosa rimada' (Gómez Manrique 1947: 16).

Pedro Salinas, on the other hand, considers it is 'la más hermosa doctrina de la conformidad con el querer de Dios' (Salinas 1947: 69). His overall judgement on the poem is highly favourable: 'Los pormenores realistas, los cambios de lugar, la escena grandiosa de la notificación y la admirable respuesta de la madre, dan [...] una extraña mezcla de movilidad narrativa, nobleza dramática y altura moral' (69). He objects, however, to the mother's quotation of Aristotle, considering it to be 'una pedante cita' (69). Kenneth Scholberg sees the influence on Manrique of the episode of the death of Lorenzo Dávalos in Mena's *Laberinto de fortuna*, remarking on the different reactions of the two mothers. He finds fault with the way in which Garcilaso's mother's expresses herself: 'Hay que admitir que el estilo demasiado literario del lamento de la madre disminuye su fuerza emotiva' (Scholberg 1984: 25), which seems a valid comment.

Alan Deyermond expresses some reservations about the poem, describing the opening stanza as 'una de las peores introducciones a un poema importante que un buen poeta de cualquier idioma haya escrito nunca' (Deyermond 1987: 99) and the ending 'bastante floja' (110). His interpretation of the messenger's words in stanza XX is strange: 'Es imposible creer que "los que pobrezillos que guardan ganados" no sufrieron tales pérdidas' (105), reading into these lines an implication that the poor do not feel the pain of bereavement in the same way as the nobility. Manrique is surely reflecting on the greater vulnerability of the warrior class, who expose themselves to more danger than those of humble estate who earn their living on the land. To say that 'la falta de simpatía humana no es sólo mimética, sino que se debe atribuir al poeta mismo' (105) is untenable, particularly when one reads stanza XXI in which the messenger makes the point that the mother comes from a long line of noble ancestors who have experienced both triumphs and misfortunes 'con gestos yguales' (Gómez Manrique 2003; l. 162). Surely Manrique is merely suggesting that Garcilaso's mother will be able to accept this latest reversal of fortune with the customary fortitude that her forebears have shown in similar circumstances. However, I think Deyermond is right in concluding that the *Defunsión* is more than just an elegy: 'es genéricamente más compleja, combinando una elegía con escenas dramáticas y con una poesía consolatoria' (Deyermond 1987: 112).

Harry Sieber alludes to the financial loss suffered by Garcilaso's family, of which there is a hint in stanza XXXV. He quotes from the mother's will in which she provided for the orphaned grandson because 'dél [Garcilaso] non quedó otra cosa' (Sieber 1965: 286). He comments that the Manrique family never forgot this slight but does not draw any political conclusions from this. There is hint of criticism of Enrique IV in stanza XXXV: 'Luego la fazienda fue toda gastada | por do más conuenía' (Gómez Manrique 2003: 361, ll. 277–78), an allusion to the fact that, according to Palencia, Garcilaso's family asked that the *encomienda* of Montizón that he had been granted should be passed on to his infant son. This request was refused by Enrique who proceeded to confer it on one of his favourites, Nicolás de Iranzo, with the result that, 'A partir de este momento el rey se mostraba cada día más odioso a la nobleza, y cada vez más favorable a los villanos' (Palencia 1998–99: I, 184).

This point is taken up and developed in some detail by Carl Atlee who concentrates on the political implications of the poem, citing the chroniclers, Enríquez del Castillo, Palencia, and especially Valera, to reveal Enrique's lack of esteem for Garcilaso (Atlee 2010: 175). In addition, Atlee analyses the literary techniques employed by Manrique to contrast Garcilaso's bravery with the king's disrespect for him, interpreting this poem as an 'implicit denunciation of Enrique IV' (169). In the light of Manrique's subsequent writings this judgement certainly rings true.

Gómez Manrique's Letter to Pedro González de Mendoza

A very different structure from that of the medieval *planctus* is to be found in Manrique's lament for the marqués de Santillana who died in April 1458. The poem itself is prefaced by a letter by Manrique to the marqués's son, Pedro González de Mendoza, then Bishop of Calahorra and subsequently Cardinal Archbishop of Toledo and Primate of Spain (Gómez Manrique 2003: 362–66). In the first paragraph he excuses himself for not writing to the Bishop before on the grounds that he himself felt in need of consolation. In fact, the poem was probably completed in 1460 since its allegorical figure Poesía, as she laments the marqués's death, remarks:

> qu'en espaçio de dos años
> tales me son fechos daños
> por esta muerte maldita. (402, ll. 896–98)

The poet pays tribute to the qualities that Santillana possessed which were of benefit to the nation: he makes a comparison between the marqués and great heroes of antiquity such as Caesar and Livy, praising him also for being the first statesman of the time to take an interest in literary pursuits as well as being a soldier, a subject that surfaces elsewhere in his writing, namely in his letter to the conde de Benavente and in the *Regimiento de príncipes*. Santillana was 'el primero de senblante prosapia e grandeza d'estado que en nuestros tyenpos congregó la çiençia con la cauallerýa e la lóriga con la toga' (363). He can think of no one else of a similar status who took an interest in literature; in fact there were many who would rebuke a knight who devoted time to such activities, but the marqués fought successfully against this attitude: 'La qual errada opinión este varón magnífico arrancó de nuestra patria' (363). Tribute is paid to his skill in commanding troops on the battlefield and his bravery in the face of danger, which were outstanding, the combination of which produced a person whose loss will be greatly felt by the people. Manrique sums up his feelings with a quotation from the Lamentations of Jeremiah 1. 1: 'Fynalmente, éste fue tanto en perfeçión bueno e prouechoso para esta rigión, que bien sin dubda ella puede dezir con Geremías que es quedada syn él como biuda señora de gentes' (363–64).

The second paragraph of this letter contains a very much more personal appreciation: he obviously looked up to the marqués as a father-figure and mentor, and recalls the favours and protection received from him and the encouragement and praise which, he claims, was undeserved. It was the marqués who encouraged him to write poetry, appreciated what he produced, and seems to have given him confidence in his own ability, thereby enabling him to shed 'el velo de la vergüeña' (364).

El planto de las Uirtudes e Poesía por el magnífico señor don Ýñigo López de Mendoza, marqués de Santillana

This poem, paying homage to the marqués de Santillana, shows the influence of one of Santillana's own compositions, the elegiac *Defunsión de don Enrique de Villena*, 'Robadas havían el Austro e Borea' (Santillana 2003: 285–94), a tribute to the classical scholar and translator of Virgil and Dante. With its many references to classical mythology, reminiscent of Dante's *Inferno*, it describes how he becomes lost in a dark, terrifying forest inhabited by monsters, culminating in a meeting with the nine Muses. There he learns of Villena's demise and joins the Muses in their lament for the marqués and many other literary figures from Homer to Villena.

Manrique's poem of 134 ten-line stanzas, 'Mys sospiros despertad' (Gómez Manrique 2003: 366–418), is a very much longer and more complex work that can be divided roughly into four sections. Unlike Santillana's plea to a pagan source of inspiration, 'Mas yo a ti sólo me plaze llamar | ¡o çithara dulçe más que la d'Orfeo!' (Santillana 2003: 286, ll. 17–18), Manrique's poem opens with an invocation to Jesus. It continues with a description of an allegorical journey, the scene set in the spring with a description of nature, unusual in Manrique's poetry. Despite the signs of renewal heralded by the season, the poet is overcome by a sense of anxiety and, driven by the need for solitude, heads for a monastery.

The second section, stanzas XII–XXXVI, shows the influence of both Dante and

Santillana with its description of the dark and terrifying valley in which the poet finds himself lost. This is in stark contrast to the scene first described: instead of the nightingale's beautiful song, he now hears the ominous cry of owls. The atmosphere is made more sinister with the presence of poisonous snakes, the discordant cries of eagles which 'por sus pechos reales | sacauan sus coraçones' (Gómez Manrique 2003: ll. 144–45), and the realization that he is trapped in this place and can find no way out. Comparing his plight with that of Jonah when swallowed by the whale, his fear grows with the increasing eeriness of his surroundings as night falls. The description is embellished with classical references: the poet senses the presence of Harpies when he would rather hear the music of Orpheus, and feels as sad as Dido when abandoned by Aeneas.

As day breaks the poet heads towards a fortress that he sees in the distance where the third and very much longer section of the narration, XXXVII–CXXX, takes place, consisting of the tributes paid to the marqués. Having entered the castle, the poet encounters seven grieving young women, three holding crosses and the other four a coat of arms each, their emblems described in some detail, revealing the noble ancestry of the deceased. At this point in stanza XLVI the poet begins to fear that the marqués has died. Rather than the pagan Muses of Santillana's poem, these seven maidens represent the Christian virtues of Faith, Hope and Charity and the cardinal virtues of Prudence, Justice, Temperance and Fortitude. The first to speak is Faith and, to pay homage to Santillana, Manrique echoes the words of his mentor who compared Villena to the final supporting column of an ancient temple:

> E bien commo tenplo a quien fallesçido
> han las sus colunpnas por gran antigor,
> e una tan sola le faze favor,
> assí don Enrique nos ha sostenido.
> (Santillana 2003: ll. 161–64)

Manrique takes Santillana's simile of the temple, creating a metaphor when Faith declares:

> Éste fue vn templo muy rico
> de nuestra congregaçión;
> en éste te çertifico
> que desde moço bien
> chico fezimos abitaçión.
> (Gómez Manrique 2003: 386, ll. 501–05)

Thus the marqués, because he embodied the three theological and four cardinal virtues from an early age, becomes the dwelling-place of the 'congregation' of the Virtues.

Faith pays tribute to two other men, both clerics who died in 1456, Alfonso de Madrigal, El Tostado and Alonso de Cartagena, who were much praised by Fernando del Pulgar for both their learning and integrity. Her praise is more extravagant when she speaks of the marqués, paying tribute to his abilities as a soldier prepared to defend the Christian faith, and claiming that he was comparable to Saint Thomas (presumably Aquinas). Hope expresses her sorrow by making comparisons between herself and female characters from Homer who suffered losses in the Trojan War. Charity pays tribute to Santillana's generosity and compassion: he was 'de los míseros abrigo, | de los hanbrientos fartura' (ll. 617–18).

The four Stoic virtues, Prudence, Justice, Temperance and Fortitude, also lament the loss of Santillana, comparing him favourably with great men of the past such as Solomon, Aristotle, Brutus and Alfonso el Sabio. Fortitude in her eulogy makes a reference to both characters from history as well as mythology, admitting to be 'nada fuerte | para comportar tristeza' (ll. 772–73). Indeed, contrary to traditional Stoic principles, rather than showing resignation to the death of Santillana, as Garcilaso's mother does to the death of her son in the *Defunsión*, she encourages the others to lament:

> Plangan comigo que plaño
> sus verdaderos amigos,
> y lloren vn mal tamaño
> e tan syn medida daño. (ll. 781–84)

The allegory is sustained when the poet meets a young woman, the personification of Poetry, who is also in mourning, and not just for Santillana, because in the last two years both Juan de Mena and Juan d'Ixar have died. She instructs the traveller to tell his audience of Santillana's genealogy and his personal attributes, which have already been praised by the Virtues. Obeying these instructions, while not failing to protest that he is unequal to such a task, Manrique proceeds to indulge in an encomium with much hyperbole of the marqués, claiming that his writing was more elegant than that of Boethius and even claiming, 'pues en los metros el Dante | ant'el se mostrara neçio' (ll. 1089–90). We are reminded again that Santillana was not only a distinguished literary figure, but also led a victorious army at the battle of Huelma in 1438 (ll. 1109). Although Manrique suggests that Pérez de Guzmán would be better suited to the task, he agrees to Poesýa's request, declaring that Santillana's death is not just a cause of grief to those who knew him but to the whole of Castile.

Although this is ostensibly an elegy, there is now a marked shift of emphasis away from personal grief and a focus on the implications of this death for Castile. Manrique expresses his concern for the nation, believing that the loss of men such as Santillana has a destabilizing effect upon society. The notion that much can be learned from men of mature years is to be found elsewhere in Manrique's poetry, for example in his *Regimiento de príncipes* when he tells the young Fernando not to listen to 'moços apasionados', but instead to heed the advice of 'onbres de discreçión, | de saber y lealtad' (633, ll. 113–14). Santillana's death, therefore, does not augur well for the future:

> E quando de los conçejos
> falleçen los cuerdos viejos,
> vezinas son las discordias
> que nunca moran concordias
> do faltan buenos consejos. (415, ll. 1236–40)

A similarly gloomy note is sounded by an unnamed Virtue who sees the immediate future as a period of sadness until someone of Santillana's qualities can be found. She expresses a negative view of the contemporary situation: sin and vice have taken a hold on all social classes, or as she says, on 'todos los tres estados' (l. 1284). She declares that she and her companions no longer have a home in the sinful society in which they find themselves. The allegorical part of the poem ends with the departure of the Virtue who has just spoken, and the closure of the castle.

In the final section of four stanzas the poet gives his own reflection on the effect of Santillana's death, saying that Castile 'tan yerma pareçia, | como sin pueblo Cartago' (ll. 1314–15). He then echoes the words, already quoted, that he spoke to Poesýa on the advisability of listening to 'ançianos | sujetos a la virtud' (ll. 1319–20) rather than to 'la loca jouentud' (l. 1317) since this was the secret of how ancient Rome prospered. The mention of ancient Rome's prosperity calls to mind the opening line of Manrique's much more polemical poem, the *Esclamaçión e querella de la gouernaçión*, 'Quando Roma prosperaua' (571), that he composed a few years later, an expression of frustration at the mismanagement of Castile's government. The forebodings expressed by the last Virtue, mentioned in the preceding paragraph, are mirrored in his use of the simile of the ship that comes to grief without its captain, an analogy with the society lacking upright men that is overrun by injustice. Finally he recalls the invocation he made at the beginning of the poem to Jesus and now asks that He may protect Castile from the evil that he fears will overcome it. This statement, like that of the Virtue who speaks in stanza CXXIX, suggests very clearly a distinct unease on the part of Manrique regarding the current state of Castilian society.

The Poem's Language

A striking stylistic feature of this poem is Manrique's figurative language and shows how, moving on from the courtly love poetry of his earlier years, he chooses images appropriate to his subject matter. Although there are few metaphors in this poem, the importance of the above-mentioned image taken from Santillana's elegy to Villena, that of the temple as a dwelling place for the Muses, should be stressed. It recurs several times, for instance when Fe laments the breaking of 'los más firmes pilares' (l. 529), alluding to the deaths of the renowned theologians, El Tostado and Alonso de Cartagena before that of the marqués. Here the metaphor seems inconsistent, since originally Santillana is referred to as the temple but now as one of its pillars. Prudencia in her lament uses the temple image in a simile: 'quedo | como tenplo sin coluna' (ll. 634–35). Manrique varies the figure of speech, referring to the Virtues' loss of Santillana, when telling Poesýa that they had lost 'las manidas | do fazían su mansión' (ll. 1039–40), while the last Virtue to speak regrets the loss of Santillana's 'mesón' where they were all made welcome (l. 1287), both variations on the notion that he was the embodiment of all virtue. In the final stanza of Manrique's reply to the Virtues both 'column' and 'temple' are used again to describe the situation. Rather than grieving for the man who has died, his focus is now on Castile's loss of a figure of such exceptional qualities and the negative consequences that are bound to ensue. Santillana has become the strongest pillar of the temple which is now seen as the Castilian nation:

> que quando la gran coluna
> quiebra, sin dubda ninguna
> se quiere caer el tenplo. (ll. 1233–35)

Still more striking is Manrique's use of more than fifty similes, which merit some close analysis. In their study of rhetoric Azaustre Galiana and Casas Rigall observe that 'la comparación y el símil establecen una analogía entre dos términos a partir de una característica que éstos comparten en cierto grado; pero [...] tienen primariamente un valor ornamental, no probatorio' (Azaustre Galiana and Casas Rigall 1997: 136–37), a statement that only partially describes Manrique's use of the simile in this poem.

Some of these similes serve to emphasize the emotions of disquiet and grief experienced by those who knew Santillana, as in stanza VII where the poet likens his unease to that of Simon Peter when his faith was challenged (Gómez Manrique 2003: 369, ll. 67–70). He conveys this sensation more powerfully in stanza IX in two linked comparisons:

> Que como el enfermo syente
> la del tienpo mutaçión,
> asý bien por consyguiente
> el infortunio viniente
> sentía mi coraçón.
> E como con tenpestad
> fuyen a la sequedad
> las aues de la marina,
> procuré por melezina
> correr a la soledad. (ll. 81–90)

In the first five lines we have an analogy between a sick man, whose physical condition makes him vulnerable to a change in the weather, and the timorous poet as he senses imminent misfortune. The second half of the stanza compares the poet's reaction to his circumstances, but retains a link with the first half: the feared change in the weather has now become a 'tenpestad'. The poet, in searching for a 'melezina' for his malaise, takes one step further than the sick man of the initial lines, because he takes action by seeking solitude, just as sea birds leave their natural habitat of the ocean and retreat inland away from the storm. To apply Robert Archer's theory of simile to this stanza, Manrique is using two images, the sick man and the sea birds, and comparing them with one referent, the poet. Although much simpler than the Marchian simile analysed by Archer, it is possible to find in these lines 'a certain amount of implicit material that might be deemed to attach itself to the literal correlatives' (Archer 1985: 58). The poet is not physically ill, but he is in a mentally fragile state. The second line of this stanza could be interpreted as a play on words: 'tienpo' referring to 'time' and therefore an allusion not only to the new era that dawns after Santillana's death, but also to the changing political climate in which the poet is living. The storm the birds try to avoid can be taken in the figurative sense, referring to the emotional turmoil in which the poet finds himself and which drives him into the wilderness and also to the turbulence that he envisages in Castilian society in the future.

Birds figure in another simile when Gómez Manrique addresses Poesýa, sympathizing with her on the recent loss of Santillana and other poets, comparing her to a falcon unable to fly after being shot down:

> Pues que fincades desnuda
> como falcón quando muda
> sus plumas al derribar,
> que las unas le falleçen
> e las otras no le creçen;
> así vos son falleçidos
> estos varones sentidos
> e otros no remaneçen.
> (Gómez Manrique 2003: 407, ll. 1043–50)

Here the community of Castilian poets is analogous to the falcon when it loses its feathers. Those that enable it to fly are the individual poets, some of whom die and are not replaced.

The poet's determination to overcome his cowardice is emphasized in stanza XIX where he uses two similes as well as antithesis in lines 186–87 to demonstrate how he overcame his fears:

> Como quien come, mirad,
> açíbar por la salud,
> fuera de mi voluntad,
> de la tal neçesidad
> delibré fazer virtud;
> e la pura couardía
> me prestó tal osadía
> que, como desesperado,
> quise fazer de mi grado
> lo que fuerça costreñía. (ll. 181–90)

Many of the similes used serve to emphasize how the death of Santillana is a loss in cultural terms to the Castilian nation. As the poet leaves the castle and the Virtues behind, the land appears desolate:

> toda sola e desierta
> la tierra d'estas donzellas,
> la qual quedaua sin ellas
> qual sin árboles la huerta. (ll. 1307–10)

The analogy between the maidens and the fruit trees implies that just as a tree provides fruit to feed us physically, the Virtues make a contribution to the spiritual and cultural nourishment of the nation. A similar comparison is made in the next stanza to reinforce this thought when Manrique remarks that without the marqués his country 'tan yerma pareçía, | como sin pueblo Cartago' (ll. 1314–15).

The nautical topos, one often used and developed in later poems, is found several times. When the poet sets out on his journey it underlines his confused state of mind:

> Como nao que se lança
> a lo fondo con fortuna,
> procurando segurança. (ll. 191–93)

Later in the poem the nautical simile has more sinister overtones when used by Temprança to express her regret at the death of a man never motivated 'por anbiçión, | con yra nin con pasyón' (ll. 753–54):

> a la ora soy quedada
> como en la mar alterada
> queda la fusta sin remos,
> a quien la mar faze guerra. (ll. 723–26)

The statement that she does not merely feel abandoned and has lost direction, but that the sea seems to be waging war against her, underlines the sentiment that the ethos of Castilian society is changing and not for the better. Conflict is also reflected in the language of jousting used in a simile by Justiçia who declares that without the marqués she has been left 'como justador syn vara' (l. 710). Finally, in the penultimate stanza the nautical simile is developed still further by the poet to express the need for a just society:

> Que como syn patrones
> se rompen çedo las fustas,
> así bien syn los varones
> de derechas intinçiones
> pereçen las cosas justas. (ll. 1321–25)

Just as ships without their captains soon come to grief, likewise the lack of men of integrity leads to a loss of justice in society. In fact, in the preceding stanza Manrique voices fears of future injustice and turbulence in society:

> que quando de las rigiones
> lieua Dios tales varones,
> manifiestas son señales
> que çerca de los vnbrales
> están las persecuçiones. (ll. 1226–30)

The *Planto* contains a number of historical, literary, mythological and biblical allusions all of which are appropriate in an elegy to a man famed for his literary pursuits and interest in the classics. Indeed, Manrique delights in parading his knowledge of history, mythology and the Bible. He compares his fear on approaching the castle's drawbridge to that of Theseus when he witnessed the death of Periteus (ll. 378–80); his anguish to that of Jonah when trapped inside the whale (ll. 166–70); his sadness to that of Dido when Aeneas leaves her (ll. 246–50). As in the *Defunsión*, there are references to the Trojan War to emphasize the grief of the Virtues whose lament is

> más dolorido que las troyanas fizieron
> la triste noche que vieron
> su gran pueblo destruydo. (ll. 512–15)

Although this poem has attracted little attention from scholars, Óscar Perea Rodríguez comments on stanzas XXII–XXX in an article on what he terms 'nocturnality', showing how Manrique emphasizes 'the night as the connection between the darkness and the fear provoked by the principle of evil' (Perea Rodríguez 2012: 301). Although I question the meaning of 'the principle of evil' (301–02), which I take to mean simply 'evil', the article explains two classical allusions made by Manrique that contribute to our appreciation of him as a vernacular humanist. One is a reference in lines 227–30 to the mariner Amyclas who transported Caesar to Italy on a stormy night, a story known in the Middle Ages by those who had read Lucan's *Pharsalia*, a translation of which Manrique had probably read in Santillana's library (302). The second is in lines 251–60, where the poet compares the insomnia he suffers during the night to that of Marcus Atilius Regulus, a Roman consul, whose torture at the hands of the Carthaginians when taken prisoner rendered him unable sleep (302). Perea Rodríguez also observes that lines 281–300 reflect Manrique's own military experience when he compares himself to the 'alcayde sospechoso' who gets up in the dark, driven by anxiety caused by the night watchmen's silence (Gómez Manrique 2003: ll. 281–82). His relief comes when the 'noturrnales lumbreras' (ll. 291–92) give way to 'las vanderas febales' (l. 294) as dawn breaks. This allusion to pagan mythology, reminding us that Apollo (or Phoebus) was connected with the sun, is immediately followed by Manrique confirming his Christian faith:

> Creo que no deseauan
> los qu'en tiniebras estauan
> con mayor ansya la luz
> que les vino por la cruz
> del Mexías que esperauan. (ll. 296–300)

Here Manrique appears to be echoing the words of the apostle Peter who, reminding his followers to remember the word of the prophets if they wish to enter the eternal kingdom, declares: 'ye do well that take ye heed, as unto a light that shineth in a dark place, until the day dawn, and the day star arise in your hearts' (II Peter 1. 19).

Although there was a veiled hint of criticism of Enrique IV at the end of the *Defunsión*, in this poem Manrique is markedly more outspoken. He exempts members of the royal family from the criticism of Castilian society uttered by the Virtue, mentioned in the preceding paragraph because, in keeping with a medieval view of kingship, she says that they are 'por nuestro Dios elegidos | para sus reynos regir' (ll. 1275–76). Although Manrique eventually opposed Enrique IV, at the time of Santillana's death events had not reached the gravity of 1465 when the king's effigy was dethroned and the young infante Alfonso was crowned in Ávila. The poet's diplomacy, or economy with the truth, can be seen in his response to Poesýa when he describes the deceased as 'leal sieruo de su rey' (l. 1218), implying that the marqués and the Mendoza family had always supported the Crown although this was not the case.

In fact we see that in this poem Manrique is beginning to use verse as a vehicle to express his disquiet at what he senses is the deteriorating ethos of Castilian society. As he pays tribute to Santillana he is almost certainly recalling his mentor's own use of both prose and verse for the same purpose. In an essay on Santillana's political poetry Jeremy Lawrance traces the development of Santillana's political writing, citing opinions that anticipate Manrique's despairing comments to the Virtues. Lawrance draws our attention to the *Qüestión fecha a Alfonso de Cartagena* in 1444 on the subject of a knight's duty to his community where the marqués expresses his disgust at:

> este tienpo así trabajoso, donde tantos escándalos, debates e bolliçios son movidos, e todos días por pecados nuestros cresçen e se aumentan tanto que ya las soberviosas flamas de la yra paresçe que llegan al çielo. (Santillana 1988: 416)

He quotes Santillana's diatribe that follows the above-quoted words in which he rails against the degeneracy of the noble class, comparing their greed, mendacity, cruelty, dishonesty and shamelessness to a list of well-known figures of antiquity. Lawrance also refers us to Santillana's *Lamentaçión de Spaña* in which he compares the current state of Spain with that of Rome during its civil war and France in its war against England. Most relevant to this study of Manrique's work is what he calls 'Mendoza's crowning example of *gravitas*', his sonnet XVIII, *Quexándose de los daños de este regno*, the last six lines of which read:

> ¿Dó es la fe, dó es la caridad,
> dó la esperança? Ca por çierto absentes
> son de las tus regiones e partidas.
> ¿Dó es justiçia, temperança, egualdad,
> prudençia e fortaleza? ¿Son presentes?
> Por çierto non, que lexos son fuïdas.
> (Lawrance 2000: 28, ll. 9–14)

Manrique was surely thinking of these lines as he composed his allegorical lament: the death of Santillana, the embodiment of the Virtues, would have a grave impact upon the Castilian nation.

Conclusion

Both the *Defunsión* and the *Planto*, written between 1458 and 1460, were composed following the death of a member of Manrique's extended family, but his approach to these two tasks is radically different. The *Defunsión* contains the four elements that constitute the traditional medieval *planctus*, but it also contains a certain amount of vivid narrative illustrating the effect Garcilaso's death has on his fellow knights and above all on his family. As a frequent advocate of the Stoic virtues, it is hardly surprising that Manrique's consolatory stanzas urge the family to bear their loss with fortitude. There is irony in the fact that it is the mother of the deceased who has to deliver this message, but it also places the focus of the poem firmly on the loss suffered by the family.

The *Planto* for Santillana fulfils a very different function. Garcilaso, although knighted, was still a young man, whereas Santillana had distinguished himself nationally both as a soldier and a man of letters. The use of an allegorical framework for the poem is a departure from the *planctus*, although three of the traditional components are included: the announcement of the death, the expression of grief and the panegyric. The lack of consolatory material is noticeable, and from stanza CXXII there is a shift of emphasis from the mere expression of sorrow to the repercussions that Santillana's death will have on the nation. The poem ends on a decidedly pessimistic note, suggesting that the marqués has left a turbulent world behind him with insufficient men to guide Castile, thus showing that political concerns can pervade even an elegy. Thus the elegy becomes a vehicle to express opinions of a political nature and anticipates future poems that Manrique will compose, some provoking controversy, such as the *Esclamación* and the *Coplas para Arias Dávila*.

CHAPTER 3

Gómez Manrique's Continuation of Juan de Mena's *Debate de la Razón contra la Voluntad*

Apart from the elegy for Santillana, Gómez Manrique produced another long work, probably in the latter part of the 1450s or early 1460s, a productive period in his literary life. This is the continuation of Juan de Mena's 'Canta tú, cristiana musa', also known as his *Debate de la Razón contra la Voluntat* (Gómez Manrique 2003: 467–552). When he died in 1456 Mena had already completed 106 stanzas, setting out the framework for the poem: a dialogue between Razón and Voluntad in which Voluntad is represented by the seven deadly sins and at the end of which Prudencia will be called upon to pass judgement. He only lived to compose exchanges between Razón and four of the sins: Pride, Avarice, Lust and Anger, but the incomplete poem also motivated Pero Guillén de Segovia and Jerónimo de Olivares to compose their own continuations. Manrique's is the longest of the three and expresses his growing interest in moral and spiritual issues. I will first summarize the content of Mena's poem and then discuss Manrique's approach.

Juan de Mena's Unfinished Poem

The topic that Mena had chosen for his last poem was one that had a long tradition behind it. Both María Rosa Lida de Malkiel and Gladys Rivera suggest that the original inspiration for the theme of the seven deadly sins might be found as long ago as the fourth century AD in Prudentius's *Psychomachia*, which tells of a battle between the personified Virtues and Sins (Lida de Malkiel 1984: 112; Rivera 1982: 14). Rivera gives a detailed account of the sources of Mena's *Coplas* (14–18), but suffice it to say that he and the authors of the continuations may have been acquainted with Prudentius's work or perhaps knew in some form Dante's *Divine Comedy* which also uses the category of the seven deadly sins. They might also have read two works on a similar theme that were produced in fourteenth-century Spain: Juan Ruiz's *Libro de Buen Amor* and Pero López de Ayala's *Rimado de Palacio*. The former contains a section on eight sins, each of which is followed by an *exemplum* (Ruiz 1988: 151–70). The latter contains a section devoted to the Ten Commandments, in which López de Ayala lists seven deadly sins, commenting on their characteristics and the harm that they cause (López de Ayala 2000: 13–23). Writing at the turn of the fifteenth century, Francisco Imperial in *El dezir a las syete virtudes* gives the seven Virtues a human form when they are introduced to him by a man he takes to be a poet; the seven sins, however, are represented by serpents. Mena's approach to the topic, as we shall see, takes a very different form from all these antecedents.

The introductory stanzas have a valedictory tone as he invokes the Christian muse, dismissing the 'musas gentiles' whom he now sees as sirens (Gómez Manrique 2003: 468, l. 9) who had lured him all his life to earthly concerns. He now takes stock of his life, welcoming his mature years as an opportunity to set his house in order:

> Venid, lisongeras canas,
> que tardáys demasïado;
> tirad presunçiones vanas
> al tienpo tan malgastado. (ll. 17–20)

He compares human life to an old house that is falling into disrepair, declaring, 'La vida pasada es parte | de la muerte aduenidera' (ll. 33–34) and resolves to focus his efforts in a more serious direction, ridding his work of 'fabulosas temas' (l. 108). In other words, he intends to reduce the frequency of his allusions to classical fables, a common feature of his earlier work. A few lines further on he commits himself to following 'la cathólica vía' in his future writing (l. 125) before explaining the structure he intends giving to this new work.

Mena chose to present Voluntad as a hideous creature 'de siete caras y bocas, | todas feas' (ll. 150–51), the seven faces each representing one of the seven deadly sins. Razón, however, is presented as a very different being with 'La su relunbrante cara | y su gesto cristalino (ll. 241–42). There appears to be no traditional order in the discussion of the seven sins: Dante, for example, treats that of Lust first and leaves Pride until last.

Soberuia

Mena chooses Soberuia to be the first sin upbraided by Razón who opens the debate, claiming that pride is the greatest of human evils and leads to perdition. Voluntad is allowed only one stanza in which she makes a five-point response in self-defence on the grounds of her knowledge, beauty, riches, lineage and religious observance (ll. 273–80). Razón replies to each of these claims, beginning by stating that the wise do not parade their knowledge; instead, in true Senecan fashion she suggests that real wisdom lies in practising moderation: 'Sea tu fundamiento | en saberte moderar' (ll. 285–86). Physical beauty is a gift that does not last and wealth is something that we cannot take with us when we die. On the subject of noble lineage Razón objects to the 'leyes de gentileza' (l. 362) that sustain the belief that a coat of arms and an ancient lineage are proof of nobility, an issue discussed elsewhere by Manrique in a dialogue with other poets. For Razón nobility is a moral concept: 'Es contrato que te obliga | a ser bueno de derecho' (ll. 371–72). The onus remains with the individual who must behave in such a way as to merit being considered noble:

> y la virtud se contrasta
> que por el linage cobras,
> si non responden tus obras
> a la tu tan buena casta. (ll. 381–84)

Soberuia's claim to piety is rejected as religious hypocrisy motivated by the desire to draw attention to herself:

> Quien finge la seruidunbre
> de soberuiosa omildat,
> no busca la claridat,
> mas quiere buscar la lunbre. (ll. 461–64)

Auariçia

Auariçia is asked why she persists in hoarding her ill-gotten gains, given that she derives no benefit from them. Like Souerbia, she gives five reasons, but in two stanzas, to defend her position: not only is she is providing for her old age and for possible reversals of fortune, but she enjoys the prestige that wealth brings, the ability to exact vengeance, and to lend money if it will be advantageous to her. Razón, however, disagrees on all five counts. She sees little point in accumulating wealth for the end of one's life and, using the nautical metaphor of a well-provisioned ship, she declares, 'con tanto lastre tu barca | çiará quando la remes' (ll. 503–04). Furthermore, material wealth does not necessarily ensure peace and security since Fortune is capable of bringing disaster to the rich:

> Seguras del su conbate
> son las casas pobrezillas,
> los palaçios y las sillas
> de los ricos más abate. (ll. 513–16)

Wealth also causes strife in families and attracts others who will covet her riches. On the subject of taking vengeance Razón assures Auariçia that this is much easier when you have nothing to lose. Perhaps what is most pertinent in Razón's invective against the miser is that she denounces the practice of usury and the cruelty of lending money at an extortionately high rate of interest:

> y encubres con maliçia
> de vsurera sotileza
> so espeçia de largueza
> la tu cruel auariçia. (ll. 557–60)

Luxuria

In eight stanzas Razón launches a blistering condemnation of Luxuria, who she claims is the enemy of chastity, demeans people of high estate, brings only short-lived pleasure but lengthy regrets, strife between married couples, and feuds amongst relatives. Illegitimacy, a consequence of female weakness, means that 'munchos fijos a sus padres | saluden por estrangeros' (ll. 671–72). Moreover, Luxuria has a debilitating effect on human beings: 'los sentidos disminuyes | e los ingenios ofuscas' (ll. 677–78).

Luxuria has six stanzas in which she makes a vigorous response: since God endowed man and the animal kingdom with the pleasure that is derived from the sexual act, not only is the natural world preserved, but the human race has gone forth and multiplied, this being particularly important in times of war, disease and natural disaster. The positive nature of human procreation is emphasized:

> por mí la vida muy cara
> reçibe forma en que dura,
> y por mí toda fechura
> al su fazedor declara. (ll. 725–28)

While conceding that some of her acts are harmful, Luxuria appeals to Razón not to portray her in such a negative light as, on balance, she does more good than harm. Lida de Malkiel, in keeping with her opinion that Mena's last work was 'un retroceso en la dirección renacentista' (Lida de Malkiel 1984: 110), asserts that Razón's unreasonable response to Luxuria reflects 'los elementos medievales, muy marcados en esta obra [...] en la línea del ascetismo cristiano' when comparing it with the *Laberinto de fortuna* (114). She considers Luxuria's defence 'como arma de la naturaleza contra la muerte, expuesta más de siglo y medio antes en el *Roman de la Rose* de Jean de Meung' (114). What is striking about this exchange is that Luxuria is given more verses to make a convincing defence and appears to gain the upper hand in the debate. It is significant that Mena's poem gives her the last word in this exchange with Razón who is dismissed and described as 'fatigada y perseguida' (Gómez Manrique 2003: l. 739).

Yra

The last of the sins that Mena writes about is Yra, and it should be noted that in this dialogue it is she who initiates the debate with Razón, who is still exhausted after her verbal tussle with Luxuria. Yra maintains that to avenge herself she does not need all the conventional trappings of war, described in picturesque terms in stanza XCV, because 'sólo coraçón y manos | me conviene demostrar' (ll. 767–68). The impatient and aggressive tone of her speech is maintained in stanza XCVII:

> Nyn atiendo la liçençia
> del ronco son de la tronpa
> o la batalla que ronpa
> porque incline mi paçiençia. (ll. 769–72)

Dismissing any conciliatory measures or truce, her final self-justificatory argument is that a man's honour cannot be satisfied by reason if no amends are made after receiving an insult (ll. 789–92). In her Stoically temperate reply Razón points to the negative effects of rage: it impairs the judgement and only plays into the enemy's hands (ll. 801–08). Instead she urges Yra to allow 'los que tienen vezes | de regir y mandar' to pass judgement in disputes (ll. 819–20). Furthermore, Razón warns Yra that she must not attack those who respect religion or who are involved with the rites of the Church, asking finally how God can forgive anyone their sins if they cannot forgive others. It is at this point that Mena's original part of the poem ends, Yra and Razón having spoken an equal number of stanzas.

Gómez Manrique's Continuation

Manrique's continuation is of 158 stanzas (501–52). He starts with a short introduction of his own in which he reflects on how death is a great leveller, treating people of all estates equally. He offers the obligatory declaration of modesty, claiming that his skills as a poet are inferior to Mena's. Like Mena, and as in his elegy for Santillana, he also rejects the Muses as his inspiration, invoking instead 'la santa graçia divina' (l. 878) but, unlike Mena, he uses a number of biblical references from both the New and Old Testaments in different ways to support both sides of the debate. He also gives Voluntad a significant role in the three dialogues that Mena was unable to write, perhaps because Mena appeared to be developing the role of Voluntad more fully in her debate with Luxuria and Yra than he did with Soberuia and Auariçia.

Gula

The first dialogue is between Razón and Gula, initiated by the latter in line 885. Her first defence is that all people need to eat, and to eat well is to look after one's health. Manrique now departs from Mena's style of defence and allows Gula to quote Christ's words from Matthew 15. 11:

> Non lo qu'entra por la boca,
> según dize San Mateos,
> faze de los justos reos,
> que lo que sale los troca. (ll. 913–16)

Obviously this quotation is deliberately taken out of context: Christ was addressing the Pharisees, taking them to task for publicly adhering strictly to certain laws while failing to examine their consciences. In the same stanza Gula attempts to boost her defence by self-righteously pointing to the folly of those who think they may achieve salvation by fasting while at the same time 'mintiendo e disfamando' (l. 919). She quotes Christ's famous saying that man cannot live on bread alone (Luke 4. 4), again deliberately misinterpreting its meaning so that it becomes an invitation to overindulgence. She finishes by maintaining that it is a greater folly to spend money on clothing than on food.

Razón opens her response to Gula by telling her that she is the enemy of both the young and the old, although it is necessary to eat in order to live: 'tú biues por comer | e comes para morir' (Gómez Manrique 2003: ll. 947–48). Moreover, she counters Gula's misuse of biblical references with three examples from the Old Testament of acts of greed that were punished or threatened with punishment: Jonathan broke his fast (1 Samuel 14. 24–25) and nearly paid the ultimate price, whilst Adam ate the fruit offered him by Eve (Genesis 3), causing them both to be condemned 'a tenebrosa prisión' (Gómez Manrique 2003: l. 974) and Lot's drunkenness caused him to father two sons incestuously, one with each daughter (Genesis 19. 30–38). Razón then returns to the claim that Gula had made, that man cannot live on bread alone, insisting on the metaphorical sense intended by Christ:

> no cuydes dezirlo, no
> por beuir sin golosinas;

> más sin palabras diuinas
> que con el pan conparó.
> (Gómez Manrique 2003: ll. 997–1000)

Finally Razón accuses Gula of being at the root of the other sins (with the exception of Enbidia), adding that she is the particular the enemy of those following a military or ecclesiastical career, the mention of the latter perhaps intended as censure of the self-indulgence of some religious communities. Gula is allowed only one stanza to respond, and Razón has the last word, praising the Stoic virtue of moderation and the avoidance of excess: 'que lo superfluo dexemos' (l. 1080).

Enbidia

The exchange between Enbidia and Razón opens with the latter observing that what distinguishes Enbidia from the other sins is the total lack of pleasure that she derives from anything. Enbidia's reply is one of the more interesting defences in this work. Firstly, while all human beings are ostensibly of the same origin, there is such a discrepancy in the way nature and fortune distribute their gifts that she can only feel aggrieved not to have been so highly favoured as others she sees around her. Secondly, those gifts that she does possess are not valued by others, and thirdly she claims that men can look back enviously to the past and emulate examples of bravery, whilst envy of the valiant will encourage the more fearful to act bravely. Envy of honours gained will inspire others to earn similar rewards, and in the same way the desire to work competitively will ennoble people (ll. 1145–52). Enbidia sees virtue in such aspirations which, she claims, are founded 'sobre peña de nobleza' (l. 1158) and should be regarded as virtuous rather than sinful. This suggestion is perhaps the most thought-provoking of the debate since Enbidia is expressing the idea that aspiration to fame is something to be praised rather than rejected as sinful. In fact, in the gloss of his own poem written for his sister, 'La péñola tengo con tinta en la mano', Manrique praises Caesar, whose example he cites in this passage, for the ambition that he displayed in wanting to equal Alexander the Great, describing his reaction at the sight of the hero's statue: 'dio vn gran gemido, como quexándose de la perezosa haraganía suya porque en la edat que en la sazón era él, ya Alixandre el mundo avía enseñoreado' (433–34, ll. 271–87).

Razón, of course, rejects all these arguments: although we are all born and die as equals, we are not all equal during our lifetime. Neither are we all endowed with the same natural gifts, but should make the most of those we have received. Even the recipients of great natural powers must still strive to lead a virtuous life in order to achieve salvation; the great talents of men such as Sampson and Orpheus did not mean that they were perfect. Those who are blessed with material wealth cannot take it with them to the next world when they die, therefore the wise man neither takes pleasure in his wealth nor frets at its loss. Where earthly honours are concerned Razón emphasizes that these are not easily won, and in any case are ephemeral. Spiritual values should be more highly prized than temporal ones because:

> más presto pasan, amigo,
> que flores de las mañanas,
> todas son cosas liuianas,
> por tienpo pereçederas. (ll. 1275–78)

These lines express a sentiment that will be found in the poem to Arias Dávila. With this in mind Razón claims that heroism in battle is less admirable than, for example, Saint Martin's act of cutting his cloak in half to share it with a poor man, a deed that guaranteed him eternal salvation. Razón rejects the glory of honours received in war, reminding Enbidia of all the death, destruction and misfortunes that result from armed conflict. She also recalls the rivalry between the brothers Cain and Abel and between Caesar and Pompey, expressing the opinion that it is actually because of envy that wars break out, citing a topical example: 'por esta son ençendidas | en Castilla grandes flamas' (ll. 1333–34).

Pereza

The last of the sins to confront Razón is Pereza who, true to her nature, is reluctant to enter into any debate with Razón on the grounds that she would rather rest. She does not believe that temporal honours and goods, the subject of the previous debate with Enbidia, are achieved through work as all the diligent achieve is to work themselves to death. Her defence only amounts to two stanzas, no doubt a deliberate decision on Manrique's part to give a portrayal of this vice that emphasizes her indolence. Razón launches into a vigorous condemnation of Pereza, firstly for being too lazy to defend herself and then for failing to heed either the material or the spiritual consequences of her idleness, saying that material rewards may be gained by those who help themselves: 'mas ayudarse conuiene | para ser reçibidor' (ll. 1399–1400). Since, however, worldly goods and honours are not considered to be of lasting value, Razón qualifies this statement by suggesting that Pereza should model herself on Fabriçio (l. 1402); this may have been Gaius Fabricius Lucindus (524n), who expelled a colleague from the Senate on the grounds that he satisfied his taste for luxury excessively. Instead, Pereza should rouse herself into activity if she wishes to achieve eternal life by following the path that Christ trod. To emphasize this point Razón uses two similes to emphasize how hard it is to save one's soul without making the necessary effort: 'como syn senbrar cojer, | e sin letras ser letrado' (ll. 1423–24).

Pereza retorts that you only have to look to contemporary Castile, full of 'ricos y muy prosperados, | sin orden, por açidente' (ll. 1431–32), to see how the efforts of the deserving are wasted, a comment that doubtless reflected Manrique's views. She sees many striving in vain to win the honours that are awarded to others who make no effort, citing the example of Trajan, a Spaniard by birth, who she claims was elected emperor without any effort on his part. Here Manrique again cites examples from the New Testament to support Pereza's defence regarding the salvation of sinners who are supposedly forgiven their past misdeeds without exerting themselves to perform good works. The robber, named in some sources as Dimas, was crucified next to Christ and achieved salvation with no effort, but merely 'con solo memento mei | que dixo con contriçión' (ll. 1463–64), according to Luke's gospel (23. 42–43). Secondly she cites Mary Magdalene who did not find instant forgiveness (Luke 8. 2) and thirdly the woman from Canaan whom Jesus himself rebukes initially when she requested that he heal her daughter (Matthew 15. 21–28).[1]

Razón rejects all these arguments outright as evil and ill-founded, accusing Pereza of causing many to take the road to perdition by listening to them. She replies to all of them except one. On the subject of worldly honours, she declares that Trajan was worthy of his election to high office and suggests he was elected 'por diuino secreto | seyendo mereçedor' (Gómez Manrique 2003: ll. 1519–20). She offers further examples of great men from the past who would not be remembered had they not exerted themselves, such as Hannibal, who would never have been able to cross mountains and swamps had he never made the effort to do so, as well as many famous heroes of ancient Rome. Where material wealth is concerned Razón assures Pereza that the idle rarely prosper and only acquire riches if they inherit them; moreover, many idlers lose what their parents have gained by dint of hard work. If Pereza wishes to prosper she must be diligent, as although Fortune has a hand in distributing riches, she is seldom supportive of idleness:

> que maguer Fortuna, quando
> le plaze, dé la riqueza,
> pocas vezes la pereza
> la fallará de su vando. (ll. 1573–76)

When discussing salvation Razón remarks that if Pereza cannot even rouse herself to strive after worldly fame and wealth, she is still less likely to achieve eternal life, something that was only made possible by Christ's incarnation and his passion. The human race is born with free will to make the choice between taking the narrow path leading to eternity or to lose all hope of salvation by following 'tras la bestial afeçión' (l. 1616). Razón also refers to the New Testament, warning that even though the faithful make the right choice, the way is still full of dangers. Here she echoes the words of 'el apóstol [...] | por su epístola segunda' (ll. 1626–27), an allusion perhaps to the second epistle of Peter in which people are exhorted to practise virtue of all kinds, and by so doing can expect to be rewarded: 'For so an entrance shall be ministered unto to you abundantly into the everlasting kingdom of our Lord and Saviour Jesus Christ' (II Peter 1. 11). Razón then reminds Pereza of the need for prayer with a reference to Christ's words in the garden of Gethsemane: 'Watch and pray, that ye enter not into temptation: the spirit is willing, but the flesh is weak' (Matthew 26. 41; Mark, 14. 38).

Razón then questions Pereza's use of biblical references to justify her stance. On the subject of Dimas, she contends that he achieved salvation not just because of his faith, but through his actions:

---

1 These two *exempla* are less obvious than the first since, unlike the robber who was crucified for theft, the gospels tell us nothing about Mary Magdalene's or the Canaanite woman's previous misdeeds.

> Que sy Dimas saluo fue
> por la fe con que creyó,
> no menos porque seruió
> con San Juan lo prouaré.
> (Gómez Manrique 2003: ll. 1665–69)

The reason for referring to Saint John is not immediately obvious because it is in Saint Luke's gospel that we are told that one of the criminals crucified at the same time rebukes the other criminal for jeering at Jesus and for suggesting that if he were the son of God he should be able to save all three of them. In fact neither robber is named in the four New Testament gospels, but here Manrique is alluding to the fourth-century Church Father, Saint John Chrysostom, who refers to the apocryphal gospel of Nicodemus in which this robber is named and his sayings reported, as Jean Joseph Gaume pointed out (Gaume 1882: 25). According to Gaume, a tradition grew up regarding Dimas who was reputed to have been in the habit of robbing travellers in the desert. Legend has it that he was on the point of robbing the Holy Family on their flight into Egypt when, becoming aware of the divine nature of the Christ child, he refrained from stealing from them and instead offered them shelter for the night in a cave (17). In Luke's version of the crucifixion Dimas declares, 'We receive the due reward of our deeds: but this man hath done nothing amiss' (Luke 23. 41). Another version of the story of Dimas's salvation is found in the final lines of the thirteenth-century *Libre dels tres reys d'orient* (Alvar, ed. 1965: ll. 225–42). On the strength of this story of Dimas's good deed, Razón then stresses the need to perform good works as well as to have faith in order to achieve salvation, citing James's epistle (2. 14–26) when she says, 'que syn las obras la fe | es como casa syn puerta' (Gómez Manrique 2003: ll. 1669–70). As for Pereza's reference to Mary Magdalene, Razón dismisses it, warning her that she should not think that she can save herself by showing sudden contrition on her deathbed. By so doing, she says, 'por ventura lançarás | la soga tras la herrada' (ll. 1679–80).

Prudençia's Judgement

A new section of the poem commences with the appearance in line 1689 of Prudençia who, as Mena had intended, is to pass judgement on the debate between Razón and Voluntad. She finds in favour of Razón, condemning Voluntad on the grounds that she is lacking in the four cardinal virtues (prudence, justice, temperance and fortitude) and the three theological virtues (faith, hope and charity). Prudençia points out that Voluntad's preoccupations are with temporal things 'lo qual pasa como un sueño | e como sonbra falleçe' (ll. 1759–60). Those who follow this way of life are mad since even the pleasures that last longest in this world will fade: 'se podreçe tan aýna | como mançana madura' (ll. 1767–68). At this point in her judgement Prudençia begins to address all men rather than Voluntad, saying that man, being a rational creature, should be able to follow Razón and distance himself from 'los brutos animales' (ll. 1777–80). She advises all men to follow the virtuous 'avnque d'estos munchos menos | que de malos fallarás' (ll. 1787–88). To achieve everlasting life, man must follow the 'camino trabajoso' (l. 1800), although it is a narrow one.

Prudençia proceeds to suggest a remedy for each individual sin by the exercise of Christian and Stoic virtues. Glossing the words of Christ in the Sermon on the Mount (Matthew 5. 3), she declares:

> Que los vmildes serán
> en los çielos ensalçados,
> los soberbios derribados
> a do siempre penarán.
> (Gómez Manrique 2003: ll. 1809–12)

The avaricious are reminded that it is not possible to take their worldly goods to the next life, whilst the lustful are told to rein in their desires with a warning to men to think not of the pleasure that is derived from this sin but to think 'después de pasado | quánto dexa desplazer' (ll. 1847–48). There is an additional warning for women who need to consider their reputations even more than men: 'por que no sus claras famas | disputen por los ryncones' (ll. 1855–56). The wrathful are reminded that justice cannot be carried out when a person is swayed by anger. The gluttonous are urged to embrace yet another Stoic virtue, that of temperance, while the envious are advised that Christian love will be a defence against the 'dardos enbidiosos' (l. 1898) they suffer, and will instead lead them to heaven. Lastly, having urged the slothful to stir themselves into action, Prudencia then makes clear that salvation is not just a matter of avoiding sin, but also requires positive action in pursuit of virtue: 'quien la gloria quisiere, | el bien faga que podrá' (ll. 1927–28), advice that Pereza has already received from Razón.

In stanza CCXLVIII a mixture of Christian and Senecan influences continues to be seen in the utterances of Prudençia when she insists on the importance of good works. Her words 'qu'en el punto que naçéys | comiença vuestro morir' (ll. 1983–84) echo those of Mena in the fifth stanza of the original poem as well as those of Seneca when he wrote to Marcia to console her on the death of her son: 'for his death was proclaimed at his birth; into this condition was he begotten, this fate attended him straightway from the womb' (Seneca 2006: II, 30–31).[2] Mena and Manrique appear to have been happy to take from Seneca those maxims that supported their own ideas and Christian teaching, probably having access to one of the compilations of sayings, many of them Senecan, that are described by Karl Blüher (Blüher 1983: 156–58).[3]

Manrique concludes this work with an address of several stanzas by Prudençia to each of the three estates of man (Gómez Manrique 2003: ll. 1993–2088). Clerics are reminded that they need to set a good example by carrying out their duties and adhering to their vows of poverty, chastity and obedience. Monarchs and aristocrats are urged to strive for peace and justice and to treat the poor and afflicted with compassion, a message that Manrique also delivers subsequently to Fernando and Isabel in his *Regimiento de príncipes*. There is also a warning to the knights of the

---

2   'mors enim illi denuntiata nascenti est; in hanc legem erat satus, hoc illum fatum ab utero statim prosequebatur'.

3   Later in the same work Seneca declares that death is not to be feared as it is a release from the sufferings of this world: 'Mors dolorum omnium exsolutio est et finis, ultra quem mala nostra non exeunt' (66), an idea that is contrary to the teaching of the Catholic Church.

realm that they should not behave in tyrannical fashion, but treat their vassals well and at the same time accept the sovereignty of the king. The message to the third estate is that they should pay their dues and live by their labours. In the advice to them, 'dexad las armas e leyes | a fydalgos e dotores' (ll. 2087–88) Manrique decries social ambitions: men should accept the status into which they were born. The final three stanzas are addressed to all men and are a reminder that we will all have to face a final judgement and that charity matters above all else:

> amarés vn solo Dios,
> e como queredes vos
> ser amados de verdat,
> a los próximos amad. (ll. 2111–14)

To sum up, Mena's last poem was clearly an ambitious project that went considerably beyond previous treatments of the same topic by Spanish poets. The fact that, rather than merely condemning the sins and their negative effects, he allows Voluntad to justify her actions strongly suggests that he was reflecting on what motivates human beings to follow their inclinations rather than listening to reason. Manrique enters into the spirit of the unfinished original, producing exchanges between Razón and Voluntad that are more complex and detailed and of a more abstract nature than Mena's. It should, however, be borne in mind that what Mena produced was very much a work in progress; had he lived longer he might have given more weight to Voluntad's defence (as Jerónimo de Olivares did in his continuation).[4]

Manrique reveals himself as well-read, referring to events and characters of ancient history recorded by classical authors such as Livy (ll. 1137–44) and the mythological Orpheus, made famous by Ovid in his *Metamorphoses* (l. 1210), a book included in the inventory of his library (Gómez Manrique 1885–86: II, 334). He shows that he is acquainted with Saint Augustine, another writer represented in his library (Gómez Manrique 2003: l. 1281) and holds up Saints Bernard and Martin as models of Christian behaviour (ll. 1282, 1285). A striking feature of his work is the wealth of biblical quotation in which he reveals himself to be well versed in both the Old and New Testaments. A particularly interesting technique that he uses in several instances is to allow Voluntad to use biblical references, including one apocryphal one, completely out of context in an attempt to support Voluntad's arguments.

Although Mena's poem is ostensibly about different forms of sin, Manrique shifts the emphasis of the debate in the exchange between Razón and Enbidia when he raises the question of one of the causes of envy, namely that of the fairness, or the lack of it, that human beings experience in their earthly life, where the distribution of natural talents, worldly goods and honours is concerned. This is highlighted first in the dialogue that takes place between Razón and Enbidia when the latter asks:

> Todos somos de una masa
> a la qual no tornaremos,
> ¿pues, por qué razón seremos

---

4   My edition of, and introduction to, Jerónimo de Olivares's continuation of Mena's unfinished poem can be read in *eHumanista*, 37 (2017), 458–97.

>   desiguales en la tasa?
>   (Gómez Manrique 2003: ll. 1105–08)

Razón has no very satisfactory answer to Enbidia, since all she can say is:

> Mira que todos yguales
> en este mundo venimos
> y asimesmo morimos,
> mas beuimos desiguales. (ll. 1189–92)

The same problem of the inequitable distribution of gifts is raised when Pereza, in similar vein, defends her idleness on the grounds that effort is not always justly rewarded and is told to use the free will that human beings possess (ll. 1621–24).

There is a certain irony in the fact that the complaint of Enbidia, quoted above on the subject of inequality, uses similar language reported to have been uttered by Gómez Manrique on an occasion when, according to the chronicler Fernando del Pulgar, he found himself quelling an angry crowd in Toledo and accusing them of being motivated by envy of their more prosperous and successful *converso* neighbours: 'todos somos nacidos de un padre e de una masa, e ovimos un principio noble' (Pulgar 1943: I, 348). The fact that he can use this argument in two contrasting contexts suggests that he believed in the concept of the common origins of all mankind. So why does Gómez Manrique devote a number of stanzas at the end of his continuation to society's three estates, urging them to fulfil the destiny in life to which they were born? Perhaps this is because he can find no better answer to such age-old problems as social inequality and the vagaries of fortune, themes he chooses to introduce into the debates with both Enbidia and Pereza when reflecting on what motivates men to sin. As a member of one of the most aristocratic families of Castile, he is relying here on the acceptance of the traditionally patrician attitude towards the existing social hierarchy, but there is also a certain element of self-contradiction to be found in the sentiments that he expresses. Although there is no doubt that he was proud of his descent, the above-mentioned speech to the Toledans includes a passage that reveals clearly that he believed that social boundaries were not impermeable: 'Vemos por experiencia algunos homes destos que juzgamos nacidos de baxa sangre, forzarlos su natural inclinación a dexar los oficios baxos de los padres, e aprender sciencia, e ser grandes letrados' (348).

The substance of Manrique's long continuation, underpinned by a wealth of biblical and literary allusions in the debates between Razón and Voluntad, almost without exception looks to the past for examples of good and bad conduct to be followed or avoided. As elsewhere in his writing, Manrique reminds us of Seneca's warning that life on earth is but a journey towards death (Gómez Manrique 2003: 547, ll. 1983–84) and that we should not value our material wealth since we cannot take it with us when we die (ll. 1985–92). The final three stanzas of his poem, when he reminds us that we must all face a final judgement and enjoins us to love God and our neighbour, demonstrate that his aim in completing Mena's poem was to offer a spiritual guide to the problem of sin.

CHAPTER 4

Cut and Thrust:
Preguntas y Respuestas (c. 1458–c. 1470)

Gómez Manrique's enthusiasm for engaging in debate has already been noted in Chapter 1 with his response to Torroella's *Maldezir de las mugeres*, a vigorous defence of the female sex. This enthusiasm is also reflected in the large number of verse exchanges, or *preguntas y respuestas*, in which he participated with friends and acquaintances, an activity that had become popular by the late fourteenth century. Antonio Chas Aguión charts the development of this genre from medieval Latin literature though to the French troubadours, and Galician-Portuguese and Catalan medieval poetry (Chas Aguión 2002: 59–87). A poet would send some verses containing a question and the addressee would reply using the same rhyme scheme and metre. This probably reflects in part the fact that dialogue was an essential part of medieval university education: a question was formulated to which a reply was required, thus sparking a debate. Judgement was pronounced by someone specifically appointed rather than by the votes of the participants. Debates included a wide range of topics: love, astronomy, theological questions and problems of human existence such as fortune, predestination and free will, death and the fleeting nature of earthly life. Not all who engaged in this activity, however, were learned men with a university training. There were also those considered *trobadores*, an attribute awarded to a 'skilled composer of original verse and music' (Weiss 1990: 30). In Castile, Alfonso de Villasandino (c. 1345–c. 1425) was a notable example of this class, who admitted to being unschooled but believed that poetic talent was a gift from God. He was highly praised by Juan Alfonso de Baena who declared him to be 'esmalte e luz e corona e monarca de todos los poetas e trobadores que fasta oy fueron en toda España' (Baena 1966: I, 16). Julian Weiss observes that as time passed Villasandino, who had depended on patronage, found himself challenged by court poets and those of the *letrado* class who did not rely on payment for composing their verses (Weiss 1990: 32). A feature of some of these fifteenth-century *preguntas y respuestas* was the use of insulting invective, a device used by Manrique in his exchanges with Juan de Valladolid.

Daniela Capra suggests that there came a time when the responses to these *preguntas* lost some of their originality and became rather formulaic, but that Manrique and his many correspondents revived the tradition, creating *respuestas* that were more than mere stock responses: 'logra una renovación de fómulas que ya habían perdido su valor y una recuperación del diálogo original' (Capra 1992: 185). She observes that the range of subjects they covered was narrower than that of their predecessors: 'falta en Gómez Manrique, la preocupación por algunos asuntos filosóficos o morales frecuentes en la poesía de debate medieval (meditaciones sobre la muerte, las siete virtudes, la trinidad de Dios)' (190). Manrique, with his conviction that the pen was as important as the sword and that literary pursuits should not be confined to the *letrados*, obviously felt that it was necessary for a knight to be able to engage in these poetic exchanges, as he says in his letter to Rodrigo Pimentel: 'que asý commo sería cosa vergonçosa a vn platero yr a preguntar a otro cómmo avía de bruñir vn plato, asý lo deue ser al caballero yr a preguntar a vn letrado cómmo ha de responder a vna requesta' (Gómez Manrique 2003: 103).

The exchanges in which Manrique participated cover a range of topics from the frivolous to the serious. Most of them are impossible to date, but it seems safe to assume that those concerning the well-worn themes of love and courtship were probably written when he was still a young man. In 'A vosotros los galantes', for example, Manrique asks Gueuara which quality is preferable in a woman: 'discreçión y bien hablar, | o syn graçia hermosura' (261, ll. 13–14). Addressing Diego de Rojas he asks whether he prefers a woman who is ugly but graceful, or one who is beautiful but stupid (215–16). He receives a reply that breaks free from the courtly code: 'a la fea, mal de teta | mate y mala saeta' (217, ll. 28–29). Diego de Saldaña asks Manrique's advice about competing with his master in courting a lady and receives a reply telling him not to entertain such an idea (217–20). There is humour to be found in a dialogue consisting of six nine-line verses initiated by Manrique, bearing the rubric 'A Johan de Maçuela que posaua en vn monesterio' (181–84) where the fifth verse alludes to 'las del velo' (l. 41), intimating that in fact this was a convent and Maçuela's motives were amorous rather than spiritual. In a similarly light-hearted dialogue (274–77) Manrique keeps Juan Álvarez Gato guessing as to the name of a woman he is pursuing. When his friend realizes her identity he warns against following 'los caminos y las sendas | por do sé c'os perderés' (ll. 15–16).

Another *pregunta* received by Manrique from Diego del Castillo (237–39) took the form of a riddle and reflects the interest both men had in classical literature:

> ¿Quién son aquellas feroçes conpañas,
> pregunto, si puedo, discreto señor,
> qu'en sus pequeñuelas y pobres cabañas
> fatigan sus cuerpos syn punto d'amor,
> y non disistiendo del grato sudor
> nos dan por engaño muy dulçe seruiçio,
> y por su galardón de vn tal benefiçio
> consiente justiçia quemar lo mejor. (239, ll. 17–24)

A close reading of this stanza strongly suggests that its author, about whose identity there is some disagreement (237–39n), was alluding to Book IV of Virgil's *Georgics*, a treatise on bees. That these creatures labour 'syn punto d'amor' echoes Virgil's observation that bees lack a sex life (*Georgics IV*: ll. 198–99).[1] Where Virgil tells us that they are deceived into rendering us their 'dulçe seruiçio' in the form of honey by the fumigating of the hive (ll. 228–30),[2] del Castillo uses the verb 'quemar' to suggest the injustice of their treatment. If he was testing Manrique's knowledge of Latin literature his interlocutor triumphs in his reply, showing his familiarity with the text:

> Abejas las nombran en nuestras Españas,
> sy yo non soy mal ynterpretador,
> a essas que moran en fieras montañas,
> en chicas choçuelas de sotil lauor;
> las quales nos prestan aquel gran dulçor
> del más admirable que rico hedifiçio,
> e, syn cometer otro malefiçio,
> alunbran a muchos con su esplendor. (ll. 17–24)

The 'fieras montañas' are Virgil's 'rugged rocks' (*Georgics*: IV, l. 203);[3] the bees' 'sotil lauor' is the care they take to construct the honeycomb from 'narcissus' tears and gluey gum from tree-bark as the first foundation of the comb' (ll. 160–62).[4] Virgil's description of the superior bees, 'Others gleam, and flash in splendour, their bodies all ablaze and flecked with equal drops of gold' (ll. 98–99),[5] is echoed in Manrique's final line.[6]

A very different but interesting and more serious dialogue, which is difficult to date, is addressed to Pedro de Mendoza.

Pedro de Mendoza

Scholars disagree as to the identity of this Pedro de Mendoza whom Manrique addresses in 'La ynmensa turbaçión' (Gómez Manrique 2003: 233–35). Vidal González remarks: 'Varios son los poetas que aparecen con este nombre en los manuscritos del siglo XV, todos ellos señores de Almazán' (233n). There is no clue in the text as to the date of this dialogue's composition, but Julio Rodríguez Puértolas thinks that Manrique was addressing Juan II's *guarda mayor* who was imprisoned on more than one occasion (Rodríguez Puértolas 1981: 191). José Luis Pérez López, however, claims that this Mendoza was a nephew of the marqués de Santillana and *guarda mayor* to Enrique IV. He quotes various instances of letters to Pedro from the marqués as well as references to other events at which they were both present (Pérez López 1994: 767–79). Perhaps it does not really matter which Pedro de Mendoza was the recipient of this poem, since Manrique and members of the Mendoza family lived in troubled times when strife between the nobility and the Crown

---

1 'necque concubitu indulgent, nec corpore segnes | in Venerum solvunt aut fetus nixibus edunt'.
2 'Si quando sedem augustam servataque mella | thesauris relines, prius haustu sparsas aquarum | ora fove, fumosque manu praetende sequacis.
3 'saepe etiam duris errando in cotibus'.
4 'narcissi lacrimam et lentum de cortice gluten | prima favis ponent fundamina'.
5 'elucent aliae et fulgore coruscant | ardentes auro et paribus lita corpore guttis'.
6 I am indebted to my husband for suggesting the *Georgics* as a source of this exchange.

was frequent, imprisonment being a misfortune that befell many a nobleman who found himself on the losing side. What makes this exchange interesting is the way in which a parody of a courtly love poem, using a stock metaphor, is used to convey a more serious message reflecting the turmoil of the time, and its recipient responds in a similar vein.

This poem of four *octavas* and a four-line *fin* reveal that Manrique is living through one of the many times of upheaval that he experienced during his life. The initial stanza, already quoted at the beginning of my introduction to this book, expresses regret at how his evenings are now taken up with constant patrols and vigils rather than reading, which he uses to excuse the quality of this piece. The second refers to his desire to study, 'El tiempo bien despendido | en las liberales artes' (ll. 9–10), and the third poses his question:

> quál vos es más molesta,
> vuestra secreta prisión
> o la vulgar detençión
> que vos es por el rey puesta. (ll. 21–24)

Here he juxtaposes the two concepts of 'prisión', one that is abstract, referring to Pedro's love interests, a reminder of the stock metaphor of the 'cárcel de amor' used so frequently in courtly love poetry of this period to express the supposed refinement and intensity of a poet's sentiments. It is in stark contrast to the unpleasant reality of the physical prison, the 'vulgar detençión' that Pedro is currently experiencing. In the following verse Manrique observes that although the two types of imprisonment are very different, they both deprive the prisoner of his freedom in their different ways, but that in answering his own question he would consider the gaoler when deciding which option he would choose.

Pedro opens his reply, 'Pues vos sobra la razón' (236–37), by flattering Manrique, saying that he is a man of abundant reason and urges him to overcome the inhumanity of the times. He adds that the period in which they are living is one which allows no man to sleep but, rather, spurs him into military action: 'a quien él falla durmiendo | fiérelo con las espuelas' (ll. 7–8). The order of the second and third stanzas appears to have been reversed as Pedro's third stanza both matches the rhyme scheme and, to some extent, responds to the content of Manrique's second.[7] In the former he observes that in the current circumstances everyone is taking up arms and that this must take precedence over literary pursuits: 'troquemos oy la çiençia | por roçín que bien corriere' (ll. 23–24). In the second verse Pedro puts a brave face on his suffering, saying that he finds no solace in poetry. It is in the fourth verse, in a quatrain strongly reminiscent of the hyperbole found in much courtly love poetry, that we see the element of parody in this exchange when Pedro declares:

> queriendo como querría
> estar en cárçel d'azero

---

7   This exchange between Gómez Manrique and Pedro de Mendoza is found in two manuscripts, MN24 and MP2, both of which reverse what seems to be the logical order of the second and third stanzas of Pedro de Mendoza's reply.

>   vn año, señor, más quiero,
>   que amando penar vn día. (ll. 29–32)

The despairing tone of the *fyn*, when he says that if he is writing nonsense it is 'por fallarme yo estrangero | d'esperança que tenía' (ll. 35–36), is also redolent of this genre while at the same time probably reflects his mood.

Superficially, this dialogue could be seen as just a parody of the courtly love poem, but Manrique's mention of Pedro's imprisonment imposed by the king, together with the sombre wording of his initial stanza and of Mendoza's final one, suggest otherwise. The serious tone is heightened by the mention of both men's interest in reading and study which must be sacrificed in the present circumstances. In an article on Manrique's dialogues with other poets Capra considers that this one, unlike most of his other exchanges, reveals 'una actitud paródica y satírica' (Capra 1992: 193). Manrique is certainly using the framework of a conventional *pregunta* specifically to parody the courtly love lyric while expressing his concern for Pedro's loss of freedom and his distaste for the gaoler. For his part, Pedro echoes the tone set by Manrique, agreeing that they live in difficult times and declaring that where love is concerned he will continue to follow 'la vida honesta' (Gómez Manrique 2003: 236, l. 13). Kenneth Scholberg comments on this poem, saying that it shows how 'el modo de pensar estaba influido, incluso en la vida sentimental, por los hechos políticos' (Scholberg 1971: 246n). I would argue, however, that in this instance political life is uppermost in the minds of the two poets and that their manner of expressing such concerns is influenced by the conventions of the courtly lyric that they both knew.

The Carrillo Circle

At some point after the death of the marqués de Santillana in 1458 Manrique joined the household of the Archbishop of Toledo, Alfonso Carrillo de Acuña, to head his private army. Carrillo was an immensely wealthy man who was also very involved in the political struggles of Castile and was fervently opposed to Enrique IV, partly due to the latter's appointment of men considered by many to be unsuitable for the important posts they came to occupy.

As Archbishop of Toledo, a city much afflicted by religious tensions, Carrillo also had an important role to play in trying to establish and maintain peace there. He is generally considered to have held an inclusive, Pauline attitude towards those of Jewish origin who converted to Christianity, unlike many Old Christians who resented the success of some *conversos* and were often suspicious about the sincerity of their conversion. According to the historian, Fray José de Sigüenza, Carrillo was a close associate of Alonso de Oropesa who became general of the Hieronymite order and had been moved to support the New Christians (*conversos*) following the riots in Toledo in 1449. In 1460 he was approached by some Franciscans who were concerned about Judaizers and their influence on the Christian community. Together they consorted with Enrique IV and it was decided that Oropesa would supervise an inquisition in the diocese of Toledo, something that Carrillo approved of but in which he declined to participate (Sigüenza 1907–09: I, 366–69). The conclusions that Oropesa drew and his opinions on the conflicts between Old and New Christians are the subject of a book that he had started to write in the early 1450s and was subsequently persuaded to finish after he had completed his inquisition. This book, bearing the title *Lumen ad revelationem gentium et gloria plebis Israel*, is dedicated to Carrillo.

In the opening dedicatory pages in which he summarizes the salient points of his book, Oropesa stresses the need for charity above all: 'la caridad es el estandarte propio de la religión cristiana por la que se reconocen los discípulos de Cristo' (Oropesa 1979: 61). He makes frequent references to Saint Paul, who reminds us that there is no difference between Jew and Greek, that all baptized Christians are one body united in Christ. He recalls a time when certain members of his order stirred up trouble and dissension by their attitude towards *conversos*: 'comenzaron a apremiar a los convertidos del judaísmo diciendo que no se los podía recibir a los honores y dignidades del pueblo de Dios en igualdad con los que se habían convertido de la gentilidad' (62). The purpose of his book, Oropesa says, is to fight

> contra la ignorancia de algunos fieles que vinieron de la gentilidad a la fe de Cristo, para hacerles ver más claro que todos nosotros, junto con aquellos que ingresaron a la Iglesia de Cristo desde el judaísmo, hemos de ser un solo pueblo en todo íntegro y perfecto, y unido en la fe en la caridad sin disparidad alguna. (76–77)

In fifteenth-century Castile this appears an enlightened attitude, but a further study of the work reveals that Oropesa had no wish to encourage the *convivencia* that had existed in previous centuries in the Iberian Peninsula. In fact his tolerance is limited to those who have embraced Christianity and he is aware of the dangers to which the faithful are exposing themselves when they have contact with Jews who continue to practise their faith. He quotes Saint Peter in the Acts of the Apostles in support of a policy of banning contact with the Jews: 'De aquí viene el que la Iglesia haya prohibido tan severamente a sus fieles que convivan con ellos, coman o beban; o que intentaran recibir medicinas de ello' (264). He disapproves of Jews holding any public office that would give them authority over Christians and thinks it particularly important that the newly converted should be kept away from practising Jews: 'Por tanto no debe haber contacto alguno de los judíos que han convertido a la fe con aquellos que todavía permanecen en sus antiguos ritos' (265).

What is striking about the men whom Carrillo gathered around him is that many of them, with the exception of Francisco de Noya, were New Christians. A number of them were men of letters and a literary circle came into being which followed on from that of the marqués de Santillana. The group attracted the attention of the chronicler Fernando del Pulgar who referred to its members as 'omes de facción' (Pulgar 1971: 62). One of the members of this circle was Pero Díaz de Toledo who had been chaplain to the marqués. Others associated included Juan Álvarez Gato, Pero Guillén de Segovia, Juan de Mazuela, Francisco de Noya, Rodrigo Cota, Juan de Valladolid and Antón de Montoro, all of whom except for

Montoro exchanged verses with Manrique, but were not necessarily members of the Archbishop's household. Montoro and Manrique were certainly aware of each other, as Montoro responded to Manrique's *Esclamaçión y querella de la gouernaçión*, and one of Manrique's replies to Juan de Valladolid is written 'en nombre del Ropero' (Gómez Manrique 2003: 341). In the case of Juan de Valladolid and Antón de Montoro their relationship with the circle was probably more tenuous and they are described by Carlos Moreno Hernández as 'bufones conversos más o menos esporádicos' (Moreno Hernández 1985: 46). The verse exchanges between Manrique and members of the circle cover a number of topics, ranging across moral issues, the nature of nobility, the current political climate, the writing of poetry, and questions about love. I classify these poems according to theme, at the same time giving some biographical details of the poets concerned.

Insecurity and Vulnerability

Pero Guillén de Segovia, who exchanged more verses with Manrique than any other poet, was born in 1413 and became *contador* to Carrillo in 1463. He was taken into the Archbishop's household after suffering ten difficult years, possibly for having shown support for Álvaro de Luna. He was almost certainly a *converso* since in the prose prologue to one of his poems he refers to the hard times he experienced, writing 'por industria me levante del suelo donde ya los menudos del pueblo me refollaban poniendome a las lanzas de todos' (Guillén de Segovia 1989: 135). Moreno Hernández quotes Américo Castro to explain that the 'menudos del pueblo' are the Old Christians responsible for the persecution suffered by so many New Christians and Jews in the fifteenth century (Moreno Hernández 1985: 28).

Guillén, despite having achieved a post in Carrillo's household, reveals a deep sense of insecurity regarding the society in which he lives in a poem addressed to Manrique, and although he does not actually pose a question, seems to seek advice. 'Nauegando los estremos' (Gómez Manrique 2003: 246–47), consists of four *octavas* and a *fin* of four lines. It contains a variety of metaphors in the first of which he sees his position as the commander of a fleet of ships, steering his vessels through distant waters, vulnerable to attacks from pirates. The allusion to 'bateles voluntarios' (l. 2) suggests that he has chosen what could be a dangerous course of action rather than having been forced into it. In such a situation the ships must not be allowed to drift, 'yerro es soltar los remos' (l. 3), and in deep water and with an unfavourable wind, the oars are 'petrechos nesçesarios' (l. 8). The first quatrain of the second verse refers to new laws being imposed by those who 'caçan con buharro' (l. 10), a hunting metaphor which likens those in authority to a hawk seeking out its prey, further heightening the poet's sense of insecurity. In the second quatrain Guillén returns to his metaphor of steering his ships, regretting that although he moors them in the most secure of havens, they are not completely safe: 'fengidos ayres no puros | las manzillan con su barro' (ll. 15–16). The third stanza defines those 'fengidos ayres', suggesting that Guillén sees much duplicity in the world around him. He reflects that those who speak openly are more supportive: 'mayor faze su partido | quien lo secreto reuela' (ll. 19–20). The second half of this stanza suggests an analogy with actors who are inconsistent in their style of speaking and there is a play on words when Guillén remarks that these actors, 'nin juntan filo con filo, | tanto rota va la tela' (ll. 23–24). The 'tela' is the subject matter of their speech, but it also has the meaning of 'fabric' or 'textile': here the implication is that the fabric has become so worn that it is impossible to mend it and fuse the broken threads, just as those in positions of power are inconsistent in their utterances. In the fourth verse he expresses dismay because he is unable to assess how his life will progress, but one thing that he feels sure of is that, without good fortune, virtue and diligence go unrewarded. This thought is echoed in the *Fin* when he writes:

> Non es bien fazer manida
> en fuzia de la Fortuna,
> nin es natural laguna
> la que finche el abenida. (ll. 31–35)

Manrique's reply to this poem, 'Mal daragar nos podemos' (248–49), offers little comfort to Guillén and is expressed in a forthright manner. He concurs with him as he responds to the points made in each stanza, admitting that they live in dangerous times and that it is difficult to protect themselves from their enemies. Rather than using the same metaphor of the ship being steered through dangerous waters used by Guillén, he employs the imagery of the battlefield to express the hostility that he feels around him. Their enemies are 'sagitarios' (l. 2) concealed in the 'frondas' (l. 6) who cannot be reached with the standard weaponry of 'las fondas | con cordeles hordinarios' (ll. 7–8). In the second verse, responding to Guillén's thoughts about safety, he reflects that those of humble birth fare better in guarding their flocks than kings who engage in warfare. He recalls having seen 'vn rey nauarro' (l. 13), presumably Juan II, who would rather have abandoned politics and followed the tenets of Epicureanism, dressed as a peasant in a sheepskin or 'çamarro' (l. 16) than continue fighting a difficult battle. In the third verse he remarks that there is no point in losing any sleep in such a corrupt world since those who have risen the highest fear their own downfall most, which is a way of telling Guillén that he has less to fear in his situation than others who have climbed higher in the world. In answer to the dismay expressed in Guillén's fourth stanza, Manrique suggests that holding out hopes for the distant future only inflicts more pain. He ends this verse by stating that 'firmeza', which might be translated as 'moral steadfastness', is a rule that applies to everyone and yet it is seldom rewarded. In the *Fin*, rather than alluding to Fortune, Manrique only emphasizes the fear that is felt by all in positions of power:

> Puedo dezir por finida
> que debaxo de la luna
> non sé tan firme coluna
> que non tema su cayda. (ll. 33–36)

Moral Questions

Another *pregunta* by Guillén, 'Sy el comienço de la cosa', bears the rubric 'a vn maestro en teología' (249–51). Óscar Perea Rodríguez suggests that these verses were intended for Francisco de Noya, another member of the Carrillo circle who had achieved the title of 'maestro en teología' in Paris (Perea Rodríguez 2007: 150). In this poem Guillén first asks what it is that produces virtue, whether this is an innate quality or something acquired and secondly, what prevents many people from acting in a moral way: whether the impediment to good behaviour is something that has always existed, or if it only arises in times of corruption. He develops these reflections in the third verse when he considers the manifestations of human weakness and poses several questions all of which show an underlying concern for sincerity. The fourth verse, couched in military terms, refers to 'aquellos tres enemigos' (Gómez Manrique 2003: 250, l. 30), with whom we do battle, presumably the world, the flesh and the devil, asking whether it is possible to save ourselves. The *fyn* uses the common metaphor of comparing life's journey with a sea voyage, but in this instance the focus is on the ship's cargo and the sustenance needed when the weather is unfavourable or the ship runs aground: 'Quál será la bitüalla | para que bien naviguemos' (ll. 37–38).

Manrique replies in 'Es hazaña virtuosa' (251–52) to the first question by saying that virtue is something acquired by habit and is refined over a long period of time. In answer to the second question he sees temptation as a battle between human frailty and the seven deadly sins which he also expresses in military terms:

> Los syete viçios valientes
> con humanas tentaçiones
> a desplegadas pendones
> son los duros conbatientes. (ll. 10–13)

In the fourth stanza he reflects that temptations appear to us 'con ábitos de amigos' (l. 30) and cannot be overcome purely by physical force:

> No de fuste nin de malla
> converná que nos armemos,
> mas a la carne sobralla,
> esta vençyda, syn falla
> los otros dos vençeremos. (ll. 32–36)

His allusion to 'los otros dos' in the final line of this verse refers to the world and the devil which will be overcome once the weakness of 'la carne' has been overcome. The metaphor of the navigation of a ship in the *fyn* mirrors that of Guillén when he states that we must not nourish ourselves with the 'pan de la canalla' (l. 37), presumably meaning ill-gotten gains, and that our ship must not carry any bad cargo: we must live our lives with integrity.

The *converso* Juan Álvarez Gato also participated in several verse dialogues with Manrique. He is reputed to have been knighted by Juan II, who died in 1454 and, since he would not have been knighted much before the age of twenty years, he was probably born around 1435 (Pescador del Hoyo 1972–73: 306–07). Early on in his career he served in the household of the Mendozas of Guadalajara and then, as a protégé of Beltrán de la Cueva, also a *converso*, he served Enrique IV. In 1466, however, he was moved to leave the king's service when Enrique IV connived with Juan Pacheco in an attempt to assassinate Pedro Arias Dávila, also known as Pedrarias. The latter survived the attack and Álvarez Gato subsequently entered the service of the Arias Dávila family (Márquez Villanueva 1960: 19). This incident no doubt brought him closer to the Carrillo circle who were united in their opposition to Enrique. Francisco Márquez Villanueva points to evidence that he very probably became a member of Carrillo's household, quoting from a poem written for Carrillo by Álvarez Gato 'en nombre de todos de su casa' (25). In this poem he names a number of men serving Carrillo including 'los Aluarez, amos que aqui estan presente' (Álvarez Gato 1928: 125, l. 9). Álvarez Gato later became *mayordomo* to Isabel I and was a friend of fray Hernando de Talavera, also of *converso* stock, who was confessor to Isabel and later, as Archbishop of Granada, opposed the establishment of the Inquisition.

A dialogue on a moral issue with Juan Álvarez Gato is initiated by Manrique in 'De vos, varón adornado' (Gómez Manrique 2003: 278). Having flattered his addressee in the first of two ten-line stanzas, he asks:

> ¿quáles males pueden ser
> que nos pueden bien hazer,
> y bienes que hagan mal? (ll. 8–10)

The second stanza forms a *cabo* in which he appears to be taking a moral stand, or at least paying lip service to one, by pointing out that many people state that poverty and adversity should be seen in a positive light and yet they expose themselves to danger as they seek prosperity, thus making themselves guilty of muddled thinking, or perhaps of hypocrisy.

Álvarez Gato's response of three stanzas, 'Dino de más memorado' (279–80), to Manrique's two, suggesting that the latter may have originally written another verse which has been lost, begins by reciprocating the compliments that Manrique has paid him. The second half of the first stanza reads:

> Males son bien y creçer
> que son por lo diuinal;
> el bien qu'es mal y perder
> es el que vino a caber
> en quien no busca lo tal. (ll. 6–10)

The obscurity of these five lines may be due to the constraints placed upon the poet to reply using the same rhyme scheme. The first two lines of this quotation appear to mean that what may seem to be adversity can grow into something good when it is divinely ordained, the implication being that suffering is good for the soul. In the final three lines Álvarez Gato declares that an acquisition considered as something good is in fact a loss when it is not sought. The reasoning behind this statement is again obscure, but it seems to mean that those who benefit from wealth and privilege acquired with no effort should not necessarily be considered truly fortunate. The reference in the first two lines of the second stanza to 'los sabios que loaron | las pequeñas facultades' suggests that Álvarez Gato thinks the wise are often in a minority and, together with those who do not conform to accepted opinions, have different views on the motivations or 'voluntades' (l. 15) that make men act as they do. Returning to the question of what is good and bad, he reflects that shrewd people did not fear misfortune and or even regard it as such, 'ni temieron las caýdas | ny las tomaron a veras' (ll. 17–18), taking the Stoics' attitude that virtue has its own reward: 'esforçando las vanderas | de las virtuosas vidas' (ll. 19–20). The use of the past tense here should be noted: although it may have been used to mirror the rhyme scheme of Manrique's verses, it also reflects the topos of regret for past times when people displayed greater moral integrity.

In his *Cabo* he flatters Manrique, remarking that it is folly for him to exchange verses with him, as it is 'como llevar agua al río | y pescados a la mar' (ll. 24–25), and in the final lines of this verse he also makes an appeal to his interlocutor:

> Vos, señor de noble seso,
> sanead tal entrevalo,
> pues tenés poder tan lleno,
> que harés de malo bueno
> como yo de bueno malo. (ll. 26–30)

His use of the word 'noble' here doubtless refers not to Manrique's aristocratic lineage but to his innate character: the imperative 'sanead', here used figuratively to mean 'to cleanse' or 'to purge', reveals a confidence in his ability to use his influence for the good of society. The word 'entrevalo', used in its abstract sense, signifies the gulf that exists between those 'personas arteras', referred to in the second stanza, and the others who are not guided by the same Stoic principles which embraced the belief that virtue is its own reward.[8] Álvarez Gato is therefore taking an uncompromisingly moral stand in his reply to what appears to have been an open question on Manrique's part with no obviously moral agenda. This preoccupation on the part of the Carrillo circle with questions on moral issues arises again in an exchange between Pero Guillén de Segovia and Manrique.

A Theological Question

Manrique exchanged several poems with Juan de Mazuela, a New Christian from Burgos who was probably born around 1415. He is known to have accompanied Alonso de Cartagena to the Council of Basel from 1434 to 1439 and at some time later became a priest and prior of the Hieronymite monastery of Santa María del Paso in Madrid. Both Diego de Valera and the *Crónica anónima de Enrique IV de Castilla* tell us that Mazuela was present when Enrique IV died in 1474, but was unable to elicit a final confession from him (Valera 1941: 292–93; *Crónica anónima de Enrique IV* 1991: II, 476–77). A dialogue initiated by Manrique was presumably written after Mazuela had embraced the religious life. Here Manrique demonstrates his interest in theological matters, reflecting the influence of *devotio moderna*, a religious movement that originated in northern Europe and whose influence

---

8 Covarrubias's dictionary gives the following definition of 'entrevalo': 'el impedimento o espacio que ay de un lugar a otro, o de un tiempo a otro'.

came to be felt in Spain. Devotional literature had begun to be produced in the vernacular, making it accessible to a wider readership; an example of this is López de Ayala's translation of the book of Job and Saint Gregory's *Moralia* into Spanish. Francisco López Estrada describes the movement as 'una corriente que pretende revisar la devoción y la piedad, con el objeto de hacerlas más vivas, con una mayor participación y conciencia del hecho religioso, sobre todo en el orden personal y subjetivo' (López Estrada 1979: 503).

In the first of three *octavas* of 'Pues vos vi sienpre maestro' (Gómez Manrique 2003: 221–22), Manrique questions his friend on two points: would Jesus have been incarnate if Adam had not sinned and secondly, if man's redemption depended upon Jesus's death. Mazuela's reply, 'Muncho más sé que ni muestro' (222–23) does not in fact answer Manrique's initial question, but assumes that he realizes that Adam's transgression was passed on to all mankind and shows the influence of Pauline thought:

> La razón está bien clara,
> por quanto Adán erró,
> al señor le conuinió
> mostrarnos acá su cara;
> pero tal muerte sofrir,
> esto fue por el contrario
> qu'Él la quiso reçebir
> con dolor estraordinario. (ll. 17–24)

As Vidal González comments, in answering this question Mazuela may have had Saint Paul's words to the Romans in mind: 'For as by one man's disobedience many were made sinners, so by the obedience of one shall many be made righteous' (Romans 5. 19). In his epistle to the Hebrews Paul also declares, 'without shedding of blood there is no remission' (Hebrews 9. 22).

On Writing Poetry

On the subject of verse composition Manrique initiates a dialogue with Guillén, sending him a poem of three nine-line stanzas, 'Tanto ha que no trobé' (Gómez Manrique 2003: 223–25), in which he bemoans his loss of skill. His use of concrete images in the three metaphors of this poem is interesting because it suggests that he sees writing poetry more as a practical craft rather than an abstract, intellectual activity. In the first stanza he imparts a sense of the struggle he is experiencing by saying that his efforts feel like engaging in combat with weapons that have become rusty through disuse. The result of this is that he finds it difficult to express any subtlety of thought and cannot resort to models found in well-known works: 'Las discreçiones remotas | no sufren obras fundadas' (ll. 8–9). In the second verse he uses a hunting image, drawing an analogy between the poet faced with the difficulties of poetic composition and the hawk that has lost its vital feathers, 'los cuchillos' (l. 11), that it needs in order to fly. Again he likens verse composition to a craft that requires the right tools, just as a blacksmith needs a hammer that is not broken to do his work. He finds it hard to produce any verse that is sufficiently polished and expresses his dissatisfaction with his efforts, suggesting that he will give up writing about matters of importance:

> Pues fallo botas las lima
> y las otras herramientas
> maltractadas, orinientas
> dexaré las obras primas. (ll. 16–19)

The third stanza, still more self-critical in tone, indicates that he is still struggling, referring to his script as 'estos pocos renglones | llenos de hartos borrones' (ll. 21–22), and ends with two questions. Firstly, he wants to know 'quándo congela Borea | lo que Austro desbarata' (ll. 24–25), intimating that the north wind or 'Borea' is a force that will help him to crystallize his thoughts from the chaos that has resulted from the influence of 'Austro', the warm wind from the south. The two final lines, despairing in tone, ask why an ugly woman should look at herself in a mirror, thus making this comparison with himself as he considers his own unsatisfactory attempts at writing poetry, and questioning why he should continue with his efforts.

Guillén's response, 'Yo que siempre reproué' (225–26), in this instance is blunt: the opening lines of his reply, 'Yo que siempre reproué | lo que fengido syntiese', give the impression that he senses a certain false modesty on the part of his interlocutor to which he takes exception. He is of the opinion that, once learned, the art of writing poetry is not forgotten, just as things that we learned long ago remain hidden in the deepest recesses of our memory or, as he puts it, 'cubiertas de gruesas motas' (l. 7). In the second verse Guillén offers encouragement, saying that the wise do not fear rivalry since any laurels they have gained will not wither. It is acceptable in the competitive ambience of the court that there should be tussles which he compares with the swordsmanship that men of Manrique's class would all practise, 'Y consienten las esgrimas | las espadas ser humientas' (ll. 15–16), thus using the same imagery of weapons of the original poem. The final stanza offers more reassurance and alludes to Manrique's mention of the North and South winds and their effect in his original poem. He develops this idea by reasoning that although the north wind does its work in winter, the succession of the seasons will not change, and therefore, just as 'la fea' can improve her appearance when she takes a look at herself, he implies that a time will come when Manrique too will be able to flourish again as a poet.

Álvarez Gato adds a reply of his own to this exchange, 'Yo, señor, ya lo dexé' (227–28), confessing in his first verse to having had the same problems with poetic composition: the more he tried, the harder it was. In the second verse he turns his attention to Manrique and flatters him by calling him 'el gran orador' (l. 10) and claiming that all others in comparison were mere 'grillos' (l. 11) who learn from him: 'çeváys a nuestro sabor | a los engeños çenzillos' (ll. 13–14). Continuing his flattery, Álvarez Gato uses a different, but traditional, metaphor to contrast their abilities:

> que las hondas y altas simas
> de las mares muy hiruientas

>   como temen las tormentas,
>   asý hazen las estimas. (ll. 15–18)

In other words, writing poetry can be compared with sailing over a stormy sea with success being equated with riding the crest of the waves. The nautical metaphor used in connection with poetic composition can be traced from classical writers: Ernst Curtius cites Virgil, Horace and Pliny amongst others who used it, commenting that it was extraordinarily widespread throughout the Middle Ages and survived into later times (Curtius 1979: 128–29). In the third stanza Álvarez Gato recalls Manrique's comparison between his progress, or lack of it, in his writing and the arrival of the north or south winds, but he sends a positive message. The winds are seasonal and when Acario, the warm wind of summer, is no longer so strong, the north wind makes its presence felt and enables the poet to achieve what he strives for, just as the ugly woman, when she looks at herself in the mirror, is able to achieve what she wants. In fact neither Guillén nor Álvarez Gato make make any constructive comments to Manrique on the difficulties of verse composition; their responses appear to reveal a desire to flatter and cement their relationship with him.

The Subject of Nobility in Fifteenth-Century Spain with Particular Reference to Diego de Valera

Another question raised by Manrique is that of the origins of nobility, found in verses addressed to Francisco de Noya. The fact that this *pregunta* attracted two other replies apart from de Noya's reflects that this was not just an issue that preoccupied those who were dissatisfied with the way in which Enrique IV hastened to ennoble many of his favourites, but a topic that had already interested a number of fifteenth-century writers. One such writer was Alonso de Cartagena, who in 1436 produced a *Discurso* in which he asserted that true virtue and honour were attributes that came from an individual's character irrespective of their ancestry or social background. Gregory Kaplan thinks that this work had considerable influence on other writers, observing:

> Cartagena's posture in the *Discurso* [...] did not take long to affect the ideology of contemporary *converso* prose. In the *Espejo de verdadera nobleza*, composed only a few years after the *Discurso* (most likely in 1441), Mosén Diego de Valera echoed Cartagena's conception of virtue and honour. (Kaplan 1996b: 55)

Diego de Valera was the son of a *converso* physician, born in 1412, therefore an exact contemporary of Manrique. He entered the service of Juan II in 1427 at age of fifteen as member of the Orden de los Donceles, which had a military role, and took part in the battle of Higueruela in 1431. He was armed as a knight in 1435 and acquired the title of Mosén in 1437. He travelled extensively in France and Bohemia on diplomatic missions for Juan II but was not afraid to oppose the king's favourite, Álvaro de Luna, and played a part in his downfall (Rodríguez Velasco 1996: 213–37). Although there is no evidence that Valera and Manrique ever corresponded with each other, as courtiers it was likely that they had contact, and the inventory of Manrique's library reveals that he had in his possession a volume listed as 'Uno pequeño de Mosen Diego de Valera' (Gómez Manrique 1885–86: II, 333). This book could have been the *Defensa de las mujeres*, but it might also have been another short tract, *Espejo de verdadera nobleza*, dedicated to Juan II, and perhaps written after Valera's return from his travels in Europe in 1438 (Rodríguez Velasco 1996: 223), although Michael Gerli suggests that it was written a decade later (Gerli, 1996: 23).

In the first of the eleven chapters of his treatise Valera seeks to define nobility and looks to writers such as Aristotle, Dante, Boccaccio and the fourteenth-century Italian jurist Bartolo da Sassoferrato. The first definition, supported by Aristotle and Boccaccio is that 'antiguas riquezas y heredamientos fazen al onbre noble' (Valera 1959a: 90). Secondly he refers to Boethius, Seneca and a number of the Church Fathers who think that 'antiguas buenas costumbres fasen al onbre noble, no curando de riqueza' and that these habits must be sustained over a long period of time for the person to be considered noble. Thirdly, nobility is thought by some to derive from valiant parents and grandparents. Valera has never seen this last opinion in any written form, but declares that it is a view commonly held by 'gente vulgar' (91). Sassoferrato, however, disagrees with all three definitions and thinks that there are three different kinds of nobility, theological, natural and civil, and it is on the latter that Valera concentrates his thoughts.

In his fourth chapter Valera defines this third category of nobility: 'La tercera nobleza es civil o política, por la qual es fecha cierta diferencia entre el noble y el plebeo (92). He emphasizes Sassoferrato's insistence on both the divine and legal nature of the monarch's rule: 'Ca los príncipes tienen el lugar de Dios en la tierra, e la ley tiene el lugar del príncipe' (92), subsequently quoting his definition of nobility as 'una calidad dada por el príncipe, por la qual alguno paresce ser más acepto allende los otros onestos plebeos' (92–93). Honour of this sort conferred by the prince must be deserved and Valera quotes Aristotle on the subject of the prince who ennobles the undeserving: 'El príncipe que da a los indignos muy pequeño loor gana; e el que da a los indignos, pierde lo que da e peca mortalmente' (93). He adds a truly Stoic sentiment when he reminds us that, no matter what honours are conferred on an individual, virtue is its own reward; as Seneca said, 'el fruto de las buenas obras es averlas fecho' (94). At the end of this chapter Valera emphasizes the role of the prince, declaring that Sassoferrato is convinced that even if a man were to live virtuously for a thousand years, he would still be a plebeian if not ennobled by the prince (94).

These thoughts lead Valera to reflect in his next chapter upon the origins of civil nobility where he refers to earlier ages when men shared everything on an equal footing and then to the time when malice in the world grew and men gradually became more grasping: 'quien pudo más ocupar quebrantando el derecho de la humanal conpañía, fizo suyo lo que primero de todos era' (95). Thus the least oppressive tyrants were held to be the noblest and 'los que la natura iguales crió, la malicia desiguales fizo' (95). He supports this with a reference to Aristotle, who asserted that only virtue and malice determined who was free and who was a slave.

In a reference to the story of the Tower of Babel, Valera reminds us that those who spoke the same language went on to choose their leader and that those closest to the leader 'fueron tenidos por nobles o fidalgos' (95). Afterwards many of the strongest won power, often helped by good fortune, and the weakest remained in servitude, although some of the latter rose to power, 'virtuosamente biviendo, otros por fuerça e tiranía e ayudándoles la fortuna' (95). One of those who belonged to the second category was Julius Caesar whom Valera considered 'primero de los tiranos' (97), a man of humble birth, helped by fortune to occupy the first imperial throne of the world. He mentions others who did likewise, rising from humble origins, as examples of the origins of nobility, showing that it is possible for some 'del polvo de la tierra ser levantados en soberanos honores' (97).

Still following Sassoferrato, Valera affirms that 'dignidad' and 'nobleza' are one and the same thing, a quality that is 'ayuntada a la persona, la qual le da alguna preheminencia' (98). Some who have this 'dignidad' have actual titles such as duke or count, whilst others acquire their nobility from their ancestors' reputation and retain it if they live 'honestamente' but lose it if they bring disgrace upon themselves (98). In a further chapter Valera refutes the common proverb 'puede el rey fazer cauallero, mas no fijodalgo' which he thinks is founded on 'poco saber e ciego conoscimiento', as the ignorant rarely respect true merit (100). Although he does not define the difference between 'cauallero' and 'fijodalgo' it can be inferred that the latter is someone who receives some recognition of his virtue; examples from the Old Testament are given of men of humble birth who were ennobled by a king, such as Joseph by Pharaoh. Valera ends this chapter by declaring that the king has the highest grade of nobility and that the closer a person is to the prince the higher his degree of nobility. There is a certain irony in this since he has expressed the opinion that those who hold the reins of power are descended originally from the more grasping elements of society, or from those who were favoured by fortune, and yet he adheres to the conviction that the monarch or prince is the noblest of all.

There are some issues that Valera feels he must deal with regarding the abovementioned chapter and one in particular is relevant in the context of discussing the poems written by *converso* members of the Carrillo circle. The question that he poses is whether 'los convertidos a nuestra Fe, que segunt su ley o seta eran nobles, retienen la nobleza o fidalguía después de cristianos' (101). In answer to this he argues that not only do *conversos* retain their noble status but enhance it on conversion as they then enjoy theological nobility, something from which they were barred beforehand. He has no doubt that there are nobles who live virtuous lives amongst the Jews and the Muslims and quotes Deuteronomy 4, which speaks of the nobility of the Jewish race. Reflecting on this, Valera asks:

> ¿en quál nasción tantos nobles fallarse pueden como en la de los judíos, en la qual fueron todos los profetas, todos los patriarchas e santos padres, todos los apóstoles e finalmente nuestra bien aventurada señora Sancta María, y el su bendito fijo Dios e onbre verdadero nuestro redenptor, el qual este linaje escogió para sí por el más noble [...] e por aquellas palabras que dixo: 'yo raigué en el pueblo honrrado y en los escogidos metí raízes'? (103)

He has little sympathy for the Jews who did not recognize the divinity of Christ: 'así los judíos, por sus pecados caídos en la incredulidad de nuestro Señor, merescieron todos los males en que están, de los quales sallir no pueden fasta ser por la gracia de Dios llamados' (104). He recalls, however, that the foundations of the Christian Church were laid when Jesus told Peter, himself a converted Jew, 'Tú eres Pedro, y sobre aquesta piedra la mi Iglesia fundaré' (105).

Valera introduces another chapter by recalling that the founders of the orders of knighthood had three considerations in mind when recruiting their members: the desire for the public good, the desire to reward virtue, and to provide the orders with worthy ministers and servants. Here the *ubi sunt* topos is much in evidence as he looks back at this time as if it was a golden age in which knights strove only to achieve noble and virtuous aims: 'la virtud ya los avía domado; bivían libres de esperança e de miedo; su final entención era sólo de gloria e de fama' (106). He reflects upon how different the ethos is now amongst those who seek to be knighted, as they are only interested in evading tax and gaining power and influence: 'Ya las costumbres de cavallería en robo e tiranía son reformadas; ya no curamos quánto virtuoso sea el cavallero, mas quánto abundoso sea de riquezas' (107). He is ashamed of the changes that he sees in the current ranks of knights: 'En tanta contrariedad son nuestras cosas a las primeras que remenbrarlo me fase vergüença' (107). Just as the habit does not make a monk, so gold does not make a nobleman.

The Three Replies to Gómez Manrique's Question on Nobility and Knighthood

Perhaps it was a consequence of reading Valera's treatise that Manrique decided to address a poem of six stanzas on the subject of nobility, 'No teniendo del saber' (Gómez Manrique 2003: 253–55), to Francisco de Noya, which elicits replies not just from Noya but also from Guillén and Rodrigo Cota. It is as 'maestre Françisco de Noya, maestro del muy exçelente Prínçipe de Castilla, Rey de Seçilia' that he is addressed by Manrique in the rubric to his *pregunta* from which we may conclude that it was written between 1469 and 1474. Manrique begins by emphasizing Noya's wisdom and knowledge, indulging in considerable hyperbole when he compares him with Virgil and Dante. Much of this poem is taken up with Manrique declaring his ignorance and his desire to learn, and it is significant that he prefaces his fourth stanza with the lines, 'Lo que no sope leyendo, | quiero saber preguntando', which certainly suggests that he had been reading on the subject of his question.

It is not until the end of the fourth verse that we learn what his *preguntas* are. The first is 'sy ovo reyes primero | que caualleros ouiese' (ll. 31–32), a question that is at the very core of the fifth chapter of Valera's *Espejo* where he writes about the origins of civil nobility. In the following verse he observes that the king has overall power 'en las tierras' (l. 35), presumably meaning he has absolute power where material things are concerned, but asks if this same power extends to matters that are as intangible as making a man a nobleman whatever his nature and disposition:

> dezid sy puede fazer
> de su poder ordinario
> noble de pura nobleza
> de qualquier su natural. (ll. 35–38)

Those words 'de qualquier su natural' strongly suggest that Manrique sees a failure to live up to his concept of nobility on the part of some of those he has seen ennobled, together with a realization that the granting of a title is little more than an empty gesture. In the *fin* he admits to having found varying answers to this question and hopes that Noya can finally give a satisfactory reply. This *pregunta* very probably mirrors the resentment felt by many of the old aristocracy at the creation of so many noble titles during the fifteenth century, a phenomenon illustrated by Roger Boase in his study of social change in late medieval Spain, *The Troubadour Revival*. Boase shows that no fewer than sixty-five titles of nobility were granted between 1430 and 1480 (Boase 1978: 159) and the promotion of men who neither possessed the sort of pedigree enjoyed by families such as the Manriques, nor demonstrated any inherently noble characteristics, was doubtless a cause of resentment on the part of the old aristocracy.

Not a great deal is known about the early life of Francisco de Noya but, according to Vidal González, he was born probably around 1415 and received the name of Noya due to an ecclesiastical appointment in Galicia (Gómez Manrique 2003: 252n). By October 1466 he was tutor or 'maestre de legir e de arts' to the young Fernando de Aragón and later a canon of Girona cathedral where he was a friend of Joan Margarit who wrote a manual for the education of the young Fernando which has not survived. He was known to have been linked with an Italian humanist, Antonio Geraldini, who played an important role in relations between Aragon and Rome (Perea Rodríguez 2007: 136–37), and was also sent on a diplomatic mission to Rome. He later held appointments in Sicily, first as Archdeacon of Siracuse, and from 1484 as Bishop of Cefalú.

Noya opens his reply to Manrique's question, 'Vuestro entero meresçer' (Gómez Manrique 2003: 255–56), with a declaration of humility where the subject of nobility is concerned, 'commo quien syn lumbre açierta | yré con dubda dubdosa' (ll. 7–8)', thus reciprocating Manrique's flattery and praising him for his lineage, intelligence, discretion and poetic ability. His answer to the question starts in the third stanza where he takes a theological approach, recalling the fall of Adam and referring to this time as 'Después qu'el gran padre nuestro | perdió la luz de la fe' (ll.17–18). He continues by reminding Manrique that subsequently the evil side of man's nature predominated so that mankind 'en saber fue ygualado | con las fyeras y jumentas' (ll. 23–24) and strife prevailed amongst the human race, again a thought very similar to that expressed in Valera's fifth chapter when he reminds us of the time when men lived in harmony with one another and shared everything they had. In the fourth stanza Noya makes it clear that it was the genuinely noble man, or *caballero*, who forced the people to live in peace with one another, established laws and chose a ruler to defend those less able to defend themselves. The qualities needed to effect these changes, 'seso, bondat, fortaleza' (l. 37) are the stuff of nobility: 'digo qu'el vero valer | no se da por secretario' (ll. 35–36). When demonstrated, however, they are to be rewarded with honours conferred by royalty. In his *fin* Noya admits that the state of knighthood has been established by kings, insisting:

> mas primero ovo en la gente
> nobleza, virtud y potençia
> e cauallero valiente
> que no real exçelençia. (ll. 45–48)

Thereby he stresses his belief in the difference between innate virtue and titular nobility.

The response from Guillén, 'Más tenéys a mi entender' (259–60), contains much flattery of Manrique, not only on the grounds of his knowledge and ability to express himself elegantly, but also for his diplomacy and skill in weathering the storms that he encounters in his life. He sees him as a leader of Castile when he echoes the words of the prophet Isaiah:

> Soys en tanto diestro
> qu'en la verga de Jesé
> al que toma algún siniestro
> sabéys tornar a la fe. (ll. 17–20)

There is no doubt in Guillén's mind that true nobility is not a quality that can be conferred on anyone, as he declares in the fourth stanza of his poem:

> y sabéys qu'el cauallero,
> syn tener quien le eligiese,
> vino ante y postrimero
> el rey que título diese. (ll. 29–31)

To emphasize the fact that nobility is an inherent characteristic he uses a comparison: base metal cannot be transformed into anything else 'porqu'en su primero ser | quedará de necesario' (ll. 35–36). The opposition to Enrique IV is obvious in the fifth verse with the declaration 'así no puede vileza | gozar de sangre real' (ll. 37–38). The final stanza of this poem reiterates the praise of Manrique and ends on a humble note with Guillén asking him to correct him if in any way he has made any omissions in his poem.

Rodrigo Cota also chose to respond to Manrique's question about nobility. A *converso* from Toledo, Cota is better known as the author of the dramatic poem *Diálogo entre el amor y un viejo* and his name has been put forward as the author of the first act of *La Celestina*.[9] He also wrote a highly satirical epithalamium out of pique when not invited to the wedding of a member of the Arias Dávila family who married a Mendoza. Although the Cota family occupied important positions in Toledo they also suffered much persecution. Rodrigo's father, Alonso, was treasurer of the city and in 1449 found himself pressurized by Álvaro de Luna into raising a tax to support Juan II's troops against the Aragonese who had invaded Castile. When the citizens rebelled against this imposition, Alonso became a target of the citizens' anger which was doubtless exacerbated by the fact of his ethnic origins and, although he survived, his house was burnt down (Cantera Burgos 1970: 10). Rodrigo and several members of the family were later to fall foul of the Inquisition (59–65).

---

9 Both Dorothy Severin (2017: 15) and Peter Russell (2007: 30–33) think it plausible that Cota wrote the first act of *La Celestina*.

In the initial stanza of his response, 'Al son del dulçe tañer' (Gómez Manrique 2003: 257–58), Cota, like the other participants in these exchanges, assumes a certain modesty, referring to 'mi torpe lengua' (l. 6) as he explains that he is inspired to write his own reply. He makes a comparison between the writing of poetry and the composing of music, observing that in making music there are some people who will strike a discordant note so that their audience may hear them and this is what he is doing in this poem. He concurs with Noya and Guillén in thinking that there were knights before kings, but that the title of knight presupposes the existence of a king to confer such a title. In the fifth stanza Cota makes plain that the quality of nobility is inherent, a 'don tan esençial' (l. 37), and not something that can be acquired from any monarch, however exalted he or she may be. In addition, the final two lines of this verse also touch on the subject of royal blood just as Pero Guillén's response does, with Cota stating that holding the royal sceptre does not dispel any of the baser traits of character in a monarch: 'ni la yngrata vileza | alinpia el çetro real' (ll. 39–40), lines that surely reflect the poet's feelings of contempt for Enrique IV.

Despite the lyrical introduction of Cota's poem, with its allusion to the 'son del dulçe tañer' in the first line, the overall tone soon becomes sombre. Manrique's *pregunta* is compared with a 'boz en cuesta riscosa' in the final line of the first stanza, suggesting that the question posed is controversial and that Manrique's opinion on the subject goes against much current thinking and is even potentially dangerous. In his third stanza Cota explains why he is choosing to make this type of reply which in the previous verse he has already admitted as discordant:

> De aqueste yerro siniestro
> que aquí no me guardé,
> algunt juÿzio muy diestro
> me pueden notar. (ll. 17–20)

The antithesis he uses in the rhyme of 'siniestro' with 'diestro' emphasizes that the point he wishes to make may be unpopular but he is confident that his own judgement is shrewd.

The second half of this third stanza deserves close attention since Cota declares that he is contributing to this debate uninvited 'entre dos tales afrentas, | fablando commo burlado' (l. 22), which indicates that he has some reason to feel aggrieved, perhaps suffering some insult or discrimination on account of his Jewish ancestry. There is no further explanation as to what has occurred, but some of the events that took place in Cota's lifetime might well throw some light upon these lines. If we assume that Cota was born between 1430 and 1440 (Cantera Burgos 1970: 21), he would have been very much aware of the events of 1449, the year of the Toledo riots and the declaration of the *Sentencia-Estatuto* which banned all New Christians from holding office in the city. In September that year Pope Nicholas V issued a bull, *Humanis generis inimicus*, that condemned the exclusion of New Christians from official posts on the grounds of their racial origins. Another bull of the same date excommunicated Sarmiento, the ringleader of the Old Christians who had fomented the hostility towards New Christians which led to the implementation of the *Sentencia-Estatuto*. Since Castile was in a state of civil war, the Crown was desirous of keeping and obtaining as many influential allies as possible. Juan II therefore thought it expedient to ask the Pope to suspend the excommunication of those who were practising racial discrimination and in 1451 Juan gave his approval to the *Sentencia-Estatuto*. A further victory for the Old Christians occurred in 1468, a year after more riots in Toledo, when Enrique IV confirmed the positions in the city of all the Old Christians holding offices previously occupied by *conversos* (Kamen 1985: 26–27). By this time Cota would have been an adult, no doubt with vivid memories of two incidents that must have been traumatic for his family and may well explain his allusion to the 'dos tales afrentas'. In the same year Carrillo condemned guilds in the city that had been created along racial lines, a move that doubtless would have been welcomed by members of his circle.

In spite of this underlying conflict, Cota's poem ends conventionally enough. His excuse of 'palabras no muy atentas' (Gómez Manrique 2003: 258, l. 24) can be taken as an indication of the self-effacing modesty which he feels obliged to express like his contemporaries and is reiterated in the final stanza where he returns to the comparison between music and poetry and refers to his poetic voice as 'mi çençerro quebrado' (l. 43). These protestations of modesty concerning the quality of his verse and the sentiments he expresses also serve to underline that he is speaking out independently. The second quatrain of this verse is apologetic, alluding to his 'seso ynprudente' and his 'lengua ynsapiente'. This reminder of his own imprudence is made more emphatic by the use of antithesis to make a contrast between his 'vana demençia' and the 'gran prudençia' of Manrique which at the same time is flattering to the latter.

Juan Álvarez Gato on the Subject of Nobility

Even though there is no evidence that he participated in this discussion about nobility, one of Manrique's poetic correspondents previously mentioned in this chapter, Juan Álvarez Gato, would almost certainly have concurred with what Noya, Cota and Guillén say in their responses. Indeed, his writing in both prose and verse reveals a more radical and developed attitude to the issue of nobility and inclusiveness than is demonstrated by these three respondents, who do little more than scratch the surface of this topic. As a *converso* he believed that all Christians were equal regardless of rank or lineage, and he makes this clear in the preface to one of his religious poems:

> Al pie dun cruçifiçio questa en Medina sobre vna pared hecha de huesos de defuntos, puso esta copla para que veamos claramente como somos todos duna masa, y que essos deuen ser auidos por mejores, que touieron mas virtudes, pus que linaje, dispusiçión y fama y rriquezas todo pereçe. (Álvarez Gato 1928: 136)

In another poem, of more than a hundred lines, he defends a certain 'moço despuelas' in the service of Alonso de Velasco, who had written some *coplas* in praise of Hernán Mexía and Álvarez Gato. The fact that some people took a negative view of Mexía's praise of the groom's literary efforts inspired Álvarez Gato to speak out, not just in defence of Mondragón, the groom, but of those of humble birth whose virtues and merits should be recognized. The opening lines of this poem read:

> Cualquier noble costunbre
> en la vida que tenemos,
> la pobreza y seruidunbre
> no le dexa arder su lunbre. (102)

There follows a condemnation of those who engage in hypocritical flattery of the rich and, in the rubric to another stanza, of the tendency to 'pregonar virtud del grande o del rrico, avnque no la tenga' (105). In the penultimate verse he speaks of both Antón de Montoro and Mondragón as he warns against the worship of gold, worldly wealth and discrimination on the grounds of birth. Of Montoro he says:

> sy bien obra el de Montoro,
> avnque pobre de tesoro
> ténganle por rrico mucho. (106, ll. 11–13)

Of Mondragón he remarks, 'sy discreto es Mondragón, | no curemos dell espuela' (ll. 17–18). In other words, Montoro's wealth lay in his talent and Mondragón's humble station in life should not detract from our appreciation of his gifts. Álvarez Gato also wrote a *prohemio* to accompany the poem for Hernán Mexía, explaining that the purpose of writing these verses was to emphasize that we should be aware of virtue when we see it and be unbiased in our acknowledgement of it, so that we should not 'atribuyr virtud o discriçión al fauoreçido o al rrico, sy no la alcança, y negalla al corrido y cuytado del pobre sy la tiene' (166–67). He cites Seneca as a model in his contention that he did not judge people on account of their outward appearance, and also reminds Mexía of the circumstances of Christ's birth: 'nuestro Redentor y Salvador [...] quiso naçer en vna pobreçilla cueva y morar en esta vida él y su bendita Madre, syn tener donde meter la cabeça, más miserablemente que ninguno' (167). He concludes with an allusion to Mondragón, saying that it is shameful that this 'fortunado y pobre varón' should be denied the praise he deserves (168).

Gómez Manrique and Juan de Valladolid on Writing Poetry

While Mondragón was fortunate to find a defender of his verse in the person of Álvarez Gato, Juan de Valladolid, yet another of Manrique's poetic interlocutors, was the subject of much negative banter and criticism. His connection with the Carrillo circle is somewhat tenuous and there is only one poem by him addressed to Manrique, but eight compositions to him by Manrique survive. Since these poems are so different in tone and content from those already discussed, I devote a separate section to them. They are of interest because they reveal some of Manrique's thoughts on the subject of writing poetry together with an ambivalent attitude towards other writers who do not originate from his social milieu. Juan Poeta, as he was also known by some, was probably born in the early 1400s in Valladolid, the son of a town crier (Montoro 1990: 130). His mother was a maidservant at an inn, according to Manrique, Antón de Montoro and Suero de Ribera. As Lorenzo Rubio González says, 'nuestro poeta fue hijo de un matrimonio de ínfima condición social y de indudable mala reputación' (Rubio González 1984: 102). Although a *converso*, we do not know whether he converted to Christianity or if his parents had already done so. He led a nomadic sort of life: Marithelma Costa lists five distinct phases, the first of which finds him in Palermo, at that time part of the kingdom of Aragon, where he worked in the customs and also as a bookbinder from approximately 1422 to 1444. Some years were spent in an itinerant lifestyle in Castile, Navarre and Italy, but by 1453 he was in Castile at the court of Juan II when he wrote a poem on the downfall of Álvaro de Luna. It seems likely that in 1455 he went to Córdoba with Juan Pacheco, marqués de Villena. Thereafter he was found in Italy, in the cities of Ferrara, Mantua and Milan before he returned to Valencia in 1470 to attend the *indulgencia general* offered by Pope Paul II (Costa 2000: 34–35). Archival research has revealed that Juan's presence was valued in Italy, where Alfonso el Magnánimo was pleased to employ him in Palermo in 1434 and offered a rise in salary when Juan returned to Sicily in 1444 (Conde Solares 2009: 40–41). In addition, he appeared in Ferrara in 1458 with a letter of recommendation from Borso d'Este to Luis Gonzaga that refers to him as a 'cortegiano del Re de Navarra' (45). In Spain his fortunes were more varied, but he was nevertheless a beneficiary of the downfall of Carlos de Viana in 1460 when he was accorded the sum of 1300 *libras*, dues which formerly had been paid to the prince (45).

Apart from the poem addressed to Manrique only seven others by Juan de Valladolid survive. Perhaps one of the best is on the death of Álvaro de Luna (ID0187, Dutton 1990–91: III, 434), composed in 1453, by which time Juan had returned to Castile and appears to have been at the court of Juan II. The poem consists of four stanzas each of eight lines and a four-line *cabo*, each stanza treating a different aspect of this momentous event. Addressing Luna in the first verse, Juan reflects on the extraordinary suddenness of the *condestable*'s downfall after such a spectacular rise to power. Thereafter the tone is moral, expressing the satisfaction of all people that justice has been meted out to a dishonest tyrant who had so overreached himself that he exercised more power than the king: 'tirano, quería robar, | y mandar más que no el rey' (ll. 21–22). The third stanza speaks of the temptations which Luna was unable to resist and of the vainglory, avarice and envy which brought about the ruin of so many citizens. Juan declares that the king was guided by God to imprison Luna and subsequently to condemn him to death. The *cabo* expresses gladness that Juan II is now effectively the monarch since he has freed himself of the influence of Luna, and he urges everyone to pay homage to him:

> Agora eres tú el rey
> magnífico & soberano
> agora cumples la ley;
> bésente todos la mano. (ll. 34–37)

Juan de Valladolid demonstrated that he was also capable of writing in typically courtly mode when he addressed two poems to the infanta María, expressing his admiration for her in the opening lines of one of these:

> No veros mes osadia
> de mis cuytas dezir

> y veros gran couardia
> y mas amar y sofrir. (ID2302, Dutton 1990–91: I, 350)

Finally, a poem bearing the rubric *Coplas de juan de valladolid o juan poeta porque vn cauallero le dio vn sayo de seda chico* (ID6768: V, 526) reveals a different aspect of his poetic ability where he develops a witty play on the word 'sayo' in response to a poem from a nobleman who sent a Jewish servant to present him with the gift of a tunic or 'sayo', saying that he and the servant would understand each other because they spoke the same language. Juan's poem is actually addressed to the 'sayo' itself and, aware of the racial overtones of the message he has received, he says, 'Vos no soys sayo ni saya | tajo francés ni morisco' (ll. 1–2). The word 'sayo' is also found in the expression 'cortarle un sayo a alguien' meaning to gossip about someone in their absence and is used in this sense in the second half of the poem, 'no sé cómo soys cortada' (l. 6), suggesting that Juan seems to want to disregard this insult and snub its sender when he says in the final lines, 'soys embiada por mote | pese atal que no soys nada' (ll. 7–8).

The style of writing in the above-mentioned poem resembles that adopted by Manrique in the verses he sends Juan de Valladolid. We cannot date these poems with any certainty, but 'Eres para loco frío' (Gómez Manrique 2003: 329–31) might come fairly early on in this sequence. It contains a mixture of racist abuse concerning Juan's Jewish ancestry, accusations of plagiarism, and negative comments on the quality of his work, together with allegations of a mercenary attitude, most of which are developed more fully in other poems. The very rubric, 'De Gómez Manrique a mosén Juan, truhán del señor Conde de Treviño, su ermano', is insulting with the epithet 'truhán' and is sarcastic in tone, since the title *mosén* was used to address members of the nobility. The use of the adjective 'loco' in the first line, however, should not be taken literally in the modern sense, as Juan was almost certainly a 'fool' in the sense of a court jester; he is also described as 'loco de quebrada' (l. 17), suggesting that he was itinerant, travelling over mountainous terrain and through ravines or 'quebradas'. There is an implication that Juan takes a roundabout route on his travels to obtain more money: 'porque te fagan el gasto | rodeas vna jornada' (ll. 19–20), followed by an accusation of avarice: 'Eres tornado correo', 'correo' meaning a 'money-bag'. That Juan is a 'muradal de los locos' (l. 26), is a further insult, since the 'muradal' was the wall outside the town where refuse was left; he is a social outcast living on the margin of society, certainly unworthy of the title *mosén*.

In four out of the poem's five stanzas there are slurs about, or allusions to, Juan's Jewish origins, some of them concerning his physical appearance: 'tienes el cuerpo de taco | la presençia de judío' (ll. 3–4) and his 'crespilla de muça, | la nariz de maestre Yuça' (ll. 10–11). In each stanza there is also criticism of either plagiarism or the quality of his poetry. In Manrique's opinion poetry must contain elegant and witty turns of phrase, or 'donayres', a word that occurs twice in this poem (ll. 15, 27). This is something that Juan rarely achieves, and when he does so his 'donayres' are lacking in originality. In a piece of extreme exaggeration, Manrique claims that Juan is only capable of producing witticisms at the time of the *jubileo*, a

Jewish festival celebrated every fifty years. His wittiest verses are at the expense of his patron, but worse still, he steals ideas from other poets:

> Eres traydor espía
> enxerido en albardán;
> nunca dizes conquerría
> syno motes que te dan. (ll. 21–24)

The implication here is that Juan insinuates himself into gatherings as a jester while noting the verses of other performers present. The fact that these allegations of plagiarism are repeatedly juxtaposed with reminders about Juan's ethnic origins leads us to surmise that plagiarism and poor quality verses are inextricably linked in Manrique's mind with Jewish origins. The lines 'No curas de capirote, | a la guisa de Judea' (ll. 13–14) are particularly telling when they immediately precede the comment 'tus donayres son de bote, | no ninguno de bolea'. According to Jeanne Battesti-Pelegrin, the word 'capirote' has various meanings, one of which she gives as 'capuche qui coiffe le docteur, le poète couronné' [a hood worn by a doctor and crowned poet] and another as 'métaphore du circoncis' (Battesti-Pelegrin 1990: 245). Here Manrique is cleverly using the two meanings of this word to express how the low quality of Juan's poetry is linked to his ethnicity, while at the same time demonstrating that he is able to produce witticisms in his verses at Juan's expense. In addition, the notion of Juan being a 'traydor espía' (Gómez Manrique 2003: 330) where poetry is concerned is developed in the next stanza when he is accused of being 'torrnado' (l. 25), implying an ambivalence in his religious allegiance. Manrique is happy for Juan to return to the Jewish faith, but he should work to merit what he is paid: 'pues primero sudas bien | aquello que se te da' (ll. 35–36). He is therefore a traitor on two counts, as a poet who appropriates the verses of others and passes them off as his own, and as an apostate who has abandoned his religion for financial gain.

The notion that the production of good poetry is the preserve of the educated nobility is reflected in 'Poeta de la nobleza' (332–34), four stanzas entitled 'Otras a el mesmo sobre convenençia que al que mejor demandase le diese el otro'. The poem is a sustained and cleverly developed insult based on the fact that he has become known as 'Juan Poeta'. The use of this moniker is highly ironic since the term *poeta* is one of praise as Santillana writes in *Prohemio e carta*:

> passaremos a Miçer Françisco Imperial, al qual yo no llamaría dezidor o trobador, mas poeta, como sea çierto si alguno en estas partes del Occaso meresçió premio de aquel triunphal e laurea guirlanda, loando a todos los otros, este fue. (Santillana 2003: 93–94)

Julian Weiss suggests that the term *poeta* implied greater erudition: 'With the examples of Dante and Jean de Meun before them, vernacular writers throughout Europe began to emulate the concept of the philosophical poet, embodied by the term *poeta*' (Weiss 1990: 14).

By addressing Juan as 'Poeta de la nobleza | e de pura hidalguía' in the opening lines of the above-mentioned poem Manrique demonstrates an arrogantly patrician attitude. Feeling that Juan is not worthy of the status of *poeta* and knowing full well that he is a man of humble birth, he taunts him, saying that he himself has so much 'hidalguía' that he could give half of it to Juan in exchange for money. He suggests that men like Juan will not go far in the world: 'pues al hidalgo syn raça [...] | no le dan pan en la plaça' (Gómez Manrique 2003: 332, 333, ll. 6, 10). The hyperbole used in the second stanza is striking since he compares the desire he feels to ask a question of Juan to the hunger that drives an eagle to accept food from someone's hand. The analogy between the king of birds swooping low to satisfy its hunger and the noble Manrique demeaning himself to beg for information from a low-born rival heightens our expectations of the question to be asked. In the third stanza he makes two more exaggerated comparisons, in one of which he sees himself driven by the same necessity as the workmen who are forced to earn their living by breaking stones. The second analogy is with the 'hambrientos ventores' (l. 24), presumably Jewish tradesmen, who are forced to take a pig to satisfy their hunger, apparently in spite of the Jewish taboo on the consumption of pork. Manrique declares at the end of this verse that he is humbling himself by knocking at the door of the enemy, an indication of his resentment at the thought of upstarts such as Juan de Valladolid insinuating themselves into social and literary circles where they do not belong. There is added irony in the way he uses the title 'mosén', normally reserved for aristocrats, when addressing Juan in stanza II, as there is also in stanza III when he calls him 'poeta muy elegante' (l. 27).

In the fourth and final stanza he returns to the comparison that he made between himself and an eagle when he refers to their different 'plumajes' (l. 34) to explain why he wants to question Juan. He extends the analogy he has already made in the second stanza by using a hunting metaphor, 'vengo de neblís' (l. 37), a 'neblí' being a type of falcon and the 'capirote' he wears can therefore be understood as the leather cap worn by the falcon when out hawking. As already stated, however, the 'capirote' also denotes poetic or academic achievement, which Manrique considers that he possesses, unlike Juan. A third meaning of this word is implied when Juan is told 'yo sufro capirote [...] | el qual vos, Juan, no sofrís', since Manrique is reminding Juan of his Jewish heritage and that he has been circumcised. It is not until the last two lines of the poem that we finally read the question to be put to Juan. The word *poeta*, used in the first line, recurs in the question: 'dezidme lo que sentís, | poeta, con este mote' (ll. 39–40), 'mote' meaning here a 'nickname'. Thus Manrique takes four stanzas, full of insults, to lead up to a question which turns out to be yet another insult.

A further poem of Manrique's to Juan de Valladolid, 'Sy de vuestra detençión' (334–36), alludes to his capture by Muslim pirates, possibly on his way to the Holy Land as a pilgrim. Lorenzo Rubio González suggests that this poem dates to around 1470, the purpose of Juan's journey being to prove his Christian credentials (Rubio González 1984: 105). Although Rubio González does not say as much, it might be assumed that this was in response to the hail of abuse that Juan received from the conde de Paredes on the subject of his presence at the *indulgencia general* in Valencia that year. The tone of the poem, entitled 'Otras trobas de Gómez Manrique a Juan Poeta quando le catiuaron los moros de allende', is mocking, as Juan is again addressed as *poeta* in the rubric (Gómez Manrique 2003: 334). In the first stanza

Manrique offers scant sympathy at Juan's plight, leaving him in little doubt as to his reaction on hearing of Juan's capture:

> vos lo podréys conoçer
> judgando por la razón
> y no por el parentesco
> caronal. (ll. 3–6)

At issue is the difference between Manrique and Juan, that of the Old and New Christian, described as 'çeçial' and 'fresco' (ll. 7–8) respectively. The wording of the second stanza encapsulates their difference in Manrique's view:

> Poeta, vos soys nouiçio,
> que quiere dezir confeso;
> yo soy antiguo profeso,
> hidalgo desde abeniçio. (ll. 9–12)

Juan is a 'confeso' meaning convert and also a 'noviçio'. The use of the word 'noviçio' here is significant: its religious connotations reflect his supposed conversion to Christianity, and its meaning of a 'beginner' reinforces Manrique's judgement of him as an unskilled poet. In contrast, Manrique identifies himself as 'antiguo profeso, | hidalgo desde abeniçio' (ll. 11–12), meaning Old Christian.

There is, however, a patronizing attempt to offer friendship to Juan by awarding him the accolade of *trobador*, emphasized by its appearance in the *pie quebrado* of line 16. Manrique doubtless considered himself a *poeta* but, having used the term ironically in addressing Juan, cannot use it of himself. These three issues of race, nobility and status in the world of the poet are all raised in this stanza and are inextricably linked for Manrique, so that he is either unwilling or unable to separate them one from another. This faint praise accorded to Juan is short-lived, as in the third stanza Manrique proceeds to insult him, reminding him, once more, that he is 'syn capirote' (l. 17). This insult is followed by pejorative comments on his poetic style which is lacking in originality and inspiration: 'no trobáys boleos, | saluo las trobas de bote' (ll. 19–20), a remark similar to those found in the poem addressed to 'mosén Juan, truhán del señor Conde de Treviño' (329–31) already discussed.

In this poem, however, Manrique goes further and puts forward the view that good poetry depends not only on originality and good breeding but also on the poet's ability to learn the craft of writing. Here he again uses the imagery of the tool used by an artisan to practise his trade in order to produce artefacts of beauty, as he does when addressing Guillén de Segovia, but he declares that Juan's verses are created using a hatchet or 'destral' rather than being elegantly fashioned with a 'lima' or file (ll. 21, 23–24). The aristocratic poet with a high opinion of his own work, however, sees this as a reason not to consider Juan as a rival as he considers his work to be trite: 'Y porque son de almazén | vuestras trobas' (ll. 25–26), and condescendingly remarks:

> Ca no fazen ningún daño
> a las mías [trobas],
> porque son gruesas y frías
> y d'estaño. (ll. 29–32)

The suggestion that Juan's verses, like objects made of cheap tin, are 'frías' is because to craft any fine artefact from metal requires heat, a comment that now explains the opening line of the first poem discussed in this section, 'Eres loco para frío' (329), that his poems are 'gruesas' implies a lack of finesse. There is another barb in the final verse of the poem when Manrique expresses regret that Juan was captured by Muslims and not by Jews because, as a renegade, he would have been amused to reacquaint himself with the practices of his youth: 'conoçiérades el ayre | de pequeño' (ll. 47–48).

Juan responds to these criticisms in the one poem that we know he addressed to Manrique, 'En loarnos syn mudança' (336–38), the rubric telling us that it was sent from Aragon. It is noticeable how in this poem Juan makes no effort to defend the quality of his verses but reacts strongly to the anti-Semitic comments. It is reminiscent of Antón de Montoro's verses which bear the title 'Montoro sobre concierto de monte a don Pedro de Aguilar' (Montoro 1990: 124) since he too explores the implications of participating in an excursion to hunt wild boar, an activity that would have been forbidden to both Jewish poets' ancestors. Montoro, never one to try to hide his ethnic origin, shows an awareness of how strongly the religious observances of his ancestors have been inculcated in him and contribute to the mixed feelings he has about accepting such an invitation, saying, 'yo me veo entre dos fuegos' (l. 4). He explains that if he shunned this event he would be considered a coward, a criticism often levelled against the Jews, and also a beggar, presumably because the 'mendigos' of this world were not accustomed to hunt. On the other hand, if he were to kill a pig, the reaction of his companions would be 'que maté a mi enemigo' (l. 8). This suggests they would consider his conversion complete and reveals how much importance was attached to such actions, indicating a public acceptance of Old Christian behaviour.

This explains, perhaps, why Juan, in contrast, is so eager to participate in such a hunt. His motives are twofold: he wants to cast off his Jewish heritage and at the same time find a way into the higher echelons of society. In the opening verse he challenges Manrique's conviction that as the son of a poor man of lowly origins he cannot engage in the aristocratic pursuit of hunting. In effect he is challenging the exclusivity of the aristocratic poet by saying that it is possible to be upwardly mobile and that nurture has a vital part to play in the making of a nobleman: 'con la notable criança, | el vil se haze hidalgo' (Gómez Manrique 2003: 336). His vivid description of the hunt, with the vigorous way in which he pursued his quarry, is calculated to impress those sceptical of his true conversion. Even more shocking to practising Jews is his account of how, having wounded the mother pig, he takes two piglets and shuts them in the synagogue. When challenged about his behaviour, he reminds his critics of the golden image of a calf that the children of Israel took to worshipping when they thought that Moses had deserted them in the wilderness and suggests that the two piglets be sacrificed in the way that Abraham sacrificed a ram that he was offered instead of his son Isaac. Furthermore, in the final stanza he suggests that God might well say, 'que no los mates del todo' (l. 55).

'Con tormenta nin bonança' (339–41), is Manrique's response to the poem just discussed. He remains unconvinced by Juan's arguments, seeing his participation in the pig-hunt as an example of the world turned upside down, although one of his jibes, 'de venados matador | vedados en el Atora' (ll. 9–10), shows an ignorance of Jewish law. In the second stanza he suggests that Juan's experience of hunting is so limited that he could not even recognize his quarry. The tone of the poem becomes darker when he regrets the fact that Juan has disobeyed the law of the Old Testament, making a comparison between Juan and 'el que murió con la soga' (l. 32), a reference to Judas Iscariot. As in previous poems to Juan, Manrique juxtaposes a statement about his ethnicity with a criticism of his style of writing: he is a 'poeta no mantüano', not to be compared with Virgil (l. 51). He continues: 'no judío ni christiano, | mas exçelente marrano' (ll. 53–54), thus leaving us in no doubt that he considers Juan to be a Judaizer and not a sincere Christian. The final lines of the last stanza remind us of the initial verse in their allusion to the chaotic state of the world turned upside down: Juan is accused of creating chaos, not just by renouncing the faith of his forebears, but in an allusion to Luke's gospel his race is deemed responsible for the betrayal of Christ: 'porque vendistes a Dios, | segunt Lucas lo deuisa' (ll. 59–60).

Manrique varies his manner of criticizing Juan in 'Señor Marqués de Villena' whose rubric reads 'De Gómez Manrique en nonbre del Ropero, contra Iohan Poeta' (341–45). El Ropero was the nickname of the *converso* poet Antón de Montoro, a contemporary of both Juan de Valladolid and Manrique and considered to have been linked to the Carrillo circle. Unlike most converts to Christianity, Montoro made no secret of his racial origins but, as I have already demonstrated when discussing his poem 'Montoro sobre concierto de monte a don Pedro de Aguilar', he often felt ill at ease among the Old Christian community despite his many protestations of the sincerity of his conversion. He and Juan de Valladolid exchanged verses over a period of twenty years, which may explain why Manrique chose to join in the literary tussle between the two writers in support of Montoro. The first line of the poem, 'Señor Marqués de Villena' shows that this piece is intended for the marqués de Villena, otherwise known as Juan Pacheco, an ambitious and duplicitous man who wielded great influence over Enrique IV. Pacheco was also a nephew of Archbishop Carrillo and sought to be on good terms with his uncle and the Manrique family, sometimes conniving with them in opposition to the king when he felt it was in his own interests to do so. Montoro lived in or near Córdoba for most of his life and it has been suggested that this poem was written in 1455 when Pacheco visited Córdoba accompanied by Juan de Valladolid, possibly for the betrothal of Enrique IV to Juana of Portugal (Rubio González 1984: 104).

Most of the charges that Manrique makes against Juan de Valladolid have already been discussed, but in this poem he adds to the criticisms he has already made on the subject of his poetic style. Mindful of the need to conform to the rules of good practice in verse composition, he now maintains that Juan does not know about rhythm and scansion, something he has not mentioned hitherto: 'Él no sabe qué es açento, | no ditongo ni mancobre' (Gómez Manrique 2003: 342, ll. 11–12). In the *Diccionario crítico etimológico castellano e hispano*, compiled by Joan Corominas and José Antonio Pascual, the word 'mancobre' is defined as 'composición poética caracterizada por jugar con varias formas de un mismo verbo o de otras palabras' (342n). Corominas and Pascual refer to Gómez Manrique's use of the word in this poem (Corominas and Pascual 1954: III, 831). Clearly Manrique thought that Juan was not capable of writing verses that contained the witty and multiple layers of meaning that were appreciated at court by the higher echelons of society, and considered that he owed his success in these quarters to his ability to recite, his 'habla podcrosa' (Gómez Manrique 2003: 342, l. 17) that made such a great impression on his audiences: 'Qu'el tono de su eloquençia, | [...] | engaña qualquier prudençia' (ll. 21, 24). It is probably the difference between the talent as a performer which Juan must have possessed, making him a rival to Montoro, and the ability to write good verse, so highly prized by the educated classes, which spurs Manrique on to making his criticisms of Juan de Valladolid since they belong to two separate traditions, those of the cultivated aristocrat and the peripatetic minstrel. Marithelma Costa expresses this idea when she writes, 'Más que al oficio del poeta — o el individuo que se maneja dentro de la palabra escrita [...] — Juan de Valladolid se vinculaba a la memorizada, improvisada y leída' (Costa 2000: 18). His praise for the way in which Juan is able to recite his verses gives Manrique the opportunity to engage in further denigrating observations about Montoro's rival, reminding us of the humble occupation of his father, a town crier who, he says, knew more about 'pregonar' (l. 26) than his son does about 'conponer' (Gómez Manrique 2003: 343). He then casts a slur on Juan's mother by calling her a whore (l. 28). Manrique does not stoop quite so low elsewhere in his verses, but since he is writing in Montoro's name, he imitates the type of insult that Montoro sometimes makes when abusing his rivals.

Since Montoro was himself of Jewish origin, Manrique cannot in this instance use racial slurs to insult Juan in the same way as he does when he writes in his own name. The only reference to his physical appearance is when he remarks on Juan's curly hair and calls him 'este crespo trauado' (l. 36). He would, however, have been aware that Montoro frequently proclaimed his Christian faith and this enables him to cast doubts on Juan's *converso* status. Having alluded to him as 'Juan Vellaco' in the first stanza (l. 6), he implies that it is inadvisable to offer him hospitality in his house and issues a warning, 'que cuyde ser otro Judas' (l. 40), which is reminiscent of the condemnation made in his reply to Juan: 'Pues soys de aquel origo | del que murió con la soga' (340, ll. 31–32). The reference to the link between nobility and literary ability is made more obliquely in stanza VI as Montoro, being a New Christian, could not insult a fellow *converso* in this way. Instead Manrique makes Montoro suggest that should Pacheco wish to grant any favour to Juan, having taken him under his wing, he can give him a coat of arms with an emblem of a toad instead of the sign he wore denoting his Jewishness. He adds that Juan should be baptized, if he has not been so already, as this will absolve him of his sin of stealing other men's prose and poetry.

Resentment at Juan's good fortune in obtaining such a patron as Juan Pacheco appears to be at the root of the conflict between Juan and Montoro at this juncture, as Manrique puts these words into the mouth of Montoro: 'a tal onbre medrar veo | con sus trobas d'almazén' (ll. 44–45). He chooses to capitalize on the poor relations between the two poets by reiterating his previous criticisms of Juan's poetic technique, using again the language associated with artisanal crafts to impart the notion that the writing of poetry is a skill that has to be learned. He comments that Juan's verses are 'forjadas de hierro viejo, | no con fuego, mas con frío' (ll. 46–47). In the second stanza he observes of his work that 'sus lauores son de cobre, | broñidas con mal asyento' (ll. 13–14), comparisons that are reminiscent of those in CXXV when Juan's verses are 'gruesas y frías | y d'estaño' (335, ll. 31–32). In the final stanza of CXXVIII the intense rivalry between Montoro and Juan de Valladolid is highlighted when, at the thought of Juan's acceptance into Pacheco's entourage, Manrique puts the following words into Montoro's mouth:

> sabed que con vn cabestro
> m'entiendo colgar, señor,
> e morir desesperado
> por ver ese muradal
> ante vuestra señoría. (ll. 73–77)

In case the reader or listener should forget who is speaking in this poem, Manrique concludes with Montoro declaring, 'adoraré mi dedal | dexando la poesýa' (ll. 79–80), reminding us that Montoro is a tailor by trade and a man of humble origins, something that he was never ashamed to admit.

It seems appropriate to mention that Juan de Valladolid and Montoro participated in a rancorous exchange of verses, provoked by a poem by Montoro, 'Juan, señor y grande amigo', which bears the heading 'Montoro a Juan de Valladolid, consejándole' (Montoro 1990: 100–02) in which Montoro makes criticisms of Juan's poetry similar to those made by Manrique. Initially Montoro's tone is conciliatory, as in the first stanza he attempts to express solidarity with Juan by offering his advice 'como de padre o de hermano' (l. 5) and reminding him that their Jewish heritage implies that they have the same problems. In the second stanza he comes to the point, insisting that audiences at court demand high standards of the performers employed, since they are composed of people 'que más saben quel saber' (l. 15) and who seek originality. Interestingly, Montoro like Manrique in 'Señor Marqués de Villena', discussed above, uses the image of the forge, saying that verses should be 'recién sacadas de fragua' (l. 17) and comments that Juan's efforts 'no tienen ni sal nin agua' (l. 20). The third stanza suggests bluntly that he should find an alternative livelihood and the fourth warns that Juan will soon find himself out of his depth in court circles, even if at present he has been befriended by 'algund galán' (l. 31) who does not understand the need to earn one's bread. The sting of this advice comes in the final stanza: Juan should follow in his father's footsteps and take up the much despised position of town crier.

The 'Respuesta de Juan de Valladolid' to this poem, 'Podéis llamar menemigo' (Montoro 1990: 103–04), contains no effort to defend his poetry but is instead a sustained attack on Montoro which shows that he has no regard for the advice offered to him: 'non vos precio más que un figo' (l. 4). In the first of the five stanzas Juan de Valladolid launches into a vitriolic attack on Montoro, calling him 'confeso, marrano, | redondo como un bodigo' and in the second claims that his rival is much reviled by others and attacked both verbally and physically. He sullies the reputation of Montoro's mother in the third verse, implying that Montoro has inherited certain traits of character from her and in the fourth pours scorn on his work, suggesting that it is he, Montoro, who should seek another way of earning his living, perhaps as a 'rapaz de carnicero' (l. 38). In the fifth verse Montoro is accused of arrogance: 'Vos presumís de gallo | con vuestro saber dinano' (ll. 41–42) and told that he is a man of little brain: 'debéis el seso enmendallo | que lo tenéis de avellano' (ll. 44–45). Finally, Juan declares that as a town crier he will be better off than Montoro will be, practising his trade of *ropero*. Another poem by Montoro, 'Noble reina de Castilla' (130) is of two stanzas, each of four lines, which is prefaced by the rubric, 'Montoro a la reina sobre que Juan de Valladolid, fijo del pregonero, dijo que había fecho unas coplas que Montoro ficiera y le enviara'. He tells the queen to 'mandar guardar la vajilla' (l. 3) because if Juan is capable of stealing what cannot be seen, he will certainly steal what is visible: 'ca quien furta lo invesibo[10] | furtará lo que paresce' (ll. 7–8).

Just as Montoro once suggested that Juan should seek another occupation (100–02), so does Manrique in a poem of just two stanzas, 'Quiérovos desengañar' (Gómez Manrique 2003: 345). He admits that Juan works hard but that his efforts are 'vn fruto que se yela' (l. 12), another reference to the lack of warmth that must be overcome to forge a good poem. Comparing verse composition again with artisanal craft, he claims that Juan does not possess an 'enguixuela' (l. 13), perhaps the handle of an adze (345n).

Another poem, 'Syendo vos tanto priuado' (346–48), probably Manrique's last poem to Juan, is ostensibly written in answer to a request for money which is refused. It gives Manrique another opportunity to criticize Juan's work, now expressed using imagery connected with building rather than forging objects from metal:

> Vuestras obras son labradas
> de gruesa manpostería;
> las mías, de cantería
> con escodas afynadas. (ll. 27–30)

Despite their inferior quality, Manrique thinks that Juan will have some success with his verses and continues by casting aspersions on his father, the town crier, and accusing him of corruption: 'trobador | de fynos cohechos' (ll. 42–43). He proceeds to smear the reputation of Juan's mother: this 'tan elegante poeta' must have a guilty secret (l. 48). Although both sides of the family were involved in trade of a low variety, somewhere along the line he surmises that some literary talent has entered the family and it is not from the town crier his father. Referring to the four 'costados' of Juan's family tree, Manrique declares:

> algo tomastes de Omero,
> escrito muy elegante,

---

10 In a footnote to her edition of Montoro's poetry Costa refers to Corominas and Pascual's *Diccionario crítico etimológico castellano e hispánico* to explain that 'invesibo' is derived from 'ver'. It should therefore be taken to mean 'invisible' in this context.

> pasando más adelante,
> el quarto, de pregonero. (ll. 57–60)

The seventh stanza and *fyn* of this poem poses a problem of interpretation when the poet turns to the question of how he should reward Juan:

> no sé qué se pueda dar,
> saluo solo vna capilla
> para que vos pongáis lüego
> no por agua, mas por fuego
> que anda cabo Seuilla. (ll. 66–70)

In trying to date this poem Vidal comments on the allusion to 'agua' and 'fuego', reminding us that the Inquisition initiated proceedings in Seville in 1481 and there is also an account of torrential rain and flooding in that city the same year. He suggests a definition of 'capilla' in line 67 as 'capa pequeña' (348n), but does not explain how a small cloak would save Juan from the ravages of flooding or the Holy Office. Márquez Villanueva seems to have agreed with Vidal, suggesting the 'capilla' was 'a two-pronged allusion to his missing foreskin and to the danger of the fledgling Holy Office' (Márquez Villanueva 1982: 399n). If in fact this poem was written in 1481, the 'capilla' could simply have been a chapel where Juan could pray and seek sanctuary. I find it hard to credit that Manrique was still engaging in verbal tussles with Juan as late as 1481, since there must have been many more pressing claims on his time as Governor of Toledo. In addition, he would have been grieving for his son and daughter, who had both died the previous year, and was probably beginning to draft the *consolatoria* that he composed for his wife.

Manrique and Antón de Montoro were not the only poets to launch verbal attacks on Juan de Valladolid. Suero de Ribera mocked him in 'O que nueuas de castilla' that bear the rubric *Coplas de Ribera a Juan Poeta, estando los dos en Nápoles* (ID6773, Dutton 1990–91: V, 527). He ridicules him cruelly on account of his father's occupation and appearance, saying that even the dogs began to bark when the *pregonero* came in sight: 'que no hay perro que nol' ladre' (l. 14). Manrique's brother Rodrigo, the conde de Paredes, was much more viciously anti-Semitic and wrote two long poems, one accusing him of becoming a Muslim when he was captured at sea by pirates, 'Si no lo quereys negar' (ID6756, Dutton 1990–91: V, 540–42) and a second on Juan's attendance at an *indulgencia general* in Valencia, 'Juan poeta en vos venir' (ID0219 V, 542–44). The second of these poems is a sustained tirade of 124 lines against Juan's presence in the cathedral of Valencia, which is seen as defiling it. In the conde's opinion, the papal bull 'se tornó con gran quebranto | escriptura del talmud' (ll. 9–10).

Clearly, while Manrique's jibes at Juan de Valladolid are pale in comparison with those of the conde de Paredes, the sentiments expressed shock the modern reader and do not sit easily beside the inclusive ethos espoused by the Carrillo circle. However, it should be borne in mind that insult and invective had long been a function of poetry, as David Nirenberg recognizes when commenting on the *Cancionero de Baena*'s poets who 'nearly all Christian, are constantly defaming one another, and the accusation of Jewishness is prominent among the charges they hurl'

(Nirenberg 2006: 402–03). Motivated by the need to earn their bread, the minstrels engaging in these verbal contests were predominantly of Jewish origin, often taking on the role of jester in a fiercely competitive arena and using their Jewishness to comic effect so that the audience would laugh at them. Even Juan Alfonso de Baena, as Francisco Márquez Villanueva observes, 'didn't mind sprinkling his *requestas* with stinging, self-mocking allusions, such as his respect for Jewish dietary laws' (Márquez Villanueva 1982: 393). Although writing a generation later, Manrique appears to continue this tradition of invective, conflating the idea that converts do not write good poetry, as Jeanne Battesti-Pelegrin puts it, 'l'affirmation formulaire dénigrante de la judaïté du convers est toujours associée à la déclaration et à la démonstration, et cela est nouveau, de son incapacité poétique' [the formulaic and denigrating assertions of the convert's adherence to Jewish customs is still associated with poetic skills that are wanting and, what is new, with demonstrating this point] (Battesti-Pelegrin 1990: 243). The claim that Manrique actually demonstrated Juan's shortcomings as a poet, however, is not really tenable as he gives no examples to illustrate the criticisms he makes.

So why did Manrique, who did not depend on writing poetry for financial gain, engage in the racial insults discussed in this chapter, especially since he had amicable exchanges in verse with other poets of Jewish origin? He made a point of supporting Montoro despite the fact that he made no secret of his ancestry and greatly admired his uncle and mentor, the marqués de Santillana, who praised the work of Rabi Santo in his *Proverbios*:

> Non vale el açor menos
> por nasçer en vil nio,
> nin los examplos buenos
> por los dezir judio. (Santillana 1984: 93)

Indeed, in his *planto* for the marqués de Santillana, Manrique refers to the *converso*, Alonso de Cartagena, whom he held in high regard as 'otro San Pablo' (Gómez Manrique 2003: 388, l. 544). Perhaps he enjoyed the opportunity to write verse in a different style from which he was accustomed and respond to Juan in a similar manner. Since so few of Juan's verses have survived we cannot pass judgement on Manrique's criticisms regarding their quality or the charges of plagiarism, although such charges were made by other poets. Perhaps we should bear in mind the fact that Juan is thought to have been to Córdoba in 1455 with Juan Pacheco, a favourite of Enrique IV, and this association could have been distasteful to Manrique (342n). Although we can pass off much of his invective against Juan as literary badinage that was not intended to be taken too seriously, the final poem addressed to Juan certainly has a sting in its tail with its apparent allusion to the impending threat of the Inquisition. Perhaps deep down, Manrique's motivation in writing as he did can be explained when he brands Juan as 'no judío ni cristiano, | mas exçelente marrano' (341, ll. 53–54). While he is supportive of Montoro who is open about his ethnicity, he is not convinced of Juan's sincerity as a convert to Christianity.

CHAPTER 5

Matters of State (c. 1463–1473)

Gómez Manrique's premonitions of political turmoil and unease regarding the way that Castile was being governed have already been noted, both in his elegy for Santillana and in his exchanges with other poets. With his growing involvement in the Castilian political scene, his disquiet is expressed with increasing intensity. In his youth he had aligned himself with the Aragonese cause, opposing Juan II of Castile and Álvaro de Luna, but on Juan's death in 1454 he and many other nobles decided to support Enrique IV. In so doing, while he had firmly nailed his colours to the Castilian mast by this stage in his career, in view of his earlier mixed allegiances, he was obviously not unsympathetic to the Aragonese cause, as demonstrated in the poem discussed below.

De Gómez Manrique quando se trataua la paz entre los señores reyes de Castilla e de Aragón e se desabinieron

Manrique's desire for unity between the two kingdoms is reflected in 'Del Señor es fecho esto' (Gómez Manrique 2003: 619–21). The poem gives us no clues as to its date, but both Vidal González (619n) and Paz y Melia (Gómez Manrique 1885–86: II, 351) suggest that it refers to negotiations that took place between Enrique IV and Juan II of Aragon in 1463. This dispute had implications beyond the Iberian Peninsula because Enrique had received overtures of friendship from ambassadors sent by Edward IV of England, who was seeking an alliance with Castile against France. Since Louis XI of France appeared to be supporting Aragon at the time, it was in Castile's interest to forge an alliance with England, thereby putting pressure on Aragon to come to an accord (Palencia 1998–99: II, 243). According to Alonso de Palencia, Diego de Valera and the *Crónica anónima de Enrique IV*, Archbishop Carrillo and Juan Pacheco were despatched to Bayonne to negotiate with the Aragonese. Manrique makes no mention of his presence in Bayonne, but all three chroniclers record that he was at Saint Jean de Luz the following month when Louis arrived to celebrate an agreement that had been reached (Palencia, 1998–99: II, 243–44; Valera: 1941: 85–86; *Crónica anónima* 1991: II, 131).

The first of the eight *octavas* of this poem confirms the wording of the rubric which intimates that discussions about peace are ongoing, since Manrique expresses a fear of the negotiations failing. He sees hostilities between two Christian states as foolish because it weakens them both and lays them open to attack from their enemies. In the second and third stanzas he suggests that such disputes should be left to pagans, whereas unity between Castile and Aragon will strengthen them both. His warning of the consequences of not following this advice reveals a very restrained, mature and prudent approach to what is happening when he says:

> y sy no fazéys lo tal,
> yo fiador
> que quien librare mejor
> libre mal.
>   (Gómez Manrique 2003: 619–20, ll. 21–24)

If 'librar' is taken here to mean to complete an action successfully, as suggested by Vidal (620n), Manrique is advocating that the best way of concluding the discussions between Castile and Aragon is to avoid any sense of triumphalism on the part of either side in order to implement an agreement successfully. His use of the *pie quebrado* in these lines, where 'fiador' rhymes with 'mejor' serves to emphasize the firmness of his convictions. Similarly, in the following verse he comments that reaching an agreement, even if difficult, is never as harmful as discord:

> que no puede ser tan mala
> la concordia
> que non faga la discordia
> mayor tala. (ll. 29–32)

Again the *pie quebrado* stresses the importance of 'concordia' and the 'tala', the prejudicial consequences, of failing to resolve their differences. The argument in favour of making peace is strengthened by the thought that a pact to cease hostilities is worth more than the uncertainty of obtaining victory. David's triumph over Goliath is cited as an example to be borne in mind: while some, like David, have been victorious in conflicts despite appearing to be the weaker party, something he attributes to the work of God, others have been successful despite being cruel and unjust. With this in mind, Manrique warns that the powerful need to be fearful and the weak even more so. Perhaps he had a premonition of what was to happen, since the king of France did not hold to the agreement that had been reached, as Diego de Valera observes:

> el rey de Francia [...] con tiránica voluntad menospreciando la conveniencia que estaua entre él y el rey de Aragón, no solamente quiso ocupar a Perpiñán, más la cibdad de Elna, y todos los lugares del condado de Ruysellón, lo qual el rey de Aragón no pudo sofrir. (Valera 1941: 86)

The final stanza of this poem is an appeal to the two sides to join forces for another reason, that of their shared ancestry: 'pues que fuystes deçendientes | de vnos anteçesores' (Gómez Manrique 2003: 621, ll. 58–59). Since Enrique IV's father, Juan II of Castile and Juan II of Aragon were first cousins, both being grandsons of Juan I of Castile, Manrique urges the two sides to set aside their differences and unite in solidarity against threats from their neighbours. His desire for an accord between the two kingdoms finally found fruition with the marriage of Isabel of Castile and Fernando of Aragon in 1469, a union that he worked hard to bring about.

The *Coplas para Arias Dávila* and Pero Guillén de Segovia's Reply

It must have been at most only a few years after writing his continuation of Mena that Manrique had occasion to compose another long poem, the *Coplas para Arias Dávila*. This time his desire to turn again to moral issues is motivated by political concerns. Arias, a *converso*, was a close advisor to Enrique IV, occupying an important and influential position at court when he became *contador mayor* to Enrique IV not long after the latter's accession to the throne of Castile. He was a controversial character who figures in various satirical poems of the period, such as the anonymous *Coplas del provincial* where he is the butt of an anti-Semitic jibe reminiscent of those made by Manrique to Juan de Valladolid: 'pues que tu pija capuz | nunca la tuvo ni tiene' (Rodríguez-Puértolas 1981: 245, ll. 165–76).

The chronicler Alonso de Palencia, who was an outspoken critic of Enrique IV and those close to him, gives us some information about Arias Dávila, claiming that he was a *converso* of humble origins who left his native city of Ávila to go to Segovia where he became a pedlar of spices amongst other things. He leaves us in no doubt about his opinion of Arias, declaring that he was selling 'cosas ínfimas robadas a otros' (Palencia 1998–99: I, 57). He also tells us that Arias bought a horse that would carry him away swiftly whenever he needed to escape the wrath of any peasant attempting to obtain justice following 'algún atropello cometido contra uno de los vecinos' (58). Arias must have attracted the attention of, and found favour with, the infante Enrique who was living in Segovia during the 1440s, since it was he who intervened to save Arias from execution when he was found guilty of committing a crime. Palencia was of the opinion that this was the turning-point in his career despite his ability to ingratiate himself with people: 'Ni siquiera con estas artes habría acrecentado sus riquezas si no hubiese cometido, según la fama, un crimen muy infame y merecedor de la prisión y pena capital' (58). A further step in Arias's rise to power was his appointment by Enrique as a tax collector and not long after Enrique's accession to the Castilian throne he was appointed *contador mayor* to the king. Since there were already two men, Juan de Vivero and Alfonso Álvarez de Toledo, who had been appointed for life to similar posts by Juan II, it seems that hostility and suspicion were aroused by this appointment (*Crónica anónima* 1991: I, 14).

As time went on Arias became a trusted counsellor to the king and a very rich man in the process, mentioned on a number of occasions in connection with the corruption of officials: the *corregidores* according to Palencia 'mejor deben llamarse *merecedores de corrección*' (Palencia 1998–99: I, 101). Encouraged by Arias to wage war against the Muslims, Enrique raised troops two years running, sending ambassadors to Rome to plead permission for the sale of indulgences to finance these campaigns. A papal bull was issued at Christmas 1456 to allow the raising of funds for this purpose and a very large sum of money was realized. According to Diego de Valera, despite the preaching of Enrique's confessor, Alonso de Espina, who declared that this should be spent on a crusade against the Muslims, 'muy poca parte se gastó en la guerra de los moros' (Valera 1941: 41). Both Valera and Palencia recount that this caused disquiet amongst the grandees of the kingdom, Palencia believing that it was the beginning of the split in the kingdom when the conde de Haro, Pedro

Fernández de Velasco, assumed the leadership of the rebels because he could rely on 'la rectitud del arzobispo de Toledo, con la fortaleza del almirante y con la magnanimidad y prudencia del conde de Alba' (Palencia 1998–99: I, 152). These events would culminate in the dethronement of Enrique's effigy and the crowning of the infante Alfonso in Ávila in 1465.

In an article on Arias Dávila, María Eugenia Contreras Jiménez examines the evidence that had survived regarding his profile. She comments on the anti-Semitic allusions to the *contador* in the satirical *Coplas de la panadera* and the *Coplas del provincial*, but points out that some researchers into his genealogy have claimed that he was of Old Christian descent (Contreras Jiménez 1985: 475–77). She also emphasizes that since Arias was so close to Enrique IV, the chroniclers' accounts vary greatly according to their political leanings, Palencia being highly critical of the king and Arias, whereas Enríquez del Castillo, an ardent supporter of Enrique, hardly mentions Arias. Rather surprisingly, Contreras makes only a rather cursory allusion to Manrique's poem, drawing no conclusions from it in the section of her article, 'Diego Arias Dávila visto por sus coetáneos' (482–86), and making no mention of the letter written to accompany it. Manrique may have experienced some satisfaction regarding his difficult relations with Arias. He was appointed governor of Ávila by the infante Alfonso after the latter had been crowned king by the rebels in 1465 and Contreras's researches at the archives of Simancas reveal that shortly after this event Alfonso wrote to Manrique to authorize him to requisition all property owned by Diego and Pedro Arias Dávila in the city and diocese of Burgos. Diego Arias died on the first day of 1466 and the following summer Manrique was instructed to collect the income derived from this property (489).

Gómez Manrique's letter

Manrique's poem was composed in response to a request from Arias who was withholding the payment from Manrique of a 'libranza', or bill of exchange, presumably for a sum of money owed by the Crown and which needed to be disbursed by the king's *contador mayor*. By setting such terms Arias was, in a sense, adding insult to injury, since he had already delayed payment to Manrique. The *Coplas* are prefaced by a letter from Manrique (Gómez Manrique 2003: 553–56) expressing no overt indignation, but noticeably lacking in any flattery despite the fact that it is addressed to a man holding an elevated position at court. Instead, it offers a series of veiled insults, beginning by saying that the request has provoked a variety of different thoughts: being asked to write a poem leads Manrique to wonder if his previous efforts were either unsatisfactory or else so very pleasing that Arias clamours for more. He uses the modesty topos in a subtle way to nudge Arias, saying that if he had to live on what he could earn by his verses and the *merçedes* granted to him by the king, he would be poor indeed: 'sería muy mal mantenido, según yo trobo e vos, señor, me libráys' (554). He claims that he does not know what has led Arias to make his request, comparing his wish to respond to 'aquella misma neçesydad que a las brauas aves faze yr al desacostunbrado señuelo' (554). In so saying he shows an awareness of being lured into uncharted territory that may ensnare him. The pretence of modesty is maintained when he describes his poem as 'esta ruda obra [...] cuyo grueso estilo vos fará manifiesta la ynorançia de su fazedor' (554). There follows a self-deprecating analogy between his supposed ignorance of literary technique and the ill-behaved nobles of ancient Rome who, according to Gaius Marius, were more disposed to teach rather than learn, thus warning Arias that the content of his poem will be didactic and implying that it will be salutary for the addressee. This letter also reflects the politically troubled times in which Manrique lived when he tells Arias that he is aware that his writings may be 'en algo más agras o menos dulçes [...] que la calidat del tienpo requiere' (555), but he declares that he lives without hope or fear and that Fortune has been favourable to him. In saying that he holds out no hopes to the future, he alludes directly to Sallust's *Conspiracy of Catiline* (555).

Thinking of the debt he is owed by the royal treasury, Manrique reminds Arias that he has served the king during 'la mayor parte de mi niñez' (555) and hopes to continue doing so, but anticipating one of the themes of the poem to come, he shows little concern for such worldly concerns. Instead, preferring to walk the moral high ground, he tells Arias that if he will not pay up he should think of some other reply to make since he, Manrique, has responded to his request. In saying that he will not be prolix, since he realizes how busy Arias is, he is perhaps hinting that not all Arias's activities are for the benefit of the Crown, and in a final protestation of modesty, begs him not to find fault with his work due its lack of aesthetic merit and flattery, but to accept it for 'la voluntad e claridad de ánimo con que [...] se fizo' (555–56).

The Coplas

This poem, 'De los más el más perfecto' (556–70), composed no later than 1465, consists of 47 nine-line stanzas, the first seven forming the introduction. Seeking divine inspiration, Manrique declares in the opening stanza:

> que sin ty prosa nin rimo
> es fundada,
> nin se puede fazer nada,
> Joanis primo. (ll. 6–9)

The last line quoted above has been interpreted by scholars in various ways, as an appeal to Christ as cousin of John the Baptist (Scholberg and Vidal González) or to John the Evangelist (Rodríguez Puértolas). Carl Atlee's claim that it is a direct reference to the first chapter of John's gospel, known in Latin as *Iohannis Primo* makes much better sense: it is an appeal to the Word Incarnate (Atlee 2007: 186–87). Atlee could have supported this claim still further by suggesting that the preceding lines reflect the wording of John 1. 3: 'All things were made by him; and without him was not any thing made that was made'. There is some subtle use of the modesty topos in the second verse of this invocation:

> Tú que das lenguas a mudos
> fazes los bajos sobir

> e los altos deçendir;
> tú que fazes conuertir
> los muy torpes en agudos,
> conuierte mi gran rudeza
> e ynorançia
> en vna grande abundançia
> de sabieza. (Gómez Manrique 2003: ll. 10–18)

The tone could initially be taken as one of humility as the poet, mindful of Christ's healing of a mute, asks for the ability to express himself with wisdom and elegance despite his 'rudeza' and 'ynorançia'. His biblical knowledge is again demonstrated in the second and third lines, reminiscent of the humble tone of the words spoken by the Virgin Mary in the Magnificat (Luke 1. 52), but also reflecting the turbulent times in which he is writing when members of the Manrique family, the 'altos' of Castilian society, were conscious of their own reversals of fortune. These lines are also an uncomfortable reminder to Arias of the meteoric rise he has experienced, after starting out in life as one of the 'bajos'.

In the following introductory stanzas there is a pretence of friendship as Arias is addressed as 'buen señor' and 'señor e grande amigo'. Some self-awareness is evident in the way the poet wishes to avoid sounding sanctimonious at the start of the fifth verse when he says, 'E no mires mis pasiones | y grandes viçios que sigo' (ll. 37–38). There is what must be an attempt at diplomatic deference when he explains the brevity of his introduction on the grounds that he knows Arias to be a man much occupied with his 'negoçiaçiones e grandes preocupaçiones' (ll. 48–49), but this could also be interpreted as a snide allusion to the time Arias devoted to the business dealings which enabled him to feather his own nest. These opening stanzas end with the injunction: 'Desde agora ten atentos | los oýdos' (ll. 62–63), leaving the reader in no doubt as to the serious nature of the content to follow.

The first section, stanzas VIII to XVII, concerns the theme of the vagaries of fortune. It opens with the words '¡O tú, en amor ermano, | naçido para morir' (ll. 64–65), a sentiment echoing the words of Seneca in his consolatory letter to Marcia on the death of her son: 'his death was proclaimed at his birth; into this condition was he begotten, this fate attended him straightaway from the womb' (Seneca 2006: 30–31).[1] This is followed by a warning that Arias should not place too much importance on worldly pleasures, goods and honours since they are ephemeral. In stanza IX Manrique uses a stock metaphor by referring to the life's problems as 'esta mar alterada' (Gómez Manrique 2003: 559, l. 73) before warning Arias how quickly the wheel of fortune can turn. There follows a reminder of the destruction of ancient cities in the past and the downfall of powerful leaders, and in stanza XII the tone becomes darker when he mentions the more recent turbulence of 'nuestras rigiones' (l. 101) and the evidence of the damage caused that still exists there, perhaps an allusion to the consequences of the first battle of Olmedo. Manrique is much more direct in the way he writes to Arias in XIII when he uses the imagery

---

[1] Mors enim illi denuntiata nascenti est; in hanc legem erat satus, hoc illum fatum ab utero statim prosequebatur'.

of a storm, again in connection with the struggles of political life:

> Que tú mesmo viste munchos
> en estos tienpos pasados,
> de grandísimos estados
> fáçilmente derrocados
> con pequeños aguaduchos. (ll. 109–13)

Political power is then likened to 'vn muy feble metal | de vedrío' (ll. 116–17), easily shattered.

Still on the subject of fortune, Manrique now reflects on the fickleness of human relationships in political circles where the respect that people show can be motivated by self-interest:

> De los que vas por las calles
> en torno todo çercado,
> con çirimonias tratado,
> no serás más aguardado
> de quanto tengas que dalles. (ll. 136–40)

Stanza XVII contains an example of this when Arias is reminded of how Álvaro de Luna, Juan II's favourite, was deserted by his supporters and met his end. If Manrique really intended this poem as a token of friendship for Arias, whom he addresses as 'grande amigo' (l. 39), this is an unfortunate remark since there is a clear parallel between him and Luna. Both men had a swift rise to power and enjoyed a close relationship with Enrique IV and Juan II respectively, who were known to lean heavily on their *privados* for advice.

The second section, stanzas XVIII to XXV, contains advice to Arias as to how he should conduct himself, with the suggestion that Arias should model himself on the *alcalde cadañero* who, knowing that his term of office lasts but a year, is at pains to be temperate in his actions so as to be judged favourably at the end of that year. This advice is reinforced with a nautical simile, comparing the state to a ship that has many oarsmen. Arias has to relate to many people, oarsmen and passengers alike, and a man who wields great power should see to it that he is not feared, but instead should try to be loved by those of good intentions, or at least not hated. In stanza XXI he spells out how this can be achieved: respect, good treatment and patience need to be shown to all walks of life. In other words, this is a call for social cohesion, which we will see expressed more forcefully in the *Esclamaçión e querella de la gouernaçión*. In the following verses Manrique takes Arias to task for failing to comply with this norm and his tone betrays the indignation of an aristocrat when he implies that Arias does not know how to behave towards members of the nobility:

> e no fagan los portales
> tus porteros
> a bestias y caualleros
> ser yguales. (ll. 195–98)

The pretence of friendship is further demolished in an allusion to the fact that Arias is considered by some to be a criminal:

> Según lo que de ti veo,
> algunos te fazen reo
> e reputan por culpante;
> mas yo dudo de tu seso
> que mandase
> que bien e mal se pesase
> con vn peso. (ll. 201–07)

As Atlee points out, the word 'peso', means both a 'balance scale' and the weight of coinage (Atlee 2007: 194), so Manrique is pointing the finger of blame at Arias and suggesting that his decisions are swayed by underhand financial considerations. Several of the chroniclers of the period make allusions to the way coins were minted; one of these was Diego de Valera who commented on Enrique's activities:

> Y mandó fazer moneda mucho más baxa que la quel rey don Juan su padre labró, y la quel rey don Enrrique su abuelo avía mandado labrar, que era mucho mejor, e mandó fundir, por aver alguna ganançia, con gran daño a sus súbditos. (Valera 1941: 64)

Alfonso de Palencia also had something to say about the decisions that Arias took regarding the minting of coins: 'La moneda sufría alteraciones y devaluaciones frecuentes en daño público, para que las rentas reales se incrementasen y luego se pagasen con ganancias de la nueva tasa del dinero' (Palencia 1998–99: I, 141). Angus MacKay explains the situation in greater detail than Atlee and traces the debasement of the coinage in reigns previous to that of Enrique IV, but both he and Atlee view the writ issued by Enrique in 1464, when he banned all minting of coins in Castile with the exception of the mint in Segovia, as an important event. MacKay explains that two weeks after this writ was issued a manifesto was produced by Enrique's opponents which refers to the alteration of the coinage and he quotes from the anonymous *Memorias de Don Enrique IV de Castilla* to reveal the intensity of feeling on the subject (MacKay 1981: 72–73). Another reference to Arias's underhand financial dealings occurs in stanza XXIV when Manrique refers to dishonest behaviour of landlords towards their workers, implying that Arias was involved in these practices also. By punishing such actions, not only will Arias win the people's affection, but he will also be at an advantage in the afterlife.

The ephemeral nature of worldly goods and honours is the theme of the third section, stanzas XXVI to XXXI. Here Manrique observes that those who rise highest and are most feared in this world are also more fearful of what they may lose. He declares that wealth and honours are only on loan to us during our lifetime, and, in so saying, he again echoes the words of Seneca: 'honours, wealth, spacious halls [...] and all else that depends upon uncertain and fickle chance — these are not our own but borrowed trappings' (Seneca 2006: 29).[2] Arias is reminded of figures from the past who rose to fame, including the legendary Midas, famous for his ability to turn everything he touched to gold, but is advised to concentrate his thoughts on 'el temor de los tormentos | infernales' (Gómez Manrique 2003: 565,

---

2   'honores, opes, amplia atria [...] ceteraque ex incerta et mobile sorte pendentia alieni commodatique apparatus sunt; nihil horum dono datur'.

ll. 251–52). Since he will take nothing with him except his shroud when he dies, he should lose no sleep over trying to obtain 'lo que tiene de fyncar | con su dueño' ll. 260–61), another reference to Arias's dishonest dealings. Palencia mentions the *ferias* at Medina where 'robos, violencias, exacciones y abusos al capricho de Diego Arias' took place (Palencia 1998–99: I, 141). This accusation is followed by an observation on the part of Manrique that the material world is like a master against whom Arias is constantly fighting: he is motivated by greed that eventually will bring regret.

The fourth and final section of the poem, stanzas XXXII to XLV (Gómez Manrique 2003: 566–70), treats the theme of the trials and tribulations of those in high office and possessors of great wealth. Having mentioned the burdens carried by kings, princes, prelates of the Church and the aristocratic armed forces, he suggests that 'los fauoridos priuados' (l. 343) of princes are also subject to the same onerous duties, this being a direct hint to Arias that he should take stock of his own situation as one who is so close to the king. Manrique refers to the constant stream of attention in the form of 'seruiçios y presentes' (l. 346) that Arias must receive in his position, implying that these are bribes and uses a particularly unpleasant simile to describe them: 'como piedras a tablados' (l. 347). Since the 'tablado' was the scaffold where a condemned man might be stoned while waiting to be executed, this line has been interpreted as a deliberate insult to Arias who was once condemned to death but saved at the last moment, reputedly by Enrique IV according to Palencia (Atlee 2007: 195; Palencia 1998–99: I, 58). He also suggests that Arias might well find the pressures of his life such that he would choose to reside somewhere humbler:

> que las tus ricas moradas
> por las choças o ramadas
> de los pobres trocarías.
> (Gómez Manrique 2003: ll. 372–74)

The final two stanzas urge Arias yet again not to place his trust in human beings or rely on temporal goods, but to think of assuring himself a dwelling-place for his soul in the hereafter. The final stanza echoes the conclusion to Christ's Sermon on the Mount (Matthew 7. 24–27) where a comparison is made between the wise man who built his house on a rock so that it survived the elements and the foolish one who built his upon sand:

> E no fundes tu morada
> sobre tan feble çimiento,
> mas elige con gran tiento
> otro firme fundamento
> de más eterna durada.
> (Gómez Manrique 2003: ll. 415–19)

Apart from the importance of the sentiments that Manrique conveys, the poem has literary qualities that merit comment: his use of the *pie quebrado* is skilful. One particularly effective example occurs in stanza IX when Arias is warned of the way the wheel of fortune can turn and change the course of our lives:

> ¡O, pues, tú, onbre mortal,
> mira, mira
> la rueda quán presto gira
> mundanal! (ll. 78–81)

The use of the rhyme of 'mortal' with 'mundanal' emphasizes human mortality, while that of 'mira' with 'gira' stresses the rapidity of the wheel's turn and the urgency of the poet's message. Moreover, the shortened seventh and ninth lines, with their interruption of the metre, underline the poet's message still further. Another striking example, again on the subject of changes in fortune, reads:

> qu'el ventoso poderío
> tenporal
> es vn muy feble metal
> de vedrío (ll. 114–17).

The rhyme of 'tenporal' with 'metal' underlines the fact that earthly power is transitory, and the fact that 'tenporal', although used adjectivally here, is also a noun meaning 'storm' is significant. These lines are also part of an extended metaphor: this stanza opens with the reflection that the mighty have often been toppled by 'pequeños aguaduchos' (l. 113), so that power is perceived as something inherently vulnerable due to the vagaries of fortune and the tempestuous nature of life at court. As Atlee remarks, this is emphasized with the antithesis in the rhyme of 'poderío' with 'vedrío', since political power can be shattered as easily as glass (Atlee 2007: 193–94).

Other figures of speech deserve comment in the way they contribute to the literary merit of the poem. Manrique first uses the rather stock metaphor of the journey through life, with the challenges that man faces, being compared to a voyage at sea with its attendant storms in stanza IX, making it plain that all people are vulnerable: 'En esta mar alterada | por do todos navegamos' (Gómez Manrique 2003: ll. 73–74). He develops this with a more original figure of speech when he declares that worldly pleasures are as transient as the spray caused by the breaking of the waves: 'no duran más que roçiada' (l. 77). Another metaphor linked to the idea of navigating our way through life occurs in stanza XV when Arias is warned of the fickle nature of those supposed friends when they realize that their friendship will reap no more benefits. Here it is not the storm they must brave; instead, as they fail to achieve their aspirations, it is as if they are becalmed because 'falleçen en el estrecho | como agua de laguna' (ll. 130–31). The nautical theme is maintained in stanza XX where the state is seen as a ship that is rowed by many but also has to carry many passengers, leading to the advice that it is imperative to forge harmonious relationships between rulers and subjects. The image of the oarsmen recurs but is used differently in stanza XXXIX when it underlines the intensity of the pressures experienced by *privados* such as Arias who, despite their material comforts, will suffer more stress than 'los remantes que tiran | en la vanda' (ll. 350–51).

There are also several imaginative and lyrical similes expressing the brevity of earthly beauty and honours and comparing these with flowers on account of their ephemeral nature, for example in VIII:

> viçios, bienes, onores
> que procuras
> pásanse como frescuras
> de las flores. (ll. 69–72)

Similarly, the value of worldly riches is short-lived: no duran más que rosas | con eladas' (ll. 232–34); again in XLVI human beings and their material wealth 'más presto que rosales | pierden la fresca verdor' (ll. 409–10). The destructive force of fire is another way that Manrique emphasizes the short-lived nature of fame, since it vanishes, 'transitoria como flama | d'aguardiente' (ll. 98–99). A similar image in the penultimate stanza is used to describe the way an increase in personal wealth can bring only a fleeting gain:

> e no son sus creçimientos
> sino juego,
> menos turable que fuego
> de sarmientos. (ll. 411–14)

This poem has been interpreted in various ways by scholars. Both Scholberg (1971) and Rodríguez-Puértolas (1981) included it in anthologies of satirical literature, the former also commenting on it in a chapter on political satire in his book *Sátira e invectiva en la España medieval* (Scholberg 1971: 246–49). Atlee's article, 'A Reassessment of the Satirical Nature of Gómez Manrique's *Coplas para Diego Arias de Ávila*' (2007), is a valuable contribution to criticism on Manrique, giving much information about the political and economic background to the times in which the poem was written. Atlee, however, does not define what he means by satire, which is generally considered to involve ridicule with a focus on features of a person's character, appearance, manner of speaking or behaviour, and exaggerating the portrayal to the point when it becomes a humorous and grotesque caricature. This poem contains neither ridicule nor humour, so I cannot agree that it is a satire, but consider it rather to be a reflection on moral values that are grounded in Christian theology and Stoic principles, combined with an implied criticism of its dedicatee and a warning of the likelihood of downfall in the future.

Although Arias was a *converso*, Manrique does not lower himself to making any jibes about his ethnicity, in spite of the fact that this section of Castilian society came in for much criticism for amassing large amounts of wealth by allegedly underhand means. It is also worth remembering that Manrique was capable of anti-Semitic outbursts, such as those he made to Juan de Valladolid. David Gitlitz, whose research shows how the Arias Dávila family retained strong ties with the Jewish community of Segovia, observes that Manrique had sufficient vision not to write an anti-Semitic poem because 'no quería arriesgar que Arias tapara sus oídos ante algo que interpretara como una típica satírica polémica anti-conversa' (Gitlitz 1996: 18). Atlee adds an interesting comment to the effect that Manrique's use of the verb 'conuertir' twice in the second stanza of his invocation is probably not coincidental and 'would have reminded the advisor of his prosperity as a New Christian and favored servant of the king' (Atlee 2007: 188). If this is a snide allusion to Arias's *converso* status, as Atlee thinks, it is only a very veiled manifestation of anti-Semitism.

This poem has to be read on two levels: not just for what it tells us about some of the players on the fifteenth-century Castilian political scene, but for its literary qualities. I have already attempted to emphasize the effective use of similes, and note that Scholberg remarks: 'Lo que más impresiona son las magníficas figuras que recalcan la fugacidad de todo' (Scholberg 1984: 35). Vidal also appreciates the poem from a double perspective: 'Sería pecar de simplismo [...] si nos quedáremos tan sólo en la crítica a la actitud de Diego Arias o la sátira política. El poema va mucho más allá, es una lección de filosofía y moral cristiana' (Gómez Manrique 2003: 62). If we ignore the admonitions directed at Arias, and focus on the central theme of the brevity of life and ephemeral value of all things temporal, the poem has a timeless and universal significance for all mankind. It is also worth noting that it has often been considered to have influenced Jorge Manrique in the composition of his famous *Coplas*.

Pero Guillén de Segovia's Response to the Coplas

Pero Guillén de Segovia reacts to Manrique's *Coplas* in the form of a prose letter and poem written as if by Arias himself. In the opening paragraph of the letter (Guillén de Segovia 1989: 144–45) he quotes Seneca to the effect that any benefits we receive should not be repaid without interest. Guillén is at pains to make clear to Manrique that he needs to be more circumspect in what he says. The words that he puts into Arias's mouth admit that he has received a moral lesson, but that it is without just cause, as he says, 'sin aver intervenido causa que permitirlo pudiese' (144). Furthermore, he reminds Manrique that the wise man is careful about the advice he offers to others and pointedly quotes Saint Gregory on the subject of those who take pleasure in hearing about the misdeeds of others: 'quel que se deleyta en oyr crymenes ajenos come las carnes de los onbres' (144). The letter shows an awareness that Arias realized that Manrique was speaking about him in the *coplas* when he declares, 'que se puede colegir que en vos, señor, dar fe aquello creyendo de my lo fablase' (144). The defensive tone of the letter continues with the reflection that Saint Thomas (presumably Aquinas), in a book that he wrote in the 'mirror of princes' genre, declared that there was nothing of so little value as the 'la gloria e el onor del favor de las gentes' (145). This is because such accolades, since they depend on human judgement, are not of lasting value, and a quotation from the prophet Isaiah, very much echoing the sentiments expressed in Manrique's *coplas*, is used to support this view: 'la gloria e favor de este mundo es como flor de feno' (145). Indeed, the voice of Arias contends that rather than making himself 'siervo de vil materia', the prudent man will ignore the vagaries of fortune and instead will do all he can to lead a virtuous life so that he 'dome o resista la feroçidad de los monstruosos actos' (145).

The poem that follows the letter, 'O soberano yntelecto' (144–56), consists of forty-seven nine-line stanzas with the rhyme scheme ABBBACdDc, mirroring Manrique's poem exactly. The first three stanzas express a mixture of flattery and assumed modesty, with an ironic invocation to God to guide him as he presumes to address a knight of such nobility. Stanzas IV–VII are defensive in that he considers that he works very hard but is fair in his dealings. He is aware of the fact that there are some people who delight in negative criticism: 'Usan del modo blasfemio | en maldezir convertido' (ll. 56–57) and urges Manrique not to heed what others may say. What is interesting here is that Guillén uses the first person plural in stanza IX:

> Quen esta vida lazerada
> donde prestados no estamos
> los que a virtud no miramos
> muchas veces murmuramos
> de la cabsa no cabsada;
> tal material no es moral
> ni satira
> mas es pasion de la Yra
> natural. (ll. 75–83)

This is a way of telling Manrique that he is addressing his comments to the wrong person. At the same time, however, Guillén softens the rebuke with his use of the first person plural, thus suggesting that we are all capable of making similar errors.

In stanza XI Arias admits that the advice offered him by Manrique is wise and in XIII notes that some men, although gifted, commit 'muy feos pecados' (l. 112) and do not exercise their free will as reason would dictate. There is a self-righteousness in much of what he says: he considers that he has always conducted himself in 'estilo moderado' (l. 169) and, commenting on the downfall of the powerful, he again uses the first person plural suggesting that all should seek to follow a virtuous life. Just as Manrique professed scorn for earthly riches, Arias echoes the same attitude, observing that death does not respect the rich and, in facing death, all social classes are equal:

> los que aran con bueyes
> de los perrlados y reyes
> ciertamente son yguales. (ll. 367–69)

He expresses the hope that his good works will assure him a place in heaven: 'ser por obras me procuro | en lo eterno conlocado' (ll. 395–96). The final stanza is polite; Arias declares that Manrique will be compensated for his efforts and that the debt that he is owed will be repaid.

Guillén obviously took great care in writing this poem and its accompanying letter. The way in which the stanzas are structured, using not just the same rhyme scheme, but the identical rhymes for each verse, reveals minute attention to detail and leads Atlee to suggest that Arias might have paid Guillén to write this response. If this is so, he interprets it as 'an acknowledgement of the impact that Manrique's *Coplas* had on the kingdom' and 'a covert admission on the part of the treasurer that he was publicly disgraced' (Atlee 2007: 197). The response of Guillén, who emerges as rather a timorous character, is intended to have a restraining influence on Manrique. Whether Guillén was paid to write by Arias or was motivated for other reasons, what is significant is that not only did Manrique display moral courage in speaking out to a man who was so close to the monarch, but he also had the satisfaction of seeing that his address in prose and verse had clearly hit its mark.

A further display of moral courage is to be found when, probably in 1465, Manrique put pen to paper and composed the poem, often referred to as the *Esclamaçión e querella de la gouernaçión*, in which he reveals his exasperation at the poor and corrupt state of government in an imaginary Castilian town, often thought to be Toledo.

The *Esclamaçión e querella de la gouernaçión*

This poem of eighteen *octavas*, 'Quando Roma prosperaua' (Gómez Manrique 2003: 571–76), stands out from the rest of Manrique's writing on account of the sense of impatience that it imparts, in contrast with the measured tones in which he usually expresses himself. Disaffection among the nobility was obviously already simmering in the early 1460s when Diego de Valera took it upon himself to write to Enrique IV on behalf of many nobles, listing five grievances. There was a general lack of governance and decisions were made without consulting the appropriate people; unsuitable appointments were being made to both ecclesiastical and secular positions and it was suspected that some of these were bought; it was difficult to gain access to the king; he did not always pay his debts; and finally, the administration of justice was corrupt (Valera 1959b: 8). Various dates have been suggested for the poem's composition, but Nicholas Round argues that 'Its markedly aggrieved tone would link it [...] with the sharply antagonistic turn taken by Spanish politics after the autumn of 1464' (Round 2013: 150). This is a reference to the group of nobles who banded together not only to complain about what they saw as Enrique IV's poor government, perceived Islamophilia and certain defects of character, but also to demand that his half-brother, Alfonso, should be named as heir to the throne in preference to his daughter Juana, whose legitimacy was questioned. All these details are recorded by the chronicler, Palencia (Palencia 1998–99: II, 293–95), and Round also refers to other sources that claim that Enrique was making gestures of appeasement in the form of financial rewards to the members of the Manrique family in early 1465 (Round 2013: 151). Enrique, however, was unwilling to meet the demands made of him, which led to the crowning of Alfonso in Ávila by the rebel nobles. These events lead Round to think that this poem was very probably written in the spring of 1465 in a final attempt to persuade Enrique to govern in a way more acceptable to the nobles. Certainly the poem could not have been written any later than 1466 since it was glossed extensively by Pero Díaz de Toledo who died during that year.

The overriding theme of these verses is the need for good government if a city is to prosper. The opening stanza refers to how ancient Rome flourished in the time of the republic and the consulate of Quintus Fabius Maximus. The second stanza is in stark contrast, with its description of an unnamed 'pueblo' where the poet lives and where 'al neçio fazen alcalde' (Gómez Manrique 2003: 572, l. 10). Although it is known that Manrique was living in Toledo at the time, there is nothing to identify this 'pueblo' or any of its inhabitants by name, although Nancy Marino suggests that the foolish mayor might be Beltrán de la Cueva, one of Enrique IV's favourites who was then at the height of his power and influence, having been appointed maestre de Santiago in 1464 (Marino 2003: 218). The poem consists of a series of what the rubric calls 'Ensienplos e sentençias', illustrating a world turned upside down, as the poet sees it, where people of inferior ability are valued more highly than the more able, and material objects of poor quality are highly prized in preference to those of real value, for example:

> ¡mirad qué gouernaçión,
> ser gouernados los buenos
> por los que no lo son!
> (Gómez Manrique 2003: ll. 22–24)

and 'fierro preçian más que oro, | la plata danla de balde' (ll. 11–12). The use of the words 'cuerdos', 'locos', and 'locura' (ll. 29, 30, 48, 54) all reinforce Manrique's exasperation at the current state of affairs which is summed up in the lines, 'Los cuerdos fuyr deurían | de do locos mandan más' (ll. 29–30). Stanza IV also has echoes of Matthew's gospel: 'que quando los çiegos guían, | ¡guay de los que van detrás!', reminiscent of Matthew 15. 14: 'And if the blind lead the blind, both shall fall into the ditch'.

Manrique's advice about how good leadership can be achieved is delivered in a series of warnings of the consequences of ineffectual government. Men in posts of responsibility need to be able to exert their authority over those under them. Without *regidores* (l. 33) and good kings (l. 79) prosperity is short-lived. Military men must be in firm command for their troops to be successful: 'las huestes sin capitanes | nunca son bien gouernadas' (ll. 39–40). Likewise, the people must be led into battle by their 'caudillos' (l. 101) if they are to fight well. Other people in different walks of life are also deemed necessary for the successful functioning of society, an example being the Church which needs its *letrados* (l. 65). Three stanzas later he states that sheep without a shepherd can do damage to property and cites the example of the Church: 'religiosos sin mayor | grandes cometen maldades' (ll. 91–92). The only other instance of criticism of the clergy by Manrique is in the *Razonamiento de vn rocín a un paje* (322–26) in which an elderly nag explains that he has been ill-used in the past, ridden by a priest who:

> más liebres en mí contadas
> el mató
> que dixo desque nació
> misas rezadas. (ll. 21–24)

The need for control on the part of those with responsibilities is seen as a way of laying firm foundations to society, as expressed in stanza VIII: 'Quanto más alto es el muro, | más fondo çimiento quiere'. This is a warning that a leader who does not manage to reach the top of this metaphorical wall is bound to fall.

In stanza VII Manrique sees a lack of justice in the anonymous 'pueblo' in question, where wrongdoing goes unpunished and services rendered are unrewarded. In the following stanza he observes that the just suffer in an unjust society where greed and self-interest prevail:

> Donde sobra la codiçia
> todos los bienes falleçen;
> en el pueblo sin justiçia
> los que son justos padeçen. (ll. 61–64)

Self-interest is also singled out for comment in VI where it is considered foolish: 'quien se guía por su seso | no va llueñe de locura' and in XI where it is seen to be dangerous: 'do rigen por afiçión | es peligrosa morada' (ll. 87–88). In X the need for justice to be carried out according to the law is expressed with the added comment, 'los reynos sin buenos reyes, | sin adversarios se caen' (ll. 79–80). The repetition of the verb 'caer', also used in VIII, makes the warning clear: a kingdom can be destroyed, not by an enemy state, but by internal unrest caused by lawlessness, which surely reflects the growing tide of dissatisfaction felt by Enrique IV's opponents.

Manrique also voices his belief in the advantages of seeking wise counsel from the elder statesmen of the realm when he declares, 'Los mançebos sin los viejos | son peligrosa metal' (ll. 69–70). This statement might seem at odds with his criticism at the start of stanza III when he complains, 'Queman los nueuos oliuos, | guardan los espinos tuertos', if one takes the 'nueuos oliuos' to refer to the younger generation of men aspiring to assume posts of responsibility. On considering stanza XIV, however, it becomes clear that what he wants to avoid is a lack of temperance and moderation:

> Es peligro nauegar
> en galea sin los remos,
> mas mayor es conuersar
> con quien sigue los estremos. (ll. 105–08)

This could be seen as another veiled criticism of the behaviour of the monarch and his followers, but also as a warning against reacting to events too impulsively.

Various images are used to stress the importance of social cohesion in the city, for example, just as a town without *regidores* will have limited success, so an uninhabited house becomes dilapidated: 'la casa sin moradores | muy prestamente se llueue' (ll. 35–36). In XI Manrique expresses the need for the town to be populated or the surrounding land will be laid waste and in XV he insists on the necessity of the different estates of society co-operating with each other:

> Los menudos sin mayores
> son corredores sin salas;
> los grandes sin los menores,
> como falcones sin alas. (ll. 117–20)

In other words, just as the 'corredores' give access to the large rooms of a house, so do the 'menudos' or lower orders of society play a supporting role by enabling their social superiors to carry out their obligations; the social hierarchy must be protected in order to maintain high standards of leadership.

As Round points out, the final couplet of the second stanza describes how those in charge of the unnamed and corrupt town 'caçan con los aguilochos | cómense los gauilanes' as evidence that the poet 'asserts a familiar class-based grievance against Enrique IV's low-born favourites' (Round 2013: 158). The opening lines of stanza IV, 'La fruta por el sabor | se conoçe su natío', echo the words of Matthew's gospel which continues: 'Do men gather grapes of thorns, or figs of thistles? Even so every good tree bringeth forth good fruit; but a corrupt tree bringeth forth evil fruit' (Matthew 7. 16–17). Manrique is referring to this biblical quotation to make a comparison between the quality of fruit harvested from a poor tree and the consequences of inadequate people in positions of responsibility to govern well in the 'pueblo'. This is yet another expression of distaste for the men in Enrique's immediate circle whom he considers to be ill-suited for the posts they occupy. In stanza XVI Manrique returns to this image of the fruit tree as the nobles' vital role is to support the monarch:

> Que bien como dan las flores
> perfeçión a los frutales,
> así los grandes señores
> a los palaçios reales.
> (Gómez Manrique 2003: ll. 121–24)

This concept is elaborated in stanza XII: 'las cortes sin caualleros | son como manos sin guantes' (ll. 95–96), suggesting that the presence of knights at court can also have a refining or moderating influence. The second quatrain of this verse makes it plain, however, that the prince should be worthy of his place at the top of the social ladder:

> e los prínçipes derechos
> luzen sobr'ellos sin falla,
> bien como los ricos techos
> sobre fermosa muralla. (ll. 125–28)

The message seems clear: Enrique is not a 'príncipe derecho' but consorts with unsuitable men rather than surrounding himself with 'los grandes señores', the very people who are plotting rebellion.

In the penultimate verse the poet returns to the subject of the first, that of ancient Rome, to remind the reader that its prosperity lasted only as long as it was well governed, but decline set in when the self-interest of its citizens took over. The final verse voices the fear that a similar fate will overcome his own 'pueblo' if the current situation continues. These final two stanzas give the poem a small degree of structure in what Round describes as a 'loose-knit, digressive, often repetitious recital of complaint' (Round 2013: 155), yet he suggests that a certain structure is to be found in the *sentencias* which end each cluster of three stanzas since they highlight one particular aspect of the poet's concern (155–56). Although this thesis seems justified in lines 23–24, where 'ser gouernados los buenos | por los que tales no son' really sums up the poem's subject matter, and lines 119–20 neatly express the need for co-operation among all strata of society, it does not always stand up to a close reading of the poem. Lines 47–48, 'quien se guía por su seso | no ua llueñe de locura', do not appear to sum up entirely the content of that stanza and the two that precede it. Similarly, lines 73–74 which start a new cluster of three stanzas, would appear to echo the final lines of the previous stanza.

Scholberg comments on the apparent lack of structure of the poem: 'este revoltijo de lugares comunes que ha confeccionado el poeta intencionadamente refleja el caos de la sociedad' (Scholberg 1984: 31), but this would have been a very innovative technique on the poet's part. Nancy Marino refers to the poem as 'una lista algo amorfa' (Marino 2003: 214). Perhaps a better key to explaining the seemingly chaotic sequence of images is to be found in Pero Díaz de Toledo's gloss on the poem where he says that Manrique's writing 'non discrepa de los santos e profetas que semejante querella quisyeron fazer a Dios' (Gómez Manrique 2003: 578). This statement suggests that the rather disjointed form of the poem follows the example available to him from the Old Testament book of *Lamentations*, a litany of verses despairing at the state of the city due to the transgressions of its inhabitants which opens with the words: 'How doth the city sit solitary, that was full of people'. Four verses later the words 'Her adversaries are the chief, her enemies prosper' would doubtless have rung true to Manrique.

The choice of vocabulary to describe this situation of 'the world turned upside down' is also indicative of the poet's reaction to what he sees, with certain key words recurring frequently to convey a sense of exasperation. Apart from the repetition of the words 'loco' or 'locura', already mentioned above, the danger of the situation is emphasized with the use of 'peligro' or 'peligroso' four times in stanzas X to XIV (ll. 76, 88, 105, 112), while 'caer' and 'caýda' occur three times (ll. 59, 80, 140) to warn of the disastrous consequences of bad government in a city. The word 'gouernar' and its cognates recur frequently (ll. 22, 23, 27, 28, 40, 75, 144). Similarly 'regir' occurs in lines 2, 87, 132 and 138, with its cognate 'regidores' in line 33. Comparisons between good government and the steering of a ship abound: no fewer than six words for ship can be found: 'nauío', 'barco', 'nao', 'galea' and 'carracas sin barquetes' (ll. 28, 76, 85, 106, 115). Particularly noticeable is the constant use of anaphora, with the word 'sin' occurring no fewer than thirty-six times between stanzas V and XVI to denote the lack of control or preparedness for action that the poet observes in this 'pueblo'. To quote Round again, this poem is a *querella* and writing in that genre 'repetition and anaphora counted for more than logical ingenuity' (Round 2013: 155).

Pero Díaz de Toledo's Reactions to the *Esclamaçión e querella*

Four responses to this poem have come down to us, by Pero Díaz de Toledo, Pero Guillén de Segovia, Antón de Montoro and Antonio de Soria. The fullest and most detailed is Díaz's voluminous prose commentary (Gómez Manrique 2003: 577–618), many times longer than the poem and probably written in late 1465 or 1466, the year of his death. This *letrado* had translated classical texts at the court of Juan II and had been chaplain to the marqués de Santillana. After the latter's death he moved to the household of Alfonso Carrillo, where he would have known Manrique.

Originally the function of a gloss on a text was explanatory, giving information to aid comprehension in the margins of a manuscript; later glosses became longer, summarizing a text's content. A further development came when the gloss became a full-blown, discursive commentary in which the author took the original text as a starting point to explore its wider implications. Some texts were glossed by their authors, one example being the *consolatoria* that Manrique wrote for his sister, Juana Manrique. The marqués de Santillana annotated his own *Proverbios* which were then expanded by Díaz to the extent that '*Los proverbios* became a theological and philosophical tract' (Weiss 1990: 129). Díaz did the same for Manrique's *Esclamaçión*, taking a sequence of *mundus inversus* images to produce a treatise.

The rubric *Yntroduçión al dezir que conpuso el noble cauallero Gómez Manrique*, is perhaps significant, suggesting a need to explain the content, and gives its author the opportunity to interpret it in the manner he chooses. Feeling the need to justify his action in writing this gloss, he asks Carrillo's permission to do so. It is plain from his comments that the poem had received a mixed reaction and some people were obviously disturbed by its content, 'interpretando la sentençia e palabras de algunas de las coplas a no sana parte, en manera de reprehensión' (Gómez Manrique 2003: 578). Others, however, supported Manrique, 'afirmando ser verdad lo en las coplas contenido e non aver cosa que calupniar en ellas' and this is the reason he gives for taking it upon himself to explain Manrique's views (578). These remarks tell us a lot about the public ambience in which Manrique wrote and the relative immediacy of the impact of his writings. Never overtly partisan, Díaz wants, he claims, to show 'quand enseñadamente escriuió [Manrique] e que su escriuir non discrepa de los santos e profetas que semejante querella quisyeron fazer a Dios de la que este cauallero muestra fazer' (578). He submitted his commentary for Carrillo's approval, asking that, if the Archbishop is satisfied, it should be circulated among his household. Díaz may have thought that he would be more adept at countering the objections to the poem's content than the Archbishop, but he takes care to add that he is sure that Manrique will also know how to explain his intentions in writing it.

Although Díaz never openly supports the sentiments aired in the poem, his comparison of Manrique with the Old Testament prophets suggests his approval of the work's content. It is significant that before embarking on his commentary he digresses and makes some reflections on the origins of poetry, citing amongst others Moses, Solomon, Homer and Virgil before mentioning Pérez de Guzmán and Santillana. The reason for this digression might be that as recently as the mid-1440s some clerics, including Alonso de Cartagena, had taken a negative view of poetry, seeking to control the reading habits of the aristocracy (Weiss 1990: 24). Díaz, however, has no reservations in this respect and offers qualified approval for Manrique whom he considers capable of producing poetry of the same quality as Guzmán and Santillana: 'sy el tienpo le da logar a continuar e continúa, yrá en el alcança a los caballeros nonbrados e publicará su yngenio de buenas e fructuosas cosas' (Gómez Manrique 2003: 581–82).

Díaz does not write a gloss on all eighteen stanzas of the poem but limits his extensive commentary to nine of them. There is some overlap in the content and I therefore discuss his comments on a thematic basis. His reactions to the complaints of Manrique are a mixture of those of a theologian offering his wisdom to a lay person and comment of a political nature which is influenced by writers both from classical antiquity and the Christian tradition. The measured tone of his learned commentary acts as a foil to the impatient tone of Manrique's verses, which become in his hands a springboard to examine in much greater detail the issues that they raise.

The Example of Ancient Rome

Two important points emerge from Díaz's gloss on the first stanza as he ponders on what it was that made ancient Rome such a great power. Firstly, early in their history, the inhabitants prospered because they were not greedy for material gain, but instead put the good of their community before all other considerations. Secondly, he reminds us that king Tarquinius was banished because the ancient Romans resented 'el yugo real' imposed upon them (583). Using the verb 'fizieron' to emphasize that the consuls who followed Tarquinius were elected by the people, he does not conceal the way in which monarchical rule was seen by the Romans: 'Aquel estado real no es auido commo la bienquerencia del que conseja, mas commo la soberbia del que enseñorea' (583).

The question of kingship arises again in the gloss on stanza V when, having admitted that the king is 'vicario de Dios en lo tenporal e tiene su lugar en la tierra' (600), Díaz asks the question, raised also in ancient times, whether it is more important to have a good king or good laws. Recalling that Aristotle held that a king was subject to human passions and could therefore err, so that it was more important to have good laws in place, Díaz insists that the king is subject to both natural and divine law. Although kings can sometimes modify laws, they cannot remove them completely, so that it is right that they should conform to them. Díaz is surely thinking here of the situation in Castile where Enrique IV had absolute power with the legacy inherited from his father Juan II and Álvaro de Luna. Angus MacKay describes how, even before their victory at Olmedo in 1445, Juan II and his favourite had summoned the *cortes* in order to impose the concept of absolute royal power (MacKay 1977: 138–39). Regarding Enrique's subsequent behaviour, MacKay remarks, 'Time and again noble factions found their plans thwarted by the king's inordinate fondness of using his absolute power' (141).

Divine Providence

Díaz takes the couplet, 'En vn pueblo donde moro | al nesçio fazen alcalde' (Gómez Manrique 2003: 572, ll. 9–10), and uses it as a starting point for reflecting on the problem of the foolish who govern and of the just and virtuous who go without reward for, or recognition of, their good qualities. Quoting Jeremiah: 'Señor, ¿por qué la carrera de los malos prospera?' (588), he takes the opportunity to launch into reflections on divine providence. As he considers this question he alludes several times to the book of Job. This book, with its story of the suffering and resignation of its protagonist, offers an example of Stoicism as embraced by certain Christians, many of them *conversos* like Díaz, who were influenced by the writings of Seneca at this time. Díaz, who translated some of Seneca's works, reminds us that Job's three friends erred when they insisted that the pain men suffer in this world is divine punishment. Job is held up as an example of a good Catholic because, after a period of despair and bitterness in the face of many disasters, he came to believe in retribution and was rewarded with prosperity in his old age.

It is perhaps noteworthy that this *converso* writer should choose a Jew as his example and use him as a role model when he lived in a society that had seen so much violence committed against Jews and *conversos* and in which the insistence on *limpieza de sangre* had caused so much havoc. Neither Manrique in his poem, nor Díaz in his gloss, mention the atrocities committed in Toledo during the pogrom of 1449. That particular episode of violence was caused by demands from Juan II for additional taxes to be raised, the chief tax collector being a family member of the *converso* poet Rodrigo Cota. As a result of the ensuing turmoil, men of Jewish origin were barred from public office by the Sentencia-Estatuto of 1449 and many others were killed or injured. Since Díaz and Manrique would have been particularly aware of these events, residing as they were in a household alongside a number of *conversos*, it is not unreasonable to suggest that the first couplet of the second stanza of the *Esclamaçión* reflects the fact that Toledo had lost many able New Christians who had played a significant role in the administration of the city.

Díaz recalls Saint Augustine's assertion that God in his wisdom so arranged matters that all men, virtuous or not, should be exposed to good and evil. Pain and suffering come to all men, but no man should feel rejected by God on seeing that the virtuous and godly also suffer. That the undeserving gain office is all part of God's plan for the world, and Díaz concludes this section of his commentary with the reflection that people get the government they deserve: 'Dios por su profundo e alto saber dispone e ordena de tales gouernadores de quales los gouernados son dignos' (596). In other words, Díaz agrees with Manrique, sharing his condemnatory view of contemporary society.

Justice

Glossing Manrique's stanzas VII and X, Díaz discusses the topic of justice and cites several writers of the past, alluding to Aristotle's conviction that justice is the greatest of all virtues (605). Perhaps his most outspoken and pertinent comment is from Saint Augustine: 'Sy la justiçia es apartada e quitada de los reynos, no son otra cosa los reynos synon grandes conpañías de ladrones, e las conpañías de ladrones no son otra cosa synon pequeños reynos' (615). Laws should be enforced by those competent to do so; justice should be seen to be done and individuals should not interpret the law to gain personal benefit at the expense of others. He responds to Manrique's warning that without a good system of justice the state will fail and advocates a pragmatic approach to the interpretation of the law, as it should be put into effect in the spirit in which it was conceived:

> la buena gouernaçión de los reynos e vniuersydades es en aver executores buenos de las leyes que las apliquen a la ynteçión del que las ordenó, e tomen entre las opiniones de los doctores aquella opinión que vieren más benigna e amiga de la ley. (614)

The Clergy

Díaz also chooses to comment on stanza IX, elaborating on the need for prelates of the Church to have sufficient knowledge to be able to defend the Catholic faith and resist heresy. Just as walls hold up a palace, so knowledge supports the Church, as Saint Jerome said: 'los labrios del saçerdote guardan justiçia e la ley se buscará e requerýa de su boca, que ángel de Dios es' (608), a clear statement of conviction about the priest's important role in society. It is not just knowledge that is needed, but experience: like Aristotle, he acknowledges many good qualities of the younger generation, but points out that Alexander the Great depended on the counsel and wisdom of old men who had seen many campaigns. He recalls the words of Sallust who said that all advisors should be devoid of 'toda yra e de toda malquerençia e de toda amistançia e de toda misericordia' (612) so that, by being unbiased, they may make good judgements.

The Three Estates and Social Cohesion

In his comments on stanzas VI and XII Díaz turns his thoughts to the structure of society where he supports the traditional view of the three estates of men: 'defensores e oradores e labradores', each having a defined role that creates a harmonious society. The nobles should be like 'los braços del rey para le ayudar e tener el reyno en paz e la execuçión de la justiçia' (616) without whose support the king would find it hard to rule. The clergy should pray for God's grace and the workers provide sustenance for all. Mindful, no doubt, of the various conflicts that were taking place in Castile during the 1460s, Díaz emphasizes the importance of obedience to the governor of a city or the leader of an army, as otherwise chaos will reign: 'Ca pueblo syn capitanes es commo cuerpo syn cabeça, dispuesto a total perdiçión' (603). If all men carried out the duties assigned to them the kingdom would prosper, a reminder of Manrique's words when he makes the comparison between a well-ordered society and a *vihuela* that has been properly strung (ll. 43–44). He interprets the final two lines of this verse, 'quien se guía por su seso | no va lueñe de locura', as meaning that it is unwise to insist unduly on one's own opinions since a man's judgement can be corrupted by personal considerations.

In the final paragraphs of his gloss on stanza XII Díaz digresses and discusses the origin of the word *corte*, the derivation supposedly being from the verb 'cortar' because 'en la corte ha de estar el espada de la justiçia que ha de cortar a todos los males e todos los tuertos e las fuerças e las soberuias que se fazen' (617), thus returning to the subject of justice. The *corte* should be frequented by those members of the first estate, as otherwise the king would find himself unable to maintain peace or justice and, looking back to Manrique's words, he says that the *corte* would be 'desnuda commo las manos syn guantes' (617). He alludes to a dialogue in one of Seneca's tragedies in which the emperor Nero is told by the author that it is right that he should be surrounded by wise men who, with the welfare of the state in mind, will advise him to grant pardons and refrain from imposing cruel punishments. Creating peace and tranquillity is 'la mayor virtud que puede aver en el prínçipe, e que los prínçipes que procuran la paz e tranquilydad en su tienpo tiene camino dispuesto e aparejado para el çielo' (617). By alluding to the notorious emperor, Díaz is distancing himself from overt criticism of contemporary events, but the implication is clear: there are parallels to be found between Nero and the current monarch. He concludes his comments by reminding us of Christ's teaching that a kingdom in which there is peace and good government will prosper and flourish, but that a divided one will fail and be destroyed.

The Responses of Guillén de Segovia and Antón de Montoro

Pero Guillén de Segovia, also a member of Carrillo's household, produced a reply of seventeen stanzas, 'Es enuidia mucho braua' (Guillén de Segovia 1989: 129–33) which follow the same rhyme scheme. In comparison with the original poem this is a restrained piece of writing. It is evident that the author is not altogether in agreement with Manrique: he is so guarded in the way he expresses himself that in places he appears self-contradictory.

In the first two stanzas he reflects on the subject of praise, flattery and adverse criticism:

> Quyen retrata de personas
> do tanta virtud sençierra
> y les roba sus coronas,
> çiertamente mucho yerra. (ll. 5–8)

He appears to be referring to the nobles' rebellious attitude towards Enrique IV, but on the other hand, he is also against praise which is not justified:

> Del consejo desadoro
> donde todos dizen dalde
> fermosura no es tesoro
> mayormente da(l)bayalde. (ll. 9)

Assuming that 'da(l)bayalde' in modern Spanish would be 'de albayalde', meaning 'white lead', a substance used in cosmetics in the Middle Ages, in this context it would imply the use of false flattery. Guillén then resorts to making an analogy with the bird kingdom when he says that he does not want to see

> falcones galanes
> que faze(n) buelos de mochos
> y presas dalcaravanes. (ll. 14–16)

The falcon is traditionally considered a noble bird, loyal to its master, which suggests that he does not wish to see the nobler members of society reduced to a more lowly rank, the equivalent in the world of birds to 'mochos' (owls) or 'alcaravanes' (curlews). He seems to be sitting on the fence, uncomfortable at the thought of criticizing the monarch, and yet apparently siding with the old nobility who are offended by the treatment they have received.

Mindful of the effect of expressing his opinions, he warns that it is unwise to speak out and make enemies within one's own circle: 'quyien de suyos fase agenos

| no govierna dyscryçión' (ll. 23–24). Excesses are to be avoided and he recalls the Stoic virtue of temperance in the fourth stanza, when he advises striving for prudent restraint. There appear to be words of warning in the fifth stanza where Guillén thinks it is unwise to speak plainly, claiming that he has seen honest people act in such a way as to cause those beneath them to suffer in long-drawn-out conflicts. In the sixth stanza he declares that those who weave subtle plots and sail against the prevailing wind are motivated by self-will rather than reason:

> amaynar deve sus velas
> quyen a viento del reves
> de voluntad bive preso. (ll. 43–45)

They must trim their sails to avoid being hurt where there is no justice. He appears to suggest to Manrique that he should be more prudent in the pronouncements that he makes in what has become an unjust society.

In stanza VII Guillén offers some thoughts on the nature of nobility that are very similar to those discussed in the previous chapter: nobility depends on the personal honour and integrity of the individual. He exhorts us to live in the present and not to become corrupted or to think of the future since we have no idea of what it has in store for us, but insists that nobility should not become corrupt even in times of crisis. Guillén reinforces the Stoic idea that virtue is its own reward, commenting that those who speak out bravely in favour of those who have been wrongly condemned achieve a pardon for them by so doing. He counterbalances this, however, in an image based on the game of chess to warn of the inherent dangers of being outspoken: 'que quyen pierde sus trebejos | recabe xaque mortal' (ll. 71–72), the 'trebejos' being the chessmen and the 'xaque mortal' checkmate.

The next three stanzas (ll. 73–96) focus on the state of the nation. Although Guillén claims to be restrained in what he is saying, he notes a change in the social atmosphere when he observes:

> vi fuscar dia sereno
> con ayre caliginoso [...]
> toros bravos fechos bueyes
> desque al yugo se retraen. (ll. 76–77, 79–80)

He implies that power has fallen into the wrong hands, and thus agrees with one of the central ideas in Manrique's original poem. He expresses his surprise and disappointment at this state of affairs by declaring, 'pues de tan alta naçión | no sespera tal errada' (ll. 85–86) and goes on to opine that nobility has become debased and tarnished: 'su vygor proçede vano | de la ley ques usurpada (ll. 99–100).

The final four stanzas contain a statement of Guillén's conviction that although there are times when silence should be maintained, there is a moral duty to speak out when it is appropriate to do so. The man who is guided by reason retains his judgement and in speaking out shows evidence of society's turmoil: 'De rebueltas y rigores | tales fablas son señales' (ll. 113–14). The moral value of standing up for your principles and not being deflected from your purpose is upheld when the poet declares:

> quien en virtuosos hechos
> mucho constante se halla
> arterios nin pertrechos
> no corrompe su batalla. (ll. 117–20)

He continues in this vein by declaring that it is fitting to pay the ultimate price for one's beliefs: 'digo ques bien porfiar | en morir sobre la fe' (ll. 123–24). Those who deny the faith are not sincere in their outward practice of religion.

Antón de Montoro responds to five of Manrique's *octavas*, the first of which is a gloss on the opening stanza, 'Quando Roma prosperaua'. Emphasizing the concept of loyalty that existed in the past but which is fast disappearing, Montoro first uses a nautical metaphor to convey the image of a ship moving backwards: 'En esos tiempos bogaba | lealtad, la cual hoy cía' (Montoro 1990: 276, ll. 1–2). He follows this by evoking the picture of a boy keeping watch while his master sleeps, strongly suggesting that the responsibilities of government are in the hands of the inexperienced due to the idleness of their superiors. In the first couplet of his second quatrain he reflects on the fact that nowadays anyone who acts with integrity only lays himself open to harm. There is a change of subject in the final two lines when Montoro draws an analogy between giving fodder to lazy animals and encouraging men who are idle, which can again be interpreted as a criticism of those holding the reins of power.

The second gloss is on Manrique's second stanza where Montoro takes the verb 'moro' in the original poem and uses it with a completely different meaning when he highlights the willingness of men to falsify their true nature for personal gain:

> Ya vimos a negro moro
> bien ponerse el albayalde,
> y a buen cristiano de coro
> parallo color de jalde. (277, ll. 1–4)

The second quatrain opens with the lines 'y muy bravos aguatochos | ahogar y dar afanes' (ll. 5–6), suggesting that people are not of sufficient courage to stand up to the upheavals they face in political life. A similar technique is used to introduce the third gloss (278) where Montoro links the word 'arroyo' of Manrique's seventh stanza to 'malvado'. In her edition of Montoro's poetry, Marithelma Costa points out that in one manuscript the first line of this gloss reads 'Las entradas del mal vado', thus maintaining the image of moving water, but completely changing the subject of the comment that he makes (278n). Montoro continues by warning that people must be prepared to act against the arrival of men intent on attack. His fourth gloss is on the third stanza 'Queman los nueuos olivos', where the parallel between ineffectual government and the 'dead wood' of the trees is retained from the original poem. The second quatrain introduces harsh criticism of the inhabitants of this imaginary town who are afraid to express their opinions frankly: 'Los naturales que ajenos | se hacen con opinión' (ll. 5–6).

The shortest gloss, 'En el tiempo que yo estaua', a single *octava* by Antonio de Soria (ID2043, Dutton 1990–91: II, 446), reveals nothing of his thoughts on the issues raised in the poem, saying that he now finds it hard to write verse because of his increasing age. Those who ask him to do so are misguided: 'mas do tú, Vejez, te entonas | todo bien se nos destierra' (ll. 5–6), which suggests that he did not wish to become involved in any controversy.

In conclusion, the *Esclamaçión* was clearly intended to cause a stir, and did so. While Antonio de Soria refrained from comment, Montoro's use of a diverse set of images in a similar style to the original poem suggests that he is supportive of Manrique. Guillén sits on the fence: his approach is that of a man who wishes to avoid further conflict and he confines himself to making a few general statements about nobility and the integrity of standing up for one's principles. It is a solemn and temperate piece of writing and, while engaging with Manrique's complaints, seeks to mollify those who have taken exception to it. The fact that Díaz chose to write such a lengthy and erudite gloss confers considerable status on the poem and on Manrique, whom he praises in his introduction (Gómez Manrique 2003: 579). By offering explanations to some of the stanzas and thereby clarifying their meaning, he clearly wishes to support Manrique and give a degree of solemnity to his message, drawing on such well-established authorities as Aristotle, Saint Augustine and Boethius.

While, as we have seen, Manrique was composing verses to engage with what to him was the bitter political reality under Enrique IV during the mid 1460s, a few years later he felt able to write two other works in a very different tone. Both were written after the marriage of Isabel to Fernando of Aragon in 1469. One is addressed to Fernando; the other is to both Fernando and his wife and is a major work concerning matters of state for them to ponder before their accession to the throne.

De Gómez Manrique al señor Prínçipe de Castilla e de Aragón, Rey de Seçilia

This poem of five *décimas*, 'Tales boluimos, señor' (Gómez Manrique 2003: 621–23), addressed to Fernando of Aragon, can be dated to 1473, by which time Fernando had married the infanta Isabel of Castile, thus creating a rapprochement between the two kingdoms. Fernando's father, Juan II of Aragon, had managed to hold on to the city of Perpignan and the area known as Roussillon, much to the regret of Louis XI of France who was now threatening to attack Perpignan and hoping that Charles of Burgundy would help him. Both Diego de Valera and the *Crónica anónima de Enrique IV* relate the events that took place and stress the bravery not only of Fernando, but also of his elderly father who refused to leave Perpignan despite the entreaties of the Aragonese and Catalans who were with him (Valera 1941: 246–61; *Crónica anónima*, 1991: II, 412–23). The French besieged the city and, although they greatly outnumbered the assembled Aragonese, Catalan and Castilian forces, were defeated.

It is not clear where Manrique was at the time of writing these verses, for if he took part in the fighting there is no mention of his presence in the chronicles. He does, however, write in the first person plural as if he went as one of the Castilian contingent to the rescue of Juan II and the Aragonese and Catalan forces, and there is a strong suggestion that he was also present when Fernando took his leave of Isabel. The intention of the poem, however, is not to discuss these events but to lavish praise upon both Fernando and Isabel.

Fernando is compared to the Trojan warrior Hector because his qualities of leadership are such that the Castilians feel themselves lost without him: 'Estamos commo galea | careçiente de patrón' (Gómez Manrique 2003: 622, ll. 11–12). Manrique extols the virtues of Isabel, emphasizes her sadness at Fernando's departure, and holds her up as a model of marital fidelity, comparing her to the turtle-dove, the stock symbol of fidelity in medieval bestiaries: 'La qual fuye las verduras | commo la tórtola faze' (ll. 21–22), and to the goddess Diana, the personification of chastity. In the final stanza Fernando is hailed as the king-to-be of Aragon and Manrique declares his support for Fernando as the future king of Castile and León. He praises him for his action in Roussillon, urging him to secure the future of that region:

> pues tomastes tal empresa
> no la dexedes represa,
> que no es para dexar,
> ni la fermosa syn par
> muy eçelente Prinçesa. (ll. 46–50)

This is a statement of confidence in the leadership of Fernando, and in making it Manrique is vindicating his active participation in promoting the marriage of Isabel and Fernando.

Much as he may have admired this young couple, he took it upon himself to write a long poem, known as the *Regimiento de príncipes*, preceded by a *prohemio* in prose, in which he offers advice on how best to govern the country when they accede to the throne. Both were written at some point after their marriage in October 1469 and before the death of Enrique IV in 1474, as the dedication to the 'Prínçipes de los reynos de Castilla e de Aragón' attests. Despite the fact that he is writing to his social superiors, he is not afraid to tell them how they may work towards self-improvement.

Gómez Manrique's *Prohemio* to the *Regimiento de prínçipes*

The *prohemio* (Gómez Manrique 2003: 624–28) explains Manrique's reasons for writing the poem: if we are to take literally what he says, he was motivated by a combination of forces. He finds it natural that men and women should feel a patriotic love of their country and, as a member of a family of ancient and noble lineage, he considers himself particularly well fitted for this task. Although he has not succeeded to any title as a younger son of a nobleman, he points out that he has, nevertheless, inherited certain attributes which can neither be passed on nor taken away in a will, namely 'el amor natural que mis pasados touieron a esta patria donde honrradamente byuieron e acabaron y están sepultados' (625). Admitting that he does not have the power that some of his family have wielded, he is still desirous of exercising some influence by offering his advice. His allusion to 'las negoçiaçiones en que la alteza vuestra de mí se ha querido seruir' (626) presumably refers to his diplomatic mission to bring Fernando and Isabel together by working with Archbishop Carrillo and Juan II of Aragon to arrange their marriage. It was Manrique who took the news to Juan II of Aragon, Fernando's father, that the terms of the alliance had been agreed between Carrillo and the Aragonese envoy Peralta.

Why should Manrique have written the *Prohemio*? Perhaps initially it was intended only to be read by Isabel and Fernando whilst the poem itself was for more public circulation. There is certainly a contradiction to be found between the two texts which might support this view. In the *Prohemio* the poet expresses the hope that the couple will be such good monarchs that the memories of both their good and bad predecessors will be forgotten, or if that is not possible, at least that they will not be spoken of. This is rather surprising since not only does the poem contain a number of stanzas on the subject of past monarchs, most of them bad, but the section on the virtue of prudence makes a point of saying that where temporal matters are concerned it is important for those in government to be mindful of the past.

The wording of the *prohemio* is more forthright than that of the poem itself particularly in what is said about the need for strong monarchs. In the *prohemio* there is overt criticism of the situation in which Spain finds itself due to the damage inflicted by a succession of weak kings; mention is made of the 'grande oprobio y difamia suya e destruyçión d'estos reynos' and the 'crudas llagas' that have been inflicted upon the nation (626). Another contradiction between *prohemio* and poem is to be found when, speaking of the inevitability of disaster that ensues with a bad government, Manrique comments: 'no ha menester vuestra alteza abtoridades ni enxemplos antiguos pues los modernos bastan asaz, sy con claros ojos mirarlos querrá la real señoría vuestra' (627). This is in contrast to the poem itself when direct references are made to monarchs of the past who brought ruin upon their kingdoms. The statement that the task the couple faces is enormous because 'con mayor dificultad se hemiendan las cosas herradas que se fazen de prinçipio' (626) seems to emphasize that Manrique is making a more direct appeal to Isabel and Fernando to consider the gravity of the political situation in which the country finds itself than he does in the poem. He alludes to the fact that he has written his work in verse, explaining that he thinks that the medium is more memorable.

The *Regimiento de prínçipes*

This poem, 'Prínçipe de cuyo nonbre', seventy-nine stanzas of nine octosyllabic lines (629–56), is conceived in the 'mirror of princes' tradition, offering advice to the young couple so that they may prepare themselves to govern wisely before they accede to the throne. Most of the stanzas are addressed to Fernando, no doubt on the assumption that he would wield greater power than Isabel when she inherited the Castilian Crown despite the terms of their marriage contract of March 1469 in which, as J. H. Elliott explains, 'it was made clear that he was to take second place in the government of the country' (Elliott 2002: 22). In the *prohemio* the poet claims to have prepared the necessary material to write a separate poem for Isabel but to have been lacking in 'el saber para le dar forma y el tiempo para la seguir' (Gómez Manrique 2003: 628). Indeed, he seems to have combined both projected poems in this single composition since the content of the advice offered in it to Isabel is certainly very different from that directed to Fernando.

Gómez Manrique's Reflections on Rulers of the Past

An analysis of the poem shows it falls into six sections. The first, of seventeen stanzas, begins with references to history in which Fernando is reminded that there have been four previous kings of the same name who have been 'justiçieros, esforçados, | dignos de gran renombre' (ll. 3–4). Reminding the young couple that monarchs who listened to those who flattered them have always brought about their own downfall, Manrique gives examples from the Old Testament, ancient history and Spanish history, such as Don Rodrigo and Pedro I, known as Pedro el Cruel. All of this justifies Manrique's attempt to exhort Fernando to avoid 'moços apasionadas' (l. 112) but instead, in order to save the country from disaster, to be guided by men of wisdom, loyalty and discretion. These will be people who will be guided by 'razón', as opposed to those governed by their impulses or desires (voluntad), seeking 'los viçios | y deleytes mundanales' (ll. 122–23).

The Theological Virtues

Manrique opens the second section, stanzas XVIII to XXIX, with what he considers the most important advice, that Fernando should be well-read, so that he may attain sufficient wisdom to 'dyçerner el byen del mal' (l. 157). The poet makes no recommendations as to what he deems suitable reading matter for a future monarch, but, to judge by the content of what follows, he was surely thinking of works with a solidly moral content. There is a reminder that although he has been born to rule he should be a faithful servant to the Lord, and should not place too much trust in his might and worldly wealth, as did Nebuchadnezzar, king of ancient Babylon, with disastrous consequences.

In the following nine stanzas, XXI–XXIX, the poet asks Fernando to reflect on the three theological virtues of faith, hope and charity. He insists that the prince should have faith in God and believe in an afterlife to achieve salvation. Those who reject such beliefs 'fazen exçesos bestiales | dignos de gran dyçiplina (ll. 201–02), which lead to civil strife and unrest, should be punished. He observes that some people exert themselves 'por byen byuir' (l. 223) whereas others do so 'por no deçendyr | al pozo luçiferal' (ll. 224–25), thus suggesting a moral superiority in those who opt to live an upright life on principle rather than solely to avoid damnation. This observation leads him to speak of the virtue of hope, namely that it is unreasonable to expect to gain salvation by faith alone, but that it is necessary to perform good works as well: 'mas obras deuéys juntar | con esta tal esperança' (ll. 233–34). He declares that to achieve happiness is impossible without charity: 'pues a qualquier miserable | deuéys ser caritativo' (ll. 248–49) and continues by quoting from 1 Corinthians 13 on the subject of love being the most important of the Christian virtues. These three virtues of faith, hope and charity are thus seen as interdependent.

The Cardinal or Stoic Virtues

In the third section, stanzas, XXX–LIV, devoted to the cardinal or Stoic virtues of prudence, justice, temperance and fortitude, it is clear that Manrique is formulating advice to influence Fernando's behaviour in such a way that he will gain the loyalty of his subjects. Where prudence is concerned, the poet reminds him again that in temporal matters Fernando should be mindful of the past, well organized about the present, and provident as regards the future. He expands what he had to say about 'moços apasyonados' in stanza XIII, hoping the prince will take advice from men considered wise and just and avoid those who in their youth behaved irresponsibly.

On the virtue of justice, Manrique urges Fernando to treat everyone equitably and not to be swayed 'por amor ni por cobdiçia' (l. 319). When making appointments he advises against giving them to 'onbres apasyonados' (l. 346) and urges him to be generous in his dealings with his subjects:

> Las penas y los tormentos
> deuéys dar syenpre menores,
> los galardones mayores
> que son los mereçimientos. (ll. 352–55)

He wants the afflicted to receive consolation and calls for a balanced attitude towards punishment, with the prince steering a course which is neither overly rigorous nor lenient.

Having promised to speak frankly in the first stanza of the poem, the tone of XLI is blunt, indicating a perception on the poet's part of two character traits he finds unattractive in Fernando. One of these is cruelty in meting out justice: 'Que ramo de crueldad | es justiçia regurossa' (ll. 361–62); the other is meanness:

> dar grandes dones syn tiento
> es cosa muy reprouada;
> mas mucho menos consyento
> que seades avariento,
> que peor es no dar nada. (ll. 365–69)

The same desire to avoid extremes is seen again in his advice on the subject of temperance, for instance, the time spent on the leisure pursuits of 'juegos, caças, montería' (l. 380) should not be excessive.

Fortitude is also considered an important attribute in a ruler: references to the many Christian saints who possessed this virtue show that Manrique's thinking is still shaped by a fusion of Christian and Stoic ideals. The theme of the constant conflict between reason and desire (*razón* y *voluntad*) is raised again with the poet claiming that there is no greater enemy than *voluntad*. The Stoic ideal of cultivating an inner strength to face the moral challenges that life will bring is clearly stated:

> que no sé mayor vytoria
> de todas quantas leý,
> ni dygna de mayor gloria
> para perpetua memoria
> que vençer el onbre a sý.
> (Gómez Manrique 2003: ll. 446–50)

Three stanzas of a *Conparaçión* follow these thoughts on fortitude to underline the message that Spain needs strong government. Manrique illustrates these verses by making two comparisons between monarchs and members of the animal kingdom. Kings who fear their subjects are not good at meting out justice; they are either like lambs fleeing from a fox or resemble insects caught in a spider's web, always vulnerable to attacks from the more powerful (ll. 460–68). To avoid comparable situations and to see that justice is done, it is moral courage that Manrique sees as necessary when he writes:

> vn coraçón tan constante
> es sin dubda menester
> que de nada no se espante. (ll. 482–84)

A Definition of True Fortitude

The influence of Stoicism is seen again in a fourth section of six stanzas, LV–LX which is subtitled 'Difiniçión del esfuerço verdadero'. Here the poet expresses the idea that true effort is not a matter of merely acting fearlessly but in suffering this fear in a selfless way if this is for the greater good. The examples he gives here are not of Christians but of heroes from antiquity who made the ultimate sacrifice to benefit their people. Death in such situations is seen as superior to living a cowardly or weak existence, the 'byuir menguado' to which Manrique alludes in stanza LV. In LVII he asserts that such an existence is not worth living when he says, 'pues con menguado biuir | el byuo se torna muerto'. In times of conflict he warns that it takes greater courage to defend one's country than to go to war and conquer since defence is necessary, but the need to conquer is not: 'al conquistar al reués | por ser cosa voluntaria' (ll. 521–22), all of which indicates a desire for self-restraint, moderation and diplomacy. Furthermore he sees truthfulness as the basis for friendship and, combined with generosity and graciousness, important for relationships with one's enemies. In so saying, Manrique appears mindful of the history of internal strife in the Iberian Peninsula and of the current hostility between those backing Isabel and Fernando as successors to the throne and their rivals who were supporting the claim of the infanta Juana, whose paternity was questionable. He is hopeful that, by putting these precepts of Stoic thought into practice, Fernando might create for himself a position of real authority. Stanza LX makes the rather optimistic observation that monarchs who are just and frank can flatten obstacles and fortresses for these will always be overcome by 'justiçia con franqueza | y con verdad esmaltada' (ll. 536–37).

Advice to Isabel

In the fifth section, LXII–LXXV, Isabel receives a very different sort of guidance from Manrique, who probably had little idea of how much influence she would wield once she became queen in her own right. The words of an *estrena* that he addressed to her in 1468, reveal his hopes for the future and his assumptions about her place in a marriage with Fernando, who had become King of Sicily that year:

> Este Dios muy soberano
> os haga reyna tenprano,
> dándovos rey por marido,
> moço, gentil y valiente,
> de los suyos bien querido,
> de los estraños temido.
> (313, ll. 11, 15–16, 19–21)

Although Manrique says he will not flatter Isabel, this is exactly what he does, and in glowing terms: God made her 'cuerda, discreta, sentyda, | en virtud esclareçida' (ll. 560–61) and physically she is of 'estrema belleza' and 'lynda proporçion' (ll. 563–64). The content of his advice is thin and lacks a logical structure, being largely of a negative kind. He uses most of these stanzas to tell her what she should not do and, contrary to his message to Fernando, he addresses her in simple language devoid of abstract concepts.

He oscillates between warning against excessive piety and failure in religious observance, interspersing these lines with thoughts on the dispensing of justice. Isabel must guard against excesses that include fasting and self-inflicted physical punishment (ll. 577–87), but be mindful that the responsibility of government 'no se da para folgar | al verdadero regiente' (ll. 593–94), spending her energies in ruling justly, equitably and without any cruelty. As with Fernando, there is an implied judgement of her character: she could be somewhat rigid in making decisions and dispensing justice. This brings her the warning: 'no se mezcle crueldad | con la tal esecuçion' (ll. 601–02). He returns to the subject of religion, urging her to reduce the time she spends in prayer, and instead to devote herself to the work of government in stanza LXVIII. In the very next stanza, however, he warns against using her time in the frivolous pursuits of 'vestyr' and 'tocar' (l. 615) rather than in prayer. In stanza LXX justice is mentioned again: Isabel's people will be more concerned about this than about her prayers, but religion is mentioned yet again in LXXI in the context of Isabel's need to set a good example by respecting both the Church and its clergy. He appears to view her as an overly devout young woman who has been brought up to do little more than to carry out the observances expected by the Church. Whereas he offers Fernando food for thought on the principles that should guide his conduct as a monarch, there is no such challenge for Isabel.

It is worth noting that Manrique follows these stanzas with a *conparaçión* in LXXII, using the word *dechados* in line 640. This word can mean simply 'example' but has the sense also of a 'sampler' or a piece of embroidery that a young girl might be expected to produce to prove herself a good needlewoman. The word *lauores* in the next line was also used in relation to working on cloth in the late Middle Ages and so when the poet enjoins Isabel to avoid 'dechados | herrados en las lauores' (ll. 640–41), he is using the simple vocabulary of domesticity which is very far removed from the abstract concepts he uses to appeal to Fernando's sense of duty. There follows an appeal to guide her people with discretion 'por la senda de razón | y no de la voluntad' (ll. 656–57). Following *voluntad* amounts to ignoring the virtue of temperance, and in case Isabel was still in any doubt, Manrique personifies the concept of 'razón' as:

> la razón es una dama
> que grandes honores ama
> y corre tras la virtud. (ll. 673–75)

The final section, stanzas LXXVI–LXXIX, is addressed to both Fernando and Isabel, with an appeal to them to think about the weighty responsibility that rests on their shoulders. The wealth and honours that they enjoy may bring a bitter aftertaste so, as servants of the Lord, they should love and fear Him if they wish in turn to be loved and respected by their subjects. Figurative language is little used in this poem, but in the penultimate stanza Manrique uses an extended nautical metaphor to compare the writing of this poem to a long sea voyage. His ship is 'menguada', or weighed down with 'buenos aparejos', suggesting the serious nature of his mission. Coming in to the harbour is equated with the realization of his hopes for the couple's future; making a landing on a beach would still enable him to convey his message:

> sy al puerto no pudiere,
> quiero salyr en la playa
> con esta fusta menguada
> de los buenos aparejos
> para tan luenga jornada,
> pero syn dubda cargada
> de verdaderos consejos. (ll. 696–702)

A striking aspect of this poem and its *prohemio* is the different mode of address that Manrique uses for the two *infantes*. The Isabel he writes for here bears little resemblance to the queen celebrated by poets and chroniclers a decade or so later. As we have seen, he couches his advice in terms of domestic duties and singles out possible failings to guard against: cruelty, frivolity and excess. The only aspect of government that he mentions in his advice to her is the dispensing of justice.

Fray Martín de Córdoba's *Jardín de nobles doncellas*

It is useful to compare Manrique's mode of address to Isabel with that of another text written before her accession to the throne, Fray Martín de Córdoba's *Jardín de nobles doncellas*. This much longer prose work was written around 1468, before Isabel's marriage to Fernando but after the death of her brother, Alfonso, who had been next in line to Enrique IV. It was also in the autumn of 1468 that Enrique bowed to pressure from Isabel's supporters and declared her to be his rightful successor, rather than the infanta Juana, at an agreement reached at Toros de Guisando. The work of

Martín, an Augustinian friar, owes much to Juan de Castrojeriz's 1344 translation into Castilian and his gloss of Aegidius Romanus's *De regimine principum*. Realizing that the next reigning monarch of Castile will be a woman, something that must have been extremely difficult to accept when the female sex was considered inherently weak, Martín sets out to convince male readers, to whom he refers as 'menos entendidos', that a woman is capable of governing on the grounds that 'del comienço del mundo fasta agora vemos que Dios sienpre puso la salud en mano dela fenbra' (Martín de Córdoba 1974: 136). We cannot be sure that Isabel ever read this work, which in its *prohemio* addresses her as 'infanta legítima heredera delos reynos de Castilla & León' (135), since no mention is made of it in the extant catalogues of her two libraries (44), but the fact that a printed edition was produced as early as 1500 (11) strongly suggests that the text aroused considerable interest.

This three-part work opens with a *prohemio* in which Martín greets Isabel by saying that he kisses her hands that are 'dignas de regir las riendas deste reyno' (135), thereby immediately showing his support for her as heir to the throne. The subsequent chapters of the first part describe how woman was created in Paradise from Adam's rib so that the human race would be perpetuated. The benefits of the sacrament of marriage, also instituted in Paradise according to Martín, are enumerated (161) and the third chapter ends with a comparison between the Virgin Mary and Isabel. All the faithful should be devoted to the Virgin, but Isabel in particular because they both have the attributes of royal lineage and virginity, and Isabel hopes to become queen, 'como la Virgen que es Reyna delos cielos, señora delos ángeles, madre delos peccadores & manto de todos los fieles' (164). This analogy between the Virgin Mary and Isabel foresees a more fully developed comparison in a poem addressed to Isabel by Fray Íñigo de Mendoza. While Martín refers to some of Aristotle's thoughts on the differences between the two sexes, it is noticeable that he omits his belief that the female is an imperfect male, then an accepted medical perception.

Martín did not intend to write a misogynistic tract in the tradition of the *maldezir* but, as Robert Archer suggests, 'Lo que le preocupa no es la intención de denigrar a las mujeres, sino la idea general que subyace en ese discurso: ¿qué son?' (Archer 2011a: 38). With this question in mind, in Part II Martín makes some generalizations about the female sex, reflecting on their good and bad qualities, so that Isabel may cultivate the former. Taking his cue from Castrojeriz, who uses three adjectives to denote the good qualities of women, 'vergonzosas: [...] piadosas e misericordiosas' (Castrojeriz 1947: II, 86), Martín claims that women are modest or 'vergonçosas' because, according to Aristotle, they seek praise and are 'flacas & temerosas de coraçón' (Martín de Córdoba 1974: 193). Their modesty is due to their fear of losing their reputation or 'vn temor de reçibir mengua' (194). The advantage that he thinks men have over women is that they are endowed with reason which acts as a restraining force when they are faced with the temptation to sin. When considering young women, however, Martín resorts to the traditional, misogynistic view of their insatiability: 'si vergüenza no las refrena del mal & las promueue al bien, yrán como bestia desenfrenada & como cauallo sin espuelas en todo mal; &

huyrán toda virtud' (195). The second good female characteristic is that of piety and thirdly he considers women to be 'obsequiosas' (203), meaning that they are compassionate and kind in their treatment of others. Martín lists three major failings of the female sex, the first being intemperance because women are 'más carne que espíritu' (210) and are not endowed with the same degree of reason as men, advice that is echoed more discreetly by Manrique to Isabel (Gómez Manrique 2003: 654, ll. 656–70). Secondly they are excessively talkative and also stubborn, again due to a lack of reason; in addition, they are fickle and inconstant. Another female characteristic that can be good or bad is that women often go to extremes in their actions, something that can be creditable or reprehensible (Martín de Córdoba 1974: 210–12).

The aim of Part III is to make recommendations as to how Isabel may overcome her innate womanly weaknesses and fit herself to become queen, one of these being that she should devote 'algunas oras del día en que estudie & oya tales cosas que sean propias al regimiento del reyno' (244). In a further chapter Martín states that although women are naturally 'flacas & temerosas', he has to admit that they can overcome this and, when they do so, 'nunca gigantes osarían atender lo que ellas cometen' (245). He illustrates this point with the examples of Judith and Holofernes and the stand that the legendary tribe of Amazon women took against Alexander. In the third chapter Martín advises Isabel that she must take stock of the natural defects she has as a woman and curb them. Although he previously stated that there were three major defects pertaining to the female sex, here he only deals with two and no mention is made of female intemperance. Isabel needs to control her urge to talk too much and to remain constant in her endeavours. By so doing, she will acquire the necessary male attributes, or 'ánimo varonil' (251) necessary to rule despite having the body of a woman.

Although there are glimpses of a positive attitude towards the prospect of a female monarch, Martín's writing reflects the ingrained misogyny of his age. His reading of the Church Fathers, such as Augustine and Jerome, whose writings had been studied and disseminated by the Church for centuries, render him incapable of casting off the accepted view of woman as a temptress. He alludes to this concept in Part I of his work when he quotes Saint Ambrose: 'Que la muger es apta armadura para tomar ánimas' (154) and in the final chapter of the *Jardín* he contradicts what he has said previously about the female attribute of 'vergüença'. He disagrees with a certain 'doctor' who thought that woman was created to serve man rather than ensnaring him and comments:

> ella (la mujer) procura la muerte alos varones. Agora por infengidos halagos, agora por lisonjas, agora por hartibles ojadas, estudian delos traer a escándalo de vituperio. Eneste dicho ha de notar la muger moça [...] que de quantas ánimas de hombres es ocasión de perder, de tantas dará razón el día del juizio; & esto es a ella importable, ca harto terná aquel día de dar razón de sí misma. (283)

Barbara Weissberger sees a close similarity between the attitudes of Manrique who refers to Isabel's need to overcome the inclination to cruelty (Gómez Manrique 2003: 652, ll. 602–03), the 'viçios senzillos' of frivolity (l. 645), and in the conflict between *razón* and *voluntad*, to make sure that temperance triumphs over excess (ll. 656–70), and that of Martín: 'Manrique's admonishments to Isabel are strikingly similar to Martín de Córdoba's in their construction of female virtue as essentially prophylactic, useful for restraining the natural propensity toward excess and vice' (Weissberger 2004: 57). Two objections can be raised against this statement. Firstly, Manrique makes no generalizations about the attributes of the female sex in this particular poem and actually sings their praises on moral grounds in his *Respuesta* to Torroella's *Maldezir de mujeres*, going to the length of claiming that some 'podrían en derredor | el mundo todo regir' (Gómez Manrique 2003: 191–202). Moreover, he makes no attempt at theological discussion on the subject of women and their virtues and shortcomings. Martín, on the other hand, writes very much as a member of his religious order and, in the words of Peggy Liss, his work is an 'extended Augustinian essay on original sin and on the descent of women from the original sinner, Eve [...] who was also held up as the source of all feminine weakness and inferiority' (Liss 1992: 70).

Weissberger also alludes to the fact that Manrique advises Isabel in stanza LXIX not to neglect her prayers in order to pay attention to her appearance or to rest, and urges her in stanzas LXXIV–LXXIV to follow the path of *razón* rather than that of *voluntad*, adding, 'Manrique tries to teach his sovereign [...] that she must work against nature as a woman' (Weissberger 2004: 58). This may well have been what he was thinking, but he does not say this in so many words. His message on this point is surely similar to the one he offered at greater length to Fernando (Gómez Manrique 2003: ll. 370–405), namely that the virtue of temperance was very important. Just as Isabel is warned against spending time on frivolous pursuits, so Fernando is advised in stanzas XLIII–XLIV not to spend too much time amusing himself in hunting and playing games (ll. 379–87). Furthermore, when extolling the virtue of fortitude to Fernando, Manrique first gives examples in stanza XLVII of male role models to follow, and then in the following stanza, surprisingly, an example of female fortitude, the eleven thousand virgin martyrs who were able to overcome their *voluntad*. Although it should be noted that they were able to do this because of their 'coraçones | de muy constantes varones' (ll. 430–31), by using such an example when addressing Fernando, Manrique is surely suggesting that the virtue of temperance is not a purely male prerogative, but something for which both men and women need to strive.

Conclusion

With the possible exception of the first work discussed in this chapter, we can be sure that these poems were all written in Manrique's mature years during the 1460s and early 1470s. Two strands of his thinking come together during this period. One is his interest in moral issues, already evident in his desire to complete Mena's *Debate*, and in some of the exchanges with other poets. The second is his political allegiance to the opponents of Enrique IV, now made manifest more boldly than hitherto. Both these strands emerge in the letter and poem to Arias Dávila where he expresses his distaste for the monarch's style of government, but the poem also has a clear focus on the transient nature of earthly life and the ephemeral value of material possessions, a fusion of his Christian and Stoic thinking. Manrique's frustration at the political situation erupts in the *Esclamaçión e querella de la gouernaçión* when he was brave enough to put pen to paper to express his exasperation at the way that he perceived that Castile was being misgoverned, well aware that in so doing he would arouse controversy.

His earlier allegiance to the Aragonese cause no doubt was a factor in his desire to seek peace between Aragon and Castile. Moreover, he had the courage of his convictions and sufficient confidence in his own position, to state this publicly, realizing that a union between the two kingdoms would make them stronger in the face of those enemies beyond the Peninsula who threatened both nations. Such a union was doubtless a strong motivating force in his desire to negotiate the marriage of Isabel with Fernando which would strengthen the bond still further between the two camps. The negative tone of the *Esclamaçión* can be contrasted with the optimism of the poem addressed to Fernando after the heroic defeat of the French, as he looks forward to seeing Fernando and Isabel as joint monarchs of Castile. Finally, in the *Regimiento de prínçipes*, he hopes that Isabel and Fernando will follow his advice based on Christian and Stoic principles, thereby bringing stability to the unified kingdoms of Castile and Aragon, the culmination of his political endeavours over nearly two decades.

CHAPTER 6

Family Consolatory and Devotional Writing

There are good reasons for believing that one of the last works that Gómez Manrique wrote was, by a long way, the most directly personal. This is the *consolatoria* composed for his wife, Juana de Mendoza, following the death of their two adult children. This was not the first consolatory piece he had written, as some twenty-five years previously he had written an even longer work to console his sister, Juana Manrique, in the midst of the suffering of her family. The two poems, while very different from one another in many ways and written at two such different periods, between them reveal yet another side to Manrique's poetic personality that we can best examine by taking them together here. It was also in the context of his immediate family that he produced his most important devotional works at different points of his life. These works, representing yet another facet of his poetic activity, are similarly rooted in Manrique's sense of family identity. For this reason these works will also be discussed here.

The Consolatory Poem for Juana Manrique

This poem without a title was composed some time between 1453 and 1458, since stanzas XX–XXI and the gloss inserted between them discuss the downfall and death of Álvaro de Luna (Gómez Manrique 2003: 439–40), and in the gloss to stanza XXVIII there is a reference in the present tense to the marqués de Santillana who did not die until 1458 (446). Juana was married to Fernando de Sandoval, the conde de Castro's son who, like many members of the high aristocracy, had provoked the wrath of Juan II by objecting to the influence of Álvaro de Luna and siding with the infantes Alfonso, Juan and Enrique de Aragón, whose armies had invaded Castile in 1429. As a result of this, in 1432, Juan II confiscated the lands that had been given to the Sandoval family and distributed them among other nobles who were loyal to him, causing much distress to Juana and her family.[1] Although Manrique is writing more than twenty years after this event, it is obvious that Juana is still resentful at what has happened to her family.

---

1   Alfonso de Cartagena dedicated his *Doctrinal de los cavalleros* to Juana's father-in-law, Diego Gómez de Sandoval, another link between these two great literary families (Archer 2011b: 69–70).

The Prose Epistle

The poem is prefaced by a prose *epístola* (419–22) in which he admits that he has delayed in responding to her request for some consolatory verses and explains why: the quality of the poetry that he would produce would not be adequate for the subject matter, since she is asking him to do something that is on a higher plane than what he self-deprecatingly calls the 'trobas de burrla' (420) that he habitually writes. As he does frequently in his writing, he expresses a sense of inadequacy which is reflected in the comparison that he makes between two such different types of literary composition when faced with the task in question: 'desmayo en el camino como onbre que, acostunbrado de pasar ríos pequeños en barcas de maromas, se vee en la fonda mar puesto sin remos e vela' (420). While Manrique does not fear well-meant, positive criticism of his efforts, he realizes that his poem will probably be read by other people, and is apprehensive about 'los escarnios de los maldizientes' (420), presumably the political rivals of the Manrique and Sandoval families.

It is out of a wish to please his sister and the fear of being considered lazy or inattentive to her wishes that he decides to put pen to paper, at the same time making excuses for his work, a 'pagiza obra', and appealing to her sense of 'beniuolençia' (421) to accept it with all its faults. He explains the rather unusual form, since his verses are interspersed with a number of glosses that he has written himself to elucidate some of the references he makes to classical sources, mindful of the fact that he is writing this for a woman. Many of these allusions are to stories he presumes to be unknown to women. The difference between the education of men and women in the fifteenth century is reflected in his comment that women like Juana are occupied with 'la conseruaçión de la virtud e a la buena gouerrnaçión de las casas de vuestros maridos en sus viriles ocupaçiones ocupados' (421–22). A treatise by Hernando de Talavera, written for María Pacheco, a contemporary of Juana's, *Do cómo se ha de ordenar el tiempo para que sea bien expendido*, describes how a noblewoman should spend her time. Chapters XI–XIII give a schedule for every waking hour of the day, most of which consists of prayer, reading devotional works, attending to the running of her house by overseeing her servants' activities, and giving audience to the poor and needy (Talavera 1911: 102–03). There is little time for leisure or cultural pursuits, but half an hour in the afternoon is permitted for 'alguna honesta música, o de alguna buena lección' (102). If Juana's life was governed by similar guidance, it is not surprising that her brother sought to explain the content of some of his verses.

The Poem

In 'La péñola tengo con tinta en la mano' (Gómez Manrique 2003: 423–48) Manrique addresses his sister in the rather ponderous *arte mayor* form and, although an older brother, he writes to her in extremely respectful terms. Rafael Lapesa attributes this to the fact that 'doña Juana estaba casada con uno de los más ricos hombres de Castilla, mientras que el poeta, a pesar de su nobilísimo linaje, no pasaba de segundón' (Lapesa 1988: 56). Indeed, the poet actually says that he thinks of his sister 'en amor sin duda más madre que ermana' (Gómez Manrique 2003: 423, l. 11) and this is reflected in his mode of addressing her, as if he were walking a tightrope between not wishing to offend her and counselling her firmly.

The thirty-stanza poem, with Manrique's own glosses inserted at intervals, can be divided thematically into five main sections. A quotation from the *Magnificat* in Luke 1. 52, 'Deposuit potentes de sede et exaltauit humiles' [He hath put down the mighty from their seats and exalted them of low degree], is placed before the first section, lines 1–55, that forms the introduction.[2] These words were no doubt intended to warn Juana that she will need to brace herself morally to read what follows, since it is the loss of her family's power and prestige which so grieves her, and they are apposite at the beginning of this poem that treats the theme of the reversal of worldly fortunes. In Luke 1. 48–53 the Virgin Mary, referring to herself as God's 'lowly servant', sings the praises of the Lord who exalts the humble and weakens the mighty and powerful. This seems an intended irony on Manrique's part, as he suggests that his sister, a woman born and married into the upper ranks of the aristocracy, should reflect upon the words of the Virgin Mary who was not of noble birth, but a role model for all women. Thus he prepares Juana to think of placing less emphasis on worldly values, so that she may accept the suggestions that he makes to her in the final section of his poem and become resigned to her circumstances. He does, however, sympathize with the loss of status suffered by her family, suggesting in the first verse that what has happened to her is 'según la costunbre del siglo mundano' (Gómez Manrique 2003: 423, l. 4). When he says that the century 'derrueca las casas de cantos e robres, | ensalça las fechas del salze liuiano' (ll. 7–8) 'casas' can be understood as 'families', an allusion to how some long-established, aristocratic lines have lost power and influence, whilst others, newly ennobled, have profited.

In his reflections on the nature of fortune in the second section of the poem (ll. 56–132) Manrique reminds his sister how fickle Fortune can be and how short-lived her benefits. As he ponders the subject of Fortune and the 'Desdichas e dichas, venturas e fados' (l. 64) that human beings experience, he concludes that 'es la Prouidençia del alta tribuna, | avnque los vocablos traemos mudados' (ll. 66–67). By using these words when discussing man's fortunes, we see an attempt to reconcile his Christian belief in the divine will with the prevailing influence of classical and in particular, Senecan, thought and preoccupation with fortune and providence. He asserts his belief that God permits such evils as war to occur because of man's sinfulness, and elaborates on this in the gloss that follows stanza VI, saying that God's secrets are 'ynotos a los muy sabidores, quanto más a los que nonada saben como yo' (426), thus admitting to a scant knowledge of theology.

In stanza VII Manrique reflects on the human condition, remarking that God, in creating man, clothed him not only physically, but allowed him to acquire 'amargas pasiones, | angustias, destierros e tribulaçiones' (ll. 86–87). These 'pasiones' are

---

2   Since Manrique's glosses are inserted in the text of the poem, all references follow the numbering of the lines in Vidal González's edition.

our 'posesiones' (l. 90); in the gloss on this verse he quotes from the Office of the Dead, reminding Juana that our life on this earth is short and full of tribulations. In the following stanza he proceeds to observe that this world with its cares and in which men toil after 'vanos onores' (l. 110) is what we inherit from our ancestors and what we bequeath to our children. He ends this verse with two lines in which he uses a nautical metaphor of life being a voyage that is difficult to navigate: 'pues no nauegamos con más fuertes remos, | nin es nuestra vela de más rezios velos' (ll. 114–15). The metaphor of the voyage is sustained and developed in stanza IX where Manrique now sees earthly life in terms of a river that has to be navigated but which is 'vn gran desuarío' (l. 139) and assures his sister that past generations experienced the same perils as long as they sailed along this river. He ends the verse by declaring that prosperity and adversity alike are short-lived:

> pues todas sus ponpas e prosperidades
> e sus infortunios e aduersidades
> non duran más qu'el blanco roçío. (ll. 130–32)

Although the metaphor of earthly life as a river has a long tradition going back to the Old Testament, it is hard not to believe that Manrique did not influence his nephew, Jorge, whose famous *Coplas*, written on the death of his father, Rodrigo Manrique, also include this image:

> Nuestras vidas son los ríos
> que van a dar en la mar
> qu'es el morir. (Jorge Manrique 1997: 172)

Furthermore, Jorge also uses the word 'rocío' to express the fleeting nature of material riches and asks, '¿qué fueron sino rocíos | de los parados? (182).

The third section of eight stanzas (Gómez Manrique 2003: ll. 133–403) is prefaced by a second quotation from the *Magnificat*: 'Esurientes inplebit bonis diuites dimisit inanes' [He hath filled the hungry with good things; and the rich he hath sent empty away] (Luke 1. 53), another reminder that privilege does not always remain with us for life. In these lines Manrique takes the opportunity to parade his knowledge, giving Juana a history lesson as he recounts the reversals of fortune that took place in ancient Greece and Rome. He reminds her of the downfall of Troy and the fact that the Greeks were not able to enjoy their triumph over that city due to the many misfortunes that overcame them subsequently, for even the great hero Ulysses was only recognized by his old dog. Significantly, Manrique makes a point of praising the faithfulness of Penelope, Ulysses's wife, and has no desire to speak ill of women in times past. He mentions the rise and fall in fortunes of Julius Caesar, Pompey and Scipio, and the fact that ultimately the latter was obliged to spend his declining years in exile 'desechado de la patria que por su braço redimió' (ll. 347–48).[3]

The fourth section of this poem (ll. 404–79) gives examples from recent Spanish history of two men who met unfortunate ends. The first is Enrique de Aragón, the son of Fernando de Antequera, King of Aragon from 1412–16. Enrique was the

---

3   Perhaps Manrique was unaware that Scipio behaved as if he were above the law towards the end of his life, refusing to answer charges of corruption and thereby falling from popularity.

younger brother of Alfonso V of Aragon and Juan II of Aragon and in Manrique's words, 'gastó su beuir en poco reposo' (l. 415). Having been made Gran Maestre de la Orden de Santiago at the age of nine, he played an important role in the early opposition to Juan II's reign in Castile in 1420, but was imprisoned and later forced into exile. He returned to Castile in 1427 and two years later he joined his brothers Alfonso and Juan in declaring war on Castile, but hostilities were averted by the intervention of their sister, María of Aragon, wife of Juan II of Castile. He spent a second period of exile residing in Naples near his brother, Alfonso, and again the three brothers were involved in armed conflict in the 'jornada de Ponza' in 1435 where they were imprisoned until the following year. Enrique was back in Castile by 1438 and participated in political struggles which culminated in the invasion of Castile by Aragonese and Navarrese forces. Wounded at the battle of Olmedo in 1445, he died a few weeks later in Calatayud. The gloss that follows stanza XIX is a eulogy to Enrique in which Manrique speaks of his 'grandísimas virtudes e buenas andanças' (l. 420) and his 'loable vida' (l. 425), thus manifesting something of his own political persuasions as he praises a man who opposed Juan II of Castile. He also reflects on the way in which Fortune, with whom Enrique had battled throughout his life, finally triumphed over him and notes the irony that Enrique was buried in Calatayud 'debaxo de las vanderas de Luna que siempre le fueron enemigas' (ll. 426–27).

Enrique's life was in marked contrast to the second example Manrique takes from even more recent history, that of Álvaro de Luna who rose to great power, had so much influence over Juan II, and 'a quien la Fortuna fue tan fauorable' (l. 438). In the gloss on stanza XX Luna's rise from comparatively lowly origins to high estate and his subsequent fall are shown as testimony of Fortune's ability in which 'la gran mouilidat de su ley confirmó' (l. 450). The poet holds this up as a warning to those who seek earthly power and it is noteworthy that he uses the first person plural of the verb when he says, 'Sin dubda grande ensiemplo a los que tras este fauor mundano corremos deue ser' (ll. 450–52), intimating to his sister that the acquisition of lands and political authority is not without its dangers. Furthermore, he doubts if the example of Luna will really deter others from seeking privilege in the future when he remarks, rather cynically, 'no cuydo estarían vn momento las sillas de las priuanças vazías sin se arrepentir los que las poseyesen fasta el pie del cadahalso llegar' (ll. 453–56). His final comments on Luna make it clear that he was opposed to him politically, when he declares that justice was done when the *condestable* was executed.

In the final section of this poem (ll. 480–83) Manrique addresses Juana's own problems. He praises her personal attributes in verse XXIII, saying that God made her 'tanto virtuosa, | que pocas se pueden con vos igualar' (ll. 482–83), mentioning the privileged position into which she was born. In the following gloss he draws her attention to two other highly virtuous women of their family, their mother and grandmother, and flatters her by saying that, even when compared with them, she is still a shining example. Perhaps this flattery is intended to soften the impact of his next verse that suggests that Juana is lacking in wisdom in her complaints about her lot, and urges her to remember that the wealth that she and her family have lost is but a temporal benefit, at the disposal of Fortune herself. He chides her for failing to see that a reversal of fortunes is a challenge to which the virtuous can rise, but can defeat the morally weak. He advocates a Stoic resignation to misfortune, particularly for someone of Juana's position in society: 'no justo es que nadie por ello sospire, | e menos los nobles de generaçión (ll. 534–35). His tone becomes more severe in the gloss that follows: it is reprehensible for those who understand about the vagaries of fortune to complain when they lose out materially and he questions the value of 'estos bienes, si tales llamar se pueden' (ll. 537–38). Manrique ends this gloss of stanza XXV by appealing to his sister to rise to the challenge she faces and to remember that adversity is only bad when you allow yourself to suffer: 'deue interuenir vuestro gran coraçón e reposado seso menospreçiando las tales aduersidades, las quales no son malas saluo a los que las sufren mal (ll. 552–55).

The lecture continues in stanza XXVI: riches and honours should be obtained honestly without sacrificing personal integrity. Their loss should not prompt a change of allegiance: 'mas si las (riquezas) perdieren, | non deuen por esso mudar sus colores' (ll. 558–59), presumably an allusion to the turbulent times in which they were living, when aristocrats would transfer their support to another faction in the hope of preferment or financial gain. After a further reminder of the ephemeral value of earthly wealth there is another gloss, seemingly based on Seneca's *De providencia* in which Manrique declares, 'Nunca fue la nobleza e virtud a perpetua pobreza condenada' (ll. 565–67). This leads him to reveal more of this thoughts on the acquisition of wealth and honour by expressing the view, which recurs frequently in his writings, that it is permissible to obtain these honestly and with a clear conscience, but that we should not hold these things too dear to us: 'mas non deuen fincarlos en los coraçones, e serán sus arcas ligeras de abrir' (ll. 570–72). Realizing perhaps that he has delivered a stern message, excessively imbued with his Stoic principles, the poet concedes that Juana's heart is not made of stone, recalling not only the sufferings of Job who bemoaned his fate for so long, but those of Jesus himself.

From this point on the work becomes more optimistic and consolatory. Manrique assures his sister that a reversal of fortune such as she has suffered is an opportunity for virtue to shine: 'que las duras aduersidades ocasión son de virtud' (ll. 602–03). She should feel strengthened in the knowledge that she is of noble birth and still has many blessings such as a husband, who has brought her no dishonour, and a son. His reminder that material wealth does not necessarily bring peace of mind is a reflection of the lawless times in which brother and sister are living when Manrique suggests that those who now inhabit the house that was once Juana's may be living in fear, perhaps 'sus reposos, viçios e riquezas por vuestros trabajos, afanes, neçesidades trocarían' (ll. 649–50). Finally he urges her to thank God for the many benefits He has bestowed upon her and to remain firm in her faith. She must show Christian resignation to God's will, as Jesus did in the garden of Gethsemane. As a final encouragement, he reminds her of the Canaanite woman in Matthew's gospel whose faith was such that her daughter was healed.

The *Consolatoria* for Juana de Mendoza

The second consolatory poem that Manrique produced more than twenty years later is especially revealing because it and its accompanying prose epistle discuss a cause of pain so much closer to home. This time the suffering is not due to the loss of status and material wealth such as that endured by his sister, but the death of two of his and Juana de Mendoza's adult children within four months of each other in 1480. Bereavement inspired Manrique to compose poetry on the occasion of the deaths of the marqués de Santillana and the knight Garcilaso de la Vega, but those poems are elegies that seek to praise the deceased and have political overtones. As Harry Sieber observes, consolatory poetry is intended to deal with the emotions experienced by those close to the deceased who survive (Sieber 1993: 158). Consequently, we learn nothing about the lives of Luis and Catalina Manrique.

The Prose Epistle

Manrique opens his letter to Juana (Gómez Manrique 2003: 448–53) quoting a saying of Scipio that he remembered from his reading of Livy: 'las cosas pasadas oluidémoslas, y si no las pudiéremos oluidar callémoslas' (ll. 5–6). This allusion seems strangely inappropriate here as Scipio was being magnanimous in forgiving, and wishing to forget, a conspiracy planned against him. In applying this Stoic principle to the deaths of his children, Manrique says that although he has spoken little about them, and then 'con grant neçesidat de remediar a sus almas' (ll. 13–14), he can never stop thinking about them. As was frequently the case throughout their lives, Juana was absent, fulfilling her duties as *camarera mayor* to Isabel la Católica while Manrique was in Toledo where he was Governor. Not only is the poem intended to bring solace to his wife, but it has also brought him comfort in the writing. He describes the therapeutic effect of composing this work, using an interesting simile: 'porque descansando en este papel como si contigo hablara, afloxase el hervor de mi congoxa, como haze el de la olla quando se sale, que por poca agua que salga auada mucho y ella no rebienta' (ll. 28–31).

He explains that the poem was started shortly after the second death, that of their daughter Catalina, but its composition was interrupted by the illness of Juana when she was attending the queen in Medina del Campo. Manrique was allowed to abandon his duties to visit her early in 1481,[4] and in this letter he explains, interestingly, that he found it hard to return to writing the half-finished work once he returned. He complains that old age has taken its toll on him and that whereas once he could compose 'en vn día quinze or veynte trobas', now things are different: 'agora en veynte días no puedo hazer media' (ll. 54, 56). As so often in his work, Manrique expresses modesty concerning his literary efforts when he alludes in his letter to 'estas pocas y malas trobas' (l. 72) and further on he says that after a huge effort he finished this piece of work, not as he would have liked but how he

---

4 Paz y Melia gives the text of the letter granting this permission (Gómez Manrique 1885–86: II, 316–17); Vidal González also quotes lines from it written in the queen's hand (Gómez Manrique 2003: 39).

was able. He was spurred on to finish the poem on two accounts: the memory many years ago of Juana reproaching him for addressing poetry to many other people but never to her. He refers to this time as 'estando en nuestros plazeres' (l. 81) and it brings him some comfort to be able to send her this poem 'en tienpo de nuestra turbaçión, por señal de amor' (ll. 84–85). The second motivation for finishing the poem was the deaths of two children of the marqueses de Moya around the same time, referring to the marquesa as 'llagada de la misma llaga que nosotros' (ll. 88–89). Otherwise known as Beatriz de Bobadilla, this lady was close to Isabel la Católica and obviously a close friend of the Manriques, and to whom Manrique professes himself 'tan afiçionado' (l. 87).

The Poem

The poem, '¡O qué materia tan dina' (453–66), of thirty-four octosyllabic *décimas*, falls into three sections, the first comprising stanzas I–XV which form a *prohemio*, almost half the entire work, and introduce us to the subject matter with an intimation in the first stanza that the poet has brought this suffering upon himself because of his sinfulness. The language is highly resonant of pain with its allusions to a 'llaga tan cruda | en parte dolorosa' (ll. 111–12) and 'tan dolorida' (l. 114), to his 'amargas afliçiones' (l. 119) and 'lágrimas caýdas' (l. 130). These feelings are expressed with increased intensity when Manrique questions how he can provide Juana with any consolation, '¿Quién hablará con el ñudo | que se haze en la garganta?' (ll. 133–34), but realizes that suffering brings wisdom, 'así da sabiduría | la congoxa y ansiedat' (ll. 151–52), and this in turn will help him to express himself, albeit in verse which will be 'apasionado' (l. 155), or full of pain, rather than well written.

Asking whom he will invoke to inspire him in this task, he allows himself to make several references to some of the gods of classical mythology, revealing that he has read Ovid's *Metamorphoses*, a copy of which he had in his library (Gómez Manrique 1885–86: II, 334). One of these references is to the daughter of Ceres, Proserpina, who was abducted by Pluto and taken to the underworld. Another, more obscure, is to 'la hija de Agenor' (l. 183) referring to Europa, whom Jupiter raped having taken the form of a bull. Manrique rejects such pagan forms of inspiration and instead will ask God's help. Even in such a situation he still feels the need to use the modesty topos when writing to his wife:

> Pues iré al Hazedor
> de los çielos estrellados
> que supo hazer letrados
> de ombres desenseñados,
> syn escuela ni dotor. (ll. 198–202)

There follow three stanzas in which the poet admits how hard it is to carry out this task, reflecting what he has said in his letter to Juana about the length of time it now took him to compose twenty lines. He returns to the very concrete images related to practising the skill of poetic composition that we saw in his verses to Juan de Valladolid:

> que las gruesas herramientas
> con que yo forjar solía
> esas obras que hazía,
> non de alta poliçía,
> todas están orinientas. (ll. 228–32)

Both time and sadness have blunted these 'tools' and there is no longer any of the posturing and superior tone that we saw in the verses addressed to his rival. The last of these three stanzas is a simile in which he compares himself to a restless horse unwilling to compete in a race; he doubts his ability to complete the task because he has lost the habit of writing verses.

Stanzas XVI–XXIV form the second section of the poem, beginning with the author's expression of anguish at the thought of his wife's distress. The tone of his writing becomes more intimate at this point and it is significant that he addresses his wife in the second person singular, thereby revealing a closeness in their relationship despite the fact that they have had to spend so much time apart. Manrique then sets out his Stoic beliefs very much as he did to his sister over twenty years previously, namely that human beings frequently mistake good for evil and vice versa. He observes that it would have been natural for Juana to have desired a more aristocratic status for her son, but how much better it was that he had died 'en su lecho, | confesado y satisfecho' (ll. 290–91), rather than having brought his own misfortune upon himself through excessive riches and ambition like the Duke of Viseu.[5] Conversely, those who have erred often turn away from evil and reform their way of life, which leads Manrique to declare:

> Pues no tengamos por males,
> ni se pueden llamar tales,
> estos que nos hazen buenos. (ll. 310–12)

Influenced no doubt by his reading of Seneca, in stanza XXII Manrique realizes that premature death need not be a cause for sadness since those who die young may be spared misfortunes and their fame and honour will not be forgotten. In his letter to Marcia, Seneca tells her, 'Think how great a boon a timely death offers, how many have been harmed by living too long!' (Seneca 2006: II, 70–71), citing the example of Pompey who survived illness in Naples only to be assassinated later in Egypt.[6] In addition, he comments, 'To your son, therefore, though his death was premature, it brought no ill; rather has it released him from suffering ills of every sort' (73).[7] Combining these Stoic sentiments with Christian teaching, he echoes the words of comfort from Luke 6. 21 for the sad and distressed:

> llama bienaventurados
> a los llorantes cuitados,

---

5 The 'duques portugueses' (l. 271) are almost certainly the Duke of Guimarães and the Duke of Viseu. The former was found guilty of conspiring (allegedly with some encouragement from the Reyes Católicos) against João II and executed in 1483; the latter was murdered by João II's own hand in 1484, also because he was plotting against him (Disney 2009: I, 135–36).
6 'Cogita quantum boni opportuna mors habeat, quam multis diutius vixisse nocuerit'.
7 'Nihil ergo illi mali immatura mors attulit; omnium etiam malorum remisit patientiam'.

> y dize que consolados
> an de ser de neçesario.
> (Gómez Manrique 2003: ll. 329–32)

The final verse of this section conveys the traditional Christian message that we should resign ourselves to the sorrows of this world in order to enjoy the 'dulçuras' (l. 341) of the afterlife.

The third section (ll. 343–442), opening with the rubric 'Consolaçión fundada sobre razón natural', tells us that excessive outpourings of grief are futile since the dead cannot be resurrected. Building on what he has already said about premature death in stanza XXII, he urges Juana to take comfort from the thought that had their children lived longer, they might have been overcome by worse misfortunes:

> de muerte más cruda
> nos podría Dios lleuar
> al hijo sin confesar,
> y si pudiera dexar
> aquella hija bïuda. (ll. 358–62)

Manrique then unburdens himself on the subject of his own guilt in a sort of *mea culpa*, since he is convinced that the deaths of his children are God's punishment for his sins, although he refrains from enlarging on what these are. Juana's grief has doubled his own distress and he asks how she can be consoled by the one who is the cause of their misfortunes: '¿cómo serás consolada | por la mano matadora?' (ll. 401–02). Since it is inevitable that Juana suffers through his own deserved punishment, he hopes that God will be especially merciful to her.

In the final two stanzas he draws consolation from his Christian faith, quoting from the Sermon on the Mount: 'Hijos de Dios llamarán | a los que fueren paçientes' (ll. 426–27). The thought that they have no living children prompts him to observe that there has been a reversal in their roles:

> ¡O qué troque tan llenero,
> si bien pensar lo queremos:
> pues que hijos no tenemos,
> que de padres nos tornemos
> hijos de Dios verdadero! (ll. 428–32)[8]

Having formerly been their children's 'anteçesores', they become their 'subçesores' (ll. 438, 442) in the next world.

In commenting on this poem, Harry Sieber remarks that by drawing on Boethius's *De consolatione Philosophae*, it 'becomes a conversation between Manrique and his absent wife' (Sieber 1993: 159). This is hardly appropriate since Juana is absent and cannot engage with what her husband has to say and we have no record of anything that she may have written. Two lines later, however, he says that the poet 'will become the philosopher who teaches Juana through his own learning process' (159), a much more accurate description of the poem's content, given that there are such clear references to Seneca's writing.

---

8   In fact they had another daughter, María, who became a nun at the enclosed Franciscan convent of Calabazanos, of whom Gómez Manrique says, 'biua se me enterró' (Carrión 1978: 578).

Ronald E. Surtz comments on stanzas VII–IX, suggesting that they are 'a sort of literacy test for its readers, beginning with Juana herself' (Surtz 2004: 54). He wonders if Juana would have known that the daughter of Agenor was Europa, or if Manrique was taking the opportunity to parade his knowledge. He finds the fact that Manrique asks for the female testimony of Proserpina and Europa 'to bear witness to the depravity of the pagan gods [by whom they were raped] and thereby to the unsuitability of seeking their aid as poetic inspiration' flattering to Juana (54). It certainly contributes to the impression we have of her as a cultivated woman who received 'una educación humanista exquisita, como muestran los autógrafos que de ella se conservan entre la documentación de la cancillería de la reina Isabel' (Rivera Garretas 2004: 24).

An Exchange of Letters between Juan de Lucena and Gómez Manrique

The extent to which Manrique's *consolatoria* for Juana was actually an exercise in Stoic self-consolation for terrible grief can be gauged by examining the correspondence between him and Juan de Lucena (Carrión 1978: 565–82). This exchange of letters probably took place at the end of 1480 or early in 1481, since there is no mention of Juana's illness or the visit her husband was permitted to make to her in Medina del Campo in the spring of 1481. The only mention of Juana is when Manrique tells Lucena that he wrote to the queen 'por incitar más su virtud para la consolación de mi muy amada muger' (579). Lucena was a priest who, having lived for a spell in Rome, returned to Spain. He undertook diplomatic missions for the Catholic Monarchs and probably became acquainted with Manrique at court.

Bearing in mind the comparatively recent deaths of three members of the Manrique family, Lucena begins his letter by praising the poet for the example of fortitude he has set: 'Y estos tan arrebatados males que la herida del vno sanaua la llaga del otro, vuestra forçada prudençia los supo y pudo tan bien tollerar que solo vos entre todos érades ovido por prudente' (575).[9] He adds that there was need to recall the Stoicism of classical writers in the face of adversity when they had Manrique as a role model in their presence. All this has changed now and, using a military metaphor, he takes him to task for failing to maintain his serenity after Catalina's death: 'Que en la lucha y en la pelea, havn que vna o dos o más bezes deruequen a su luchador, si enflaqueçido cahe a la postre, no gana el preçio de fuerte' (575).

Lucena continues by accusing Manrique of being weak and effeminate, 'asý vos mostrays fembra, regando la cara con lágrimas, con las vnyas rasgando las hazes' (575), and likening his reaction to that of Job in his misfortunes. Amongst other examples, he reminds him of Cato's bravery in performing his duties immediately after the death of his only son, adding that many people forget their grief in a short space of time. He tells him to cease mourning, to behave not as those without belief

---

9 Gómez Manrique's brothers Rodrigo and Fadrique died in 1476 and 1479 respectively. His nephew, Jorge, also died in 1479; Lucena appears to think that Jorge was Fadrique's son rather than Rodrigo's.

in the afterlife, but instead to remember that 'partiremos desta vida que muere para nos hallar puestos en la que nunca muere y juntos en aquella espaçiosa y más que espaçiosa ciudat de nuestro Dios moremos siempre con Jesu Christo (576).

Manrique admits to finding himself in a quandary as to whether he should reply to this letter; couching his response in language with frequent images that reflect his military past, he begins by comparing himself to a cowardly knight who cannot decide whether to launch himself into the fight or flee the battlefield, since he would either appear discourteous or expose his weakness. It is plain that he is offended by the letter and, wishing to refute its 'infamias', he tells Lucena, 'no vos marauilleys por que me quexe de vos y alabe a mí' (577). He speaks of the cumulative effect of his children's deaths coming after that of his brothers and nephew: 'aquellas afliçiones cuyos rastros, havnque no poco ni mucho ni nada desfechos, algo estauan rematadas o holladas de las postreras esquadras del dolor de las muertes de los hijos' (577). He denies indulging in lamentations as Lucena has accused him, but having ministered to his daughter in her final days 'en tan gran soledat', he admits to having shed 'algunas demasiadas lágrimas que la humanidad no pudo resistir' (578) and reminds Lucena that even Jesus was reported to have wept on several occasions. Using the language of war again, he describes his heart as 'lombardeado de las gruesas piedras' to the extent that 'no fuera marauilla que con esta cayera en los yerros de que me culpays' (578) because even an experienced jouster can fall after suffering previous setbacks.

Manrique describes how, despite being physically weakened after this latest tragedy to the extent that, 'obe de estar dos días en la cama que apenas me podía rodear', he roused himself sufficiently to go about his business 'porque no se atribuyesse la disposiçion de la persona a flaqueza de corazón' (579). He ends his letter saying that he has two reasons to complain to Lucena, firstly because he accused him wrongly. Secondly, as a 'tan indocto cauallero' defending himself against Lucena, whom he generously calls 'otro Tulio', he is forced to praise his own behaviour, which is 'ageno de toda virtud' (580). Despite his indignation, Manrique thanks Lucena for writing to him, graciously remarking, 'mejor señal de verdadera amistad son las amorosas represiones más que las demasiadas alabanças entre los verdaderos amigos' (580).

Other Poems for Juana de Mendoza

The *consolatoria* was not the only poem Manrique addressed to Juana. There are at least two other works, both very different generically.[10] One of these is a ten-line *estrena*, the first two lines of which express his devotion to Juana with a surprising degree of hyperbole: 'Amada tanto de mí | e más que mi salvaçión' (Gómez Manrique 2003: 295). This is not the love of courtly verse of which he wrote much in his youth, but perhaps an appreciation of her in later life which, he explains, is 'más por la virtud de ti | que por ninguna pasión' (ll. 3–4).

---

10   Another poem, of twelve lines, 'Vyéndovos tanto penada' (117) may also have been composed for Juana de Mendoza as its content echoes that of the *consolatoria* addressed to her.

The other poem requested by Juana, '¡O tú, reyna, que beata', is one of several religious compositions on the subject of the Virgin Mary entitled 'Los cuchillos del dolor de Nuestra Señora puestos en metro por Gómez Manrique a ynistançia de doña Juana de Mendoça, su muger' (283–87). The poem consists of fifteen verses of *octavas* which are based on a traditional way of saying the rosary, recalling seven incidents in the life of the Virgin that brought her great sorrow. The 'cuchillos' or 'wounds' are the events in Jesus's life that caused her suffering, most but not all of which are authenticated in the gospels. The first four verses of the poem are introductory and in praise of Mary and her purity.

In the fifth verse Manrique describes the first 'cuchillo' that Mary experienced when Jesus was presented at the Temple and Simeon spoke:

> y fabló por profeçía
> qu'el infante
> vn cuchillo muy tajante
> sería. (ll. 37–40)

This is a reference to Luke 2. 35, also alluded to in the *Representaçión del Nasçimiento de Nuestro Señor*, as discussed below. The second wound, in stanza VI, is founded on Matthew's gospel which tells us that Joseph learned in a dream that he should flee with Jesus and Mary to Egypt because Herod was intent on killing the child. The following verse, again based on Luke 2. 41–50, refers to the occasion when Jesus, at the age of twelve, remained in the Temple and caused his parents great anguish because they thought that he was lost. Jesus's arrest, the fourth wound, is the subject of stanza VIII and the fifth, in stanza IX, is an allusion to the account of the crucifixion according to John 19. 26–27. On seeing his mother and the disciple, thought to be John the Evangelist, standing at the foot of the cross, Jesus said, 'Woman, behold thy son!'. The deposition from the cross is the subject of stanza X and Mary's participation in Jesus's burial that of XI. In the latter Manrique departs from the account found in the gospels which recounts that it was Joseph of Arimathea who buried Jesus, and according to John's gospel, he was helped by Nicodemus. This departure from what is written in the gospel has to be seen as poetic licence in order to convey the intensity of Mary's grief.

Stanza XII, the first of the four final verses of the poem, praises Mary for her fortitude and it is interesting to note how this is described, the implication being that this is not a typically female characteristic:

> y la tu pura flaqueza
> femenil
> fue conuertida en veril
> fortaleza. (ll. 93–96)

The final three verses form a prayer to the Virgin in which Manrique asks that she may save him from damnation and help him not to sin in thought or deed. In the last verse Mary is addressed as 'Entera consolaçión | en nuestros grandes conflitos' (ll. 113–14), demonstrating that she is seen as a source of comfort for the afflicted.

The style of this poem is reminiscent of much of Manrique's love poetry. The use of the *pie quebrado* in the sixth and eighth lines, causing an interruption of the metrical form, helps to emphasize the feelings expressed as in the first stanza, for example:

> ¡O Virgen senper intacta,
> por quien dixo Salomón:
> "Pura donzella",
> toda eres toda bella
> en perfectión! (ll. 4–8)

Mary's purity is underlined and the rhyme of 'perfectión' with 'Salomón' reminds us of Solomon's wisdom. The use of the *pie quebrado* is also used in combination with antithesis to heighten the dramatic effect of the poem. An example of this is in the quotation from stanza XII in the paragraph above where 'femenil' (l. 94) rhymes with 'veril' in the next line and 'flaqueza' (l. 93) with 'fortaleza' (l. 96). Anaphora is another figure of speech found in stanza XIV with the repetition of 'Líbrame' at the beginning of the first and fifth lines when the poet is praying to the Virgin that she may guide him away from sin.

The two Juanas were not the only members of the poet's family to enjoy the fruits of his literary efforts. The family was very devout and two of Manrique's sisters became nuns at the Real Monasterio de Nuestra Señora de la Consolación de Calabazanos, founded by their mother, Leonor de Castilla, near Palencia. One of these sisters, María, asked her brother to write a nativity play for the nuns to perform at Christmas.

La Representaçión del Nasçimiento de Nuestro Señor

This short play (660–74) dates to some time between 1458 and 1468, since the dedicatory rubric states that it was written 'a instançia de doña María Manrique, vicaria en el monesterio de Calabazanos' (660). This community moved to Calabazanos in 1458 (Surtz 1983a: 19–20) and in 1468 María was promoted from *vicaria* to the position of abbess (Gómez Manrique 2003: 660n). The play, the earliest dramatic work in Spanish by a known author, is seen by scholars as marking an important point in the evolution of medieval theatre, since traditionally any religious dialogue was very much part of, and linked to, the celebration of the liturgy and based on close reference to biblical material. At Christmas, for instance, the *Officium pastorum*, an enactment of how the shepherds received the news of Christ's birth and their visit to Bethlehem, might be inserted into the liturgy. The *Siete Partidas* of Alfonso X had stipulated that a church was intended as a house of prayer, but certain dramatic activities were permitted:

> Pero representaciones ay que pueden los clérigos fazer así como de la nascencia de Nuestro Señor Jesu Christo en que muestra como el ángel vino a los pastores, e les dixo como era Jesu Christo nacido. [...] Tales cosas como estas que mueven al ome a fazer bien e a aver devoción en la fe pueden las fazer. (Álvarez Pellitero 1990: 23–24)[11]

---

11   Ana Álvarez Pellitero quotes from Alfonso X's *Primera partida*.

In the words of Ana Álvarez Pellitero, 'la pieza significa un enriquecimiento en comparación con el enjuto esquema del *Officium pastorum* (108–09). The text, firmly rooted in biblical and apocryphal sources together with some additions to the Nativity story of Manrique's creation, is very much more than a simple celebration of the Nativity, since there are also frequent allusions to Christ's passion and suffering. It should be borne in mind that Manrique was writing for a community of *clarisas*, the female branch of the Franciscan order, and that scholars have noted that the linking of the Nativity and the Passion is a feature of Franciscan spirituality.

The play consists of 180 lines in seven scenes, the first six composed in octosyllabic verse, Manrique's preferred metre, but with variations in the rhyme scheme. The first scene, of three *octavas*, opens with Joseph who laments that Mary appears to have been unfaithful to him since she is expecting a child which is not his. Matthew's gospel hints at Joseph's doubts: 'Then Joseph her husband, being a just man and not willing to make her a publick example, was minded to put her away privily' (Matthew 1. 19). In Manrique's play, however, Joseph is concerned for his own reputation, which is emphasized in the rhyme scheme by his self-description of 'desuenturado' and 'desonrrado' (Gómez Manrique 2003: 660, ll.1, 4). His misgivings also feature in some of the apocryphal gospels (660n). Not only is Joseph portrayed by Manrique as apprehensive, but also as ignorant, when in the final two lines of this verse he declares somewhat prosaically, 'dizen que d'Espíritu Santo, | mas yo d'esto non sé nada' (ll. 7–8). Mary's prayer to God that Joseph, in his 'ceguedad' and 'sinpleza' (ll. 15, 16) may be enlightened, is of one of Manrique's additions to the biblical story and serves to create dramatic tension: the temporal and the spiritual worlds meet as she experiences a conflict between her duty to God and loyalty to her husband. Her prayer is answered when an angel appears to Joseph, reminding him of Isaiah's prophecy (ll. 20–24; Matthew 1. 20–23). Manrique emphasizes Joseph's 'sinpleza' again in the angel's opening words:

> ¡O uiejo de munchos días,
> en el seso, de muy pocos,
> el prinçipal de los locos! (ll. 17–19)

This is the sole appearance of Joseph in the play, but his depiction as an ignorant, foolish, elderly man is found elsewhere in medieval European literature. Johan Huizinga observes, when writing of the fourteenth-century French poet, Eustache Deschamps: 'The curiosity with which Joseph was regarded is a sort of reaction from the fervent cult of Mary. The figure of the Virgin is exalted more and more and that of Joseph becomes more and more of a caricature' (Huizinga 1965: 163).

Departing from the order of events as told in Luke's gospel, in scene II, after the birth of Jesus, Mary expresses her devotion to God, echoing the words of the Magnificat (Gómez Manrique 2003: 662, ll. 37–40; Luke 1. 46–47). In the next stanza we see the influence of Franciscan spirituality when Manrique again departs from the details of the nativity story known in the synoptic gospels, portraying Mary as already aware of the pain that she will suffer when Jesus dies to redeem the sinners of this world by his own sacrifice (ll. 43–45). According to Luke's gospel, Mary and Joseph had no intimation of the child's future until Jesus was presented in the Temple and Simeon blessed the family. Speaking to Mary of the child's destiny in life, Simeon ends by saying, 'Yea, a sword shall pierce through thine own soul too' (Luke 2. 35). Thus Manrique telescopes the events of the holy family's life. By juxtaposing Mary's expression of joy at her son's birth and the pain that his death will bring, Manrique emphasizes the nobility of her soul as she vows to bring up her child with due reverence and endure her suffering with no loss of faith. It is noticeable in stanza VI how Manrique again uses his rhyme scheme to full advantage with 'plazer' and 'padeçer' (ll. 41, 44) and 'pecadores' and 'dolores' (ll. 45, 48).

The third scene continues the story of Christ's birth according to Luke (2. 8–17) with the angel's announcement to the shepherds in a single *octava*. Manrique embellishes the story by adding a brief conversation among the shepherds. They are depicted as simple, rustic people, expressing themselves in tercets and everyday parlance:

> Dime tú, ermano, di,
> si oýste alguna cosa,
> o si viste lo que vi
> Vna gran boz me semeja
> de vn ángel reluziente
> que sonó en mi oreja.
> (Gómez Manrique 2003: 664, ll. 65–70)

When we see the shepherds in the next scene, in the presence of Jesus, each one speaks a verse of seven lines in praise of the child. They appear transformed by their experience, spiritually enlightened, expressing themselves in language of a more cultivated register; moreover, they show an awareness of the child's destiny as the Saviour of mankind:

> munchas graçias te fazemos
> porque quesiste, Señor,
> la nuestra carne uestir,
> en la qual muy cruda muerte
> as por nos de reçebir. (ll. 97–101)

A further departure from the gospel story occurs in scene V when three angels visit Mary and declare their devotion to her. Gabriel, the angel of the Annunciation, will be her loyal ambassador. Michael, who will also accompany her and Jesus, speaks of his victory over 'las huestes luçiferales' (l. 114), a reference to the battle he and his angels won against the bad angels who were cast out of heaven (Revelation 12. 7–9). Raphael, who will be her pageboy, echoes the words originally spoken by the mother of John the Baptist, Elizabeth, and included in the Ave María, '¡O mater Christe, | bendicha entre las mugeres!' (Gómez Manrique 2003: 666, ll. 127–28; Luke 1. 42).

Scene VI is in striking contrast to the scenes that precede it: the action is no longer mimetic, but allegorical. In a radical departure from the gospels, rather than introducing the Magi who bring their gifts to the infant, Manrique creates an ironical twist to the action with the presentation of the chalice of the Last Supper together with the instruments of torture that will be used at the crucifixion. The link between the Nativity and the Passion, of which the audience has already received hints, is now made manifest with this juxtaposition of the Nativity scene with the personification of these objects. The scene opens with an *octava*, spoken by the chalice, a symbol of the central tenet of Christian belief, who tells the infant that he must drink from this cup to redeem mankind, thus foretelling Jesus's act at the Last Supper with the words:

> ¡O santo niño, naçido
> para nuestra redençión!
> Este cáliz dolorido
> de la tu cruda pasión
> es neçesario que beua
> tu sagrada majestad
> por saluar la vmanidad
> que fue perdida por Eua. (ll. 129–36)

The rope that tied Jesus to a column, the whip with which he was lashed, the crown of thorns, the cross, the nails and, finally, the lance that pierced his side when on the cross follow, each reciting a quatrain. The lance echoes the words of the prophet Zechariah:

> Con esta lança tan cruda
> foradarán tu costado,
> e será claro, sin duda,
> lo que fue profetizado. (ll. 157–60; Zechariah 12. 10)

The final scene is a lullaby, sung in chorus by the nuns as they address the infant. Here Manrique changes the metre to one of six syllables, which is typical of the *villancico*. That this is no ordinary lullaby, however, is made clear in the first verse that contains an obvious reference to Christ's manhood and death:

> Callad vos, Señor,
> nuestro redentor,
> que vuestro dolor
> durará poquito. (ll. 161–64)

The second verse contains an appeal to the angels to console the child, suggesting that the infant is aware of his destiny. The third and fourth verses allude to Israel's captivity in Egypt and their exodus from that land. The lullaby ends joyfully with the nuns encouraging each other to sing, since they are all 'esposas | del Jesú bendito' (ll. 179–80), thus emphasizing, to quote Alan Deyermond, what links 'el tiempo histórico de la obra — la vida terrenal de Jesús — con el tiempo actual de su primer público' (Deyermond 1992: 292).

This play has probably received more attention from scholars than other works by Manrique. Ronald E. Surtz, in an article on Franciscan influence on medieval Castilian theatre, notes that, in common with other plays and poems written by or for Franciscans, it 'develops a devotional or theological motif popularized by Franciscans' (Surtz 1983b: 141). In the case of the *Representaçión* the motif is the connection between the Incarnation and Redemption. He quotes from two

Middle English lullabies, compiled by a thirteenth-century Franciscan friar, and from a Nativity poem by a contemporary of Manrique's, Ambrosio Montesino, also a Franciscan, to demonstrate this link. He considers the presentation of the instruments of torture to the infant in scene VI to be 'the play's principal anomaly' because it is unusual to see the juxtaposition of the two dogmas enacted on the stage (142–43). In a footnote to his article he comments that pictorial representations of this juxtaposition were also rare, citing just two examples (150). Although Deyermond responds to this with two further examples, he agrees that Manrique is unlikely to have been inspired by iconographic tradition. The implication is that Manrique was doing something innovative in composing this scene. Deyermond and Surtz both suggest that it might well have been the inspiration in 1509 for a sermon preached by the Franciscan nun, Sor Juana de la Cruz, who speaks of the Virgin Mary seeing in a vision the cross and the instruments of torture brought to her by angels descending from heaven (Deyermond 1992: 294; Surtz 1983b: 144).

Deyermond's article on the *Historia sagrada y técnica dramática* of the play contains a detailed analysis of the biblical and apocryphal sources that Manrique used: 'incluye de una manera u otra casi toda la "historia humanae salvationis"' (Deyermond 1992: 291). This is an allusion to the *Speculum Humanae Salvationis*, an illustrated work of popular theology that first appeared in the early fourteenth century and concentrated on the theory of typology: certain events narrated in the Old Testament (types) prefigured others in the New Testament (antitypes). The *Speculum* was translated from Latin into several vernacular languages. Manrique was perhaps aware of this text, as the *Representaçión* contains examples of typology, as Deyermond emphasizes. One example is the reference to Eve's sin in the book of Genesis: her eating of the forbidden fruit marks the entry of sin into the world (type), which is redeemed by Christ's sacrifice (antitype), as explained in the above-quoted lines spoken by the chalice (Gómez Manrique 2003: ll. 133–36). Another typology is found in two verses of the lullaby of the final scene that refers to Israel's captivity in Egypt and the exodus from that land:

> Este fue reparo
> avnque l'costó caro,
> d'aquel pueblo amaro,
> cautiuo en Egito.
>
> Este santo dino,
> niño tan benino,
> por redimir vino
> el linaje aflito. (ll. 169–76)

The Israelites' bondage and subsequent freedom from slavery prefigures Christ's redemption of mankind by freeing the human race of sin. Deyermond takes the concept of typology a step further when he comments, 'se extiende en la Edad Media para incluir la historia de la Iglesia y la vida del cristiano', calling this concept a 'retrotipo' for want of a recognized term (Deyermond 1992: 303). Interpreting the final scene of the play, he notes that the lullaby sung by the nuns ends with the lines 'pues somos esposas | del Jesú bendito' (ll. 179–80), and reminds us that in scene V Mary is greeted by Gabriel with the words:

> Dios te salue, gloriosa,
> de los maytines estrella,
> después de madre donzella
> e antes que fija, esposa. (ll. 105–08)

Thus he sees the relationship of the nuns as brides of Christ, an accepted concept in conventual spirituality, as the 'retrotipo' of Mary's relationship with God, which means that the Franciscan sisters can enter into 'la cadena tipológico' (304).

Harry Sieber's article, redolent of the literary criticism of the '60s and '70s, stresses the importance of the dramatic structure and symmetry of this work. He observes that the play is structured in such a way that scenes including three characters are interspersed with a scene or scenes in which a sole character performs a monologue, until the sixth scene where the chalice and the six allegorical figures representing Christ's martyrdom appear. His article contains four diagrams (Sieber 1965: 120, 121, 123, 125) to illustrate this symmetry which he considers to be of great importance to an appreciation of the play. Whether Manrique composed his play with so great a preoccupation with structure and symmetry is debatable. The way in which he introduces the themes of birth, salvation and devotion shows how closely they are linked one to another and does not depend on an appreciation of the numbers of characters who appear in each scene. What seems more pertinent is how the focus of the play oscillates between two realms, the spiritual and the temporal, particularly in the first four scenes.

Another article, by Stanislav Zimic, emphasizes the importance of Joseph's role in this play, declaring that following the appearance of the angel to Joseph in the first scene, all further action 'debe considerarse como la visión de José en un nivel diferente' (Zimic 1977: 360). To underline what he terms the 'comunidad íntima de lo terrestre y lo divino' he refers to parallels with European painting, citing El Greco's *El entierro del conde de Orgaz* (362). Moreover, he claims that Joseph's doubt 'está implícitamente en todas las escenas sucesivas y es en efecto, el común denominador de todas ellas' (363). While there can be no doubt that the spiritual and temporal worlds meet in each scene, this emphasis on Joseph's importance seems rather far-fetched since he makes but one brief appearance in the first scene and no further reference is made to him. The central theme is the story of man's salvation which Manrique has conveyed skilfully.

A more recent article, building on the work of both Deyermond and Surtz by Nicasio Salvador Miguel, covers some of the same ground, but his research also points to some of the sources from which Manrique may have drawn. He notes that the description of Joseph as an old man appears in apocryphal works such as the *Protoevangelio de Santiago* and the *Evangelium pseudo Matthaei*, suggesting that the latter was probably known to Manrique (Salvador Miguel 2012: 146). He also observes that this depiction of Joseph becomes commonplace and found in works by Íñigo de Mendoza and Ambrosio de Montesino among others. Artists, such as Botticelli, depicted Joseph as an elderly man. Piero della Francesco, an exact contemporary of Manrique, portrays him as ageing and grey-haired in his painting of the Nativity (National Gallery, London), but Salvador Miguel has found an Iberian example in the altarpiece of the monastery of San Esteban de Bañolas in the province of Girona, which dates to the mid-fifteenth century (150). He also makes the point that the adoration of the angels in scene V, which does not figure in the gospels, appears in literary texts, Íñigo de Mendoza being one example, and in iconography (154).

There is evidence of much archival research in this article regarding the female members of the Manrique family who joined the community of Calabazanos. Apparently María Manrique, who asked her brother to compose a nativity play, only professed as a nun after her marriage to Rodrigo de Castañeda was annulled (136). Salvador Miguel surmises that while living with her family, and subsequently with her husband, she would have been accustomed to a literary environment where 'además de la poesía cancioneril, los momos, el teatro profano y otras fiestas, circulaba el teatro religioso como una forma extendida de asueto y devoción' (165). In addition he alludes to the fact that when she first professed, it was at Santa Clara de Astudillo, which was founded in 1354, and thinks it very likely that during the season of Advent and Christmas there would have been 'prácticas poéticas, asociadas de algún modo a la liturgia, de las que serían muestra las canciones polifónicas en romance que [...] se han copiado en un par de duernos' (167). These 'duernos' have been named as the *Cancionero musical de Astudillo* by Pedro Cátedra, after the convent in which they are housed, although there is no concrete evidence that they were actually compiled at Astudillo (167). Cátedra's opinion regarding this material is quoted by Salvador Miguel: 'Cátedra considera "indudable" que esos poemas "debieron ser fundamentales en la nueva fundación" de Calabazanos e incluso apoya que la *Representación* de Gómez Manrique significaría una "renovación de algo previo"' (167–68). Since María moved to Calabazanos when it was founded in 1458, her request to her brother can be seen as a step towards establishing a practice with which she had previously been familiar. Salvador Miguel emphasizes that many of the sisters of Astudillo were from aristocratic families who vied with each other and the court to promote their cultural interests, establishing libraries and becoming patrons in the fields of literature, art and music (169–70). We must conclude that María, in her request to her brother, was imbued with the same cultural interests of so many other members of her family and her ancestors. It is extremely gratifying that the community of Calabazanos, although enclosed, now allows their chapel to be used every year to welcome the public to four performances of the *Representaçión* shortly before 25 December, with the sisters singing the *villancico* that forms the final scene.

Other Religious Works

The theme of salvation is treated in other poems, although we do not know if they were written for family members. In the *Coplas fechas para la semana santa* (674–78) the Virgin Mary appeals to men and women of all three estates to join with her in grieving since Jesus died to redeem them. In the second scene Saint John echoes what she has said and reminds us that Judas, who betrayed Jesus, should also be mourned. In the third scene John first expresses his distress to Mary Magdalen and then tells the Virgin Mary to be courageous and accompany him to the place where

Jesus is buried. The language of this short piece is highly charged emotionally, with much use of anaphora.

A *décima*, the *Troba fecha a Santo Tomé* (282), is dedicated to the doubting Thomas. The tautology '¡O qué duda tan dudosa | fue la de Santo Tomé!' (ll. 1–2), declares that the Resurrection should never be doubted. Antithesis in the third and fourth lines demonstrates that, by showing he doubted, Thomas enabled the doubters to strengthen their faith. The three verbs, 'nasçió', 'murió' and 'resçuçitó', in the past tense, emphasize the poet's belief in these events, whereas the final verb of the poem, 'resurgiremos', rhyming with 'dudemos', in the future tense, affirms Manrique's belief in the afterlife.

Conclusion

A striking feature of the two consolatory poems is how the personal and public aspects of the Manrique family's lives seem to be inextricably linked. This is particularly true in the case of the poem written for Juana de Mendoza which, while it was inspired by a profoundly emotional reaction to personal tragedy, contains references to current political events in Portugal. One can only conclude that even what seems to us a deeply personal matter, concerning the poet's immediate family, cannot be separated from the shifting, and often treacherous, world of politics, revealing how intensely public they felt their lives to be. Moreover, Manrique found that he had to defend himself against the criticisms of Lucena, which appear to have been founded on rumour, another intimation that his private life was minutely scrutinized. Despite all this, the poet's faith, demonstrated in his devotional writing, and his Stoic convictions appear to remain unshaken.

Thus we see two strands of Manrique's poetic persona come together in this chapter: his Christian and Stoic convictions and his devotion to family. I think it is safe to say that in the poems discussed in this chapter he reveals more to us about his private life than most poets who were his contemporaries. While he wrote a number of poems to male relations, often of the *pregunta y respuesta* type, it cannot be denied that the two *consolatorias* and the *Representaçión*, all written for women, occupy an important place in his *oeuvre*, suggesting that he appreciated, and wished to contribute to, the cultural life of educated women.

CONCLUSION

Gómez Manrique stands out from his contemporaries as a poet in several ways. Where countless others would have abandoned verse outside the context of courtly practices, Manrique turned poetic composition into a vehicle that enabled him to reflect on and address many facets of his complex and unceasingly difficult existence. Certainly his poetic trajectory could be said to follow a fairly foreseeable pattern for an early modern nobleman who managed, against all odds, to reach old age: love poetry as a young courtier, elegies for dead comrades, and then the turning to moral and devotional themes in his mature years, exploring, in his case, a combination of Christian and Senecan ideas. But while his productivity as a poet spans so many years, there is little sense that poetry was for him a purely literary endeavour, or an attempt to emulate the great literary models of his age, or that he wrote with the judgement of posterity in mind. On the contrary, he presents himself as a man of his time, of the political moment, or of the immediately lived experience of his contemporaries. These aspects mark him out from other more talented and learned poets like Santillana or Mena.

In general terms, he would have seen himself as supporting and participating in the current trend of some members of the nobility and more lowly placed *letrados* in his century in the face of the dominance of clerical literacy. He would have learned early from his relative, the marqués de Santillana, whom he admired greatly, that there was no reason why the courtly and military areas of expertise that he developed should be mutually exclusive, and this is reflected in his known work: a sizeable body of courtly love poetry alongside a substantial volume of more weighty and varied compositions. He realized, however, the difficulties of combining arms and letters in practical life: there are occasions when he regrets that his military commitments do not permit him the leisure to extend his wide reading further, notably in his *pregunta* to Pedro de Mendoza, quoted at the beginning of this book, which appears to have been composed during a military campaign (Gómez Manrique 2003: 234–35). Similarly, his administrative and political duties hindered him from retaining, let alone developing, his skills in poetic composition, as he makes clear in the poem he addresses to Guillén de Segovia (223–25). Likewise, in the letter to his wife that accompanies the *consolatoria* (448–53) written for her following the death of two of their children, he complains about how much longer it now takes him to compose any verses than when he was a young man. Perhaps it is because of these difficulties that literary emulation, or even the desire to distinguish himself as a writer, does not seem to be at the forefront of his ambitions.

Rather, leaving aside his courtly love poetry, what is evident in his work is almost always a pragmatic and dutiful engagement through verse with the events and issues that confronted him at every turn. This is certainly the primary specific function of the writing of verse for Manrique. For him poetry, supported sometimes by prose, was the medium for conveying an intellectually based public response to the events in his own political, military and family life, and of evaluating the issues that arose from them.

Debate with others would have been a second function of verse-writing for him: there are numerous compositions of this kind, some of them trivial and addressed to friends, but others on major issues of his time such as the nature of true nobility, discussed by him with three correspondents, or the substantial and influential reply to Torroella's misogynistic *Maldezir de mugeres* (191–202). Verse was also a platform from which to promote his own political views. This was particularly relevant in the turbulent times of fifteenth-century Castile, and Manrique took the opportunity to stir up controversy when he disseminated in his *Esclamaçión e querella de la gouernaçión* (571–76) his accusations of what he saw as rampant corruption and maladministration. It does not seem too much of an exaggeration to suggest that this aspect of his writing was a kind of fifteenth-century forerunner of what today we term social media.

His verse sometimes performed a fourth function too: that of writing for the sake of family members, notably in times of crisis, in order to console them. Indeed, on one occasion when composing a consolatory poem for his wife after the loss of two of their adult children, in the letter accompanying the poem, Manrique admits to experiencing the therapeutic effect of writing. He also offered them devotional works for their own use, notably *Los cuchillos de dolor* (283–86), also composed for his wife, at her request. I have already argued that his detailed response to the misogyny of Torroella's *Maldezir* was more than a mere defence of the courtly code. His respect for the opposite sex is made manifest in the number of poems he wrote for female relatives. Some of these are merely *estrenas*, but the fact that several, such as the two *consolatorias* and *La Representaçión del nasçimiento de Nuestro Señor* (660–68), composed at the request of his sister, are of major significance is a reflection of his regard for educated women and his recognition of their literary and intellectual interests as well as their spiritual welfare.

It is precisely because the first three specific functions I have identified above are so publicly oriented that an understanding of the social, political and economic background in which Manrique lived and wrote is so fundamental to an appreciation of his work and the interpretation of it. His aristocratic birth and descent on his mother's side from Enrique II, giving rise to the family motto, 'Non venimos de reyes sino los reyes de nos', all suggest much about how the Manriques saw themselves. Times, however, were changing and the fortunes of many long-established families suffered various vicissitudes, often brought about by their own rebelliousness. An example of this is Manrique's sister, the condesa de Castro, which is why he addressed a consolatory prose epistle and poem to her (419–48). On the other hand, when Manrique found himself in 1460 living in the Archbishop of Toledo's household, commanding Carrillo's private army, he came into contact with a number of men, often *conversos*, who were not of the same social class but with whom he appears to have enjoyed engaging in debate, and this was a very fruitful period in his literary life. Social class and politics were inextricably linked: Enrique IV's promotion of recently ennobled men had caused resentment among the old aristocracy, not least Don Gómez. Then came the sudden and unexpected death of the infante Alfonso and the constitutional crisis which arose with the prospect of a woman on the throne. This event was a major landmark in Manrique's life, leading to his unequivocal support for the infanta Isabel as the heir to Enrique IV and opposition to the claims of the infanta Juana, an issue in which he found himself deeply involved and which ultimately resulted in his composition of the *Regimiento de prínçipes* (629–56).

This inextricable link between real events and his trajectory as a poet makes it all the more important to attempt to consider his work, as I have done here, within a chronological framework, albeit a loose one. This framework allows us to trace the development of his thought and the changing nature of his preoccupations. The early work, consisting of love poetry, offers little thematic interest and is typical of a young knight wishing to carve out a courtly identity by displaying basic poetic skills, skills which he developed and refined over the course of his production in great metrical variety and with the deployment of an extensive range of rhetorical resources. The elegy for Garcilaso is an expression of his respect for a man of his own class who paid the ultimate sacrifice in a campaign against the Muslims. In this poem Manrique simultaneously casts an image of himself both as a knight who was present at the battle and as a poet who is able to write an elegy that reveals an acquaintance with classical literature. Near the end of it the first glimmering of his disapproval of the favouritism of Enrique IV towards men of lower rank can be detected, reflecting the beginning of a transition to politically oriented writing. This disapproval is markedly more apparent in the *planto* for Santillana, very probably written a little later in 1460. Here, while he develops the genre of elegy further within an ambitious allegorical framework and focuses on his homage to Santillana's literary legacy, we find allusions to what the poet considers to be the deteriorating political scene in Castile due to the lack of men of integrity, such as the marqués, in positions of power and influence.

It is when Manrique joins the household of Archbishop Carrillo that his literary output of substantial works begins to increase significantly, and there is growing evidence of his intellectual curiosity. Mixing with a number of men who were *letrados*, most of them *conversos*, and who did not therefore bring with them the same preconceptions and sense of entitlement to wield power and influence, he engages with them on a wide variety of subjects. These included the difficulties they encountered in verse composition and various moral or theological problems. Perhaps most pertinent of all is the exchange on the nature of true nobility, in which his correspondents assert that it is a quality not automatically passed down from one generation to the next, but one that is inherent in certain individual people. The fact that it was Manrique who initiated the discussion strongly suggests that he was beginning to question the assumptions of his own class on this matter.

It was also during this period of his career that he began to write at greater length on moral issues. Surrounded by other men of letters, he aspired to complete Juan de Mena's unfinished *Debate de la Razón contra la Voluntad* (467–552), an ambitious project in which he claimed, like the other poets who wrote continuations to Mena's poem, the right to discuss the religious and ethical matters which not so many decades before might have been the province of clerics alone. This phase of his career saw the composition of what many judge to be his finest poem, the *Coplas para Arias Dávila* (556–70), a work with a strongly moral theme, the writing of which was motivated primarily by political concerns. Before the end of his time with Carrillo there came the radical change of tone we see in the *Esclamaçión e querella de la gouernaçión* (571–76), a manifestation of what is by now his anger and deep frustration.

The need for diplomacy as a way to solve Castile's problems, however, carried greater weight than the urge to rebel and cause havoc. A tension starts to arise between the persona of what Nicholas Round has termed a '*caballero sabio*, eager to use his cultural and poetic accomplishments to improve the moral state of the realm, and the son of a notoriously assertive family of warring grandees' (Round 2013: 158). The 'warring grandee' element of Manrique manifests itself, for instance, in the elegy for Garcilaso, when he lauds the young Garcilaso for launching into a skirmish against a group of Muslims near Granada; yet despite the fact that he was involved in military action for many years, this is the only concrete reference in his poetry to any personal engagement on the battlefield. It should be noted that by the time he embarks on his continuation of Mena's *coplas* on the seven deadly sins, probably written during the same decade, Manrique allows Razón to remind Enbidia that war is the cause of much devastation and personal tragedy. The desire for peace and reconciliation between Castile and Aragon is made manifest and advocated in forceful terms in 'Del Señor es fecho esto' (Gómez Manrique 2003: 619–21), a poem which very likely dates to 1463. This tension was resolved in Manrique's mature years when he channelled his energies into his role of statesman and felt justified, on account of his ancient and distinguished lineage, in advising Isabel and Fernando on how to conduct themselves as monarchs in his *Regimiento de prínçipes*. His patriotism is reflected in this poem as he looks to the future, hoping to see justice, peace and social cohesion, the lack of which had previously motivated him to write the *Esclamaçión*.

Another ideological tension, more difficult to gauge, can be observed in Manrique's poetic production, namely the anti-Semitism that manifests itself in his writings to Juan de Valladolid, despite the fact that the Carrillo circle was known to have an inclusive ethos and counted a number of *conversos* in its membership. As *corregidor* of Toledo he lived through some violent upheavals in the city, one of which occurred in 1478. By this time Archbishop Carrillo had shifted his allegiance from the Catholic Monarchs to Afonso V of Portugal, who had designs on the Spanish throne. Together with a large number of disaffected citizens who resented both the success of Toledo's *conversos* and the recent imposition of another tax, Carrillo plotted to overthrow Manrique. Francisco Márquez Villanueva believed that Manrique was well disposed towards New Christians, describing him as 'uno de los pocos que mantuvieron la cabeza fría en todo referente al pavoroso problema de los conversos' (Márquez Villanueva 1960: 164). This is borne out in Fernando del Pulgar's *Crónica de los reyes católicos* in which he reports the speech, allegedly made by Manrique, as he faced an angry and rebellious crowd of Old Christians (Pulgar 1943: II, 343–51). Upbraiding those present for threatening to continue Toledo's long history of insurrection and violence, he impresses upon them the fact that they are mistaken in believing that noble birth and lineage are necessary to hold major office. Perhaps the most important statement reputedly made by Manrique is, 'todos somos nacidos de una masa, e ovimos un principio noble'; he follows this by asserting that many men of 'baxa sangre' rise to distinguish themselves in diverse walks of life (348).[1] His oratorical skills were sufficient to quell that rebellion.

The *converso* problem recurred in 1484–85 as the establishment of the Inquisition in Toledo approached and this time it was the New Christians who caused problems for Manrique. The chronicler, Alfonso de Palencia, in his *Guerra de Granada*, recounts how the city of Seville had suffered financially as a consequence of the arrival of the Inquisition, as many Jewish men resorted to fleeing with what valuables they could carry and burying the rest in the hope of returning when it might be safe. As a result there was a dearth of gold and silver in Andalusia and insufficient money to pay the troops or maintain the garrison at Alhama, so that the monarchs had to 'recurrir a los pechos' (Palencia 1998: 116). Manrique must surely have felt very torn between his long-standing allegiance to the Catholic Monarchs and the ensuing economic damage to Toledo if its New Christian citizens followed the example of those in Seville when they faced the coming of the Inquisition. With this in mind Manrique, whom Palencia describes as 'el noble y prudentísimo Corregidor', was at least able to delay the start of proceedings in his city (117; Gómez Manrique 2003: 40). Around the same time some *conversos* were suspected of plotting an insurrection; several were executed on Manrique's orders, but then he relented and merely fined them rather leniently and the Inquisition went ahead. Presumably he was motivated by the desire to avoid an outcome in which the city became depopulated (Netanyahu 2001: 1161).

Ana Gómez-Bravo takes the view that Manrique's attitude towards the Inquisition, which ultimately he supported, was 'more in tune with his virulent diatribes against *converso* poets Juan Poeta or Montoro' (Gómez-Bravo 2013: 52).[2] She also points out that Manrique's wife, Juana de Mendoza, as *camarera mayor* to the queen, stood to benefit financially and received large sums of money from the Inquisition in Toledo, as the research of María-Milagros Rivera-Garretas establishes (52; Rivera Garretas 2007: 145, 172). Whatever Manrique thought privately about the Holy Office we shall never know, but rather than taking this negative view of Manrique,

1   Much of the content of this speech, expressed in very similar language, can also be found in a letter by Pulgar bearing the rubric 'Para un su amigo de Toledo' (Pulgar 1929: 69–74).
2   There is no evidence that Gómez Manrique addressed any poem to Antón de Montoro. One of Manrique's poems to Juan de Valladolid, however, actually bears the rubric 'De Gómez Manrique en nonbre del Ropero, contra Iohan Poeta' (Gómez Manrique 2003: 341–45). Montoro was often referred to by the sobriquet 'El Ropero' and was also critical of Juan de Valladolid. See chapter 4.

we need to bear in mind that he lived and worked alongside many *conversos* whom he obviously admired, and appreciated the role they played in life of the city of Toledo. The inconsistency he showed in dealing with those who rebelled in 1485 is surely a manifestation of the very real dilemma he faced while discharging his administrative duties and living in a society plagued by violence and intolerance.

This study has involved a great deal of close analysis of Gómez Manrique's poetry. What have we learned from engaging with it in such detail? In the first place, I hope it reveals how carefully structured and considered much of his work is, how closely it responds to and interweaves with the ideas of a good number of his contemporaries who rarely expressed themselves at such length. It is from such detail that we acquire a better sense of the intense intellectual and ethical engagement of Manrique with whatever concrete event urged him to write, or whatever abstract concept the event called up in his well-stocked mind.

Clearly, Manrique was a devout Christian, but what is striking is the biblical knowledge that comes to the fore in his moral and religious writing. A number of his verses contain lines that echo those of the New Testament, but it is in his continuation of Mena's *Debate de la Razón contra la Voluntad* and the *Representaçión del Naçimiento de Nuestro Señor* that references to both Old and New Testaments abound, and he also shows an awareness of apocryphal texts. We cannot tell whether he knew sufficient Latin to read the Vulgate or works such as Ludolph of Saxony's *Vita Christi*, but he no doubt heard many a sermon in the vernacular that would have familiarized him with the biblical sources to which he alludes. In addition, it should be borne in mind that Manrique lived for a considerable period of time in Toledo in Archbishop Carrillo's household which brought him into close contact with *letrados* and clerics, notably Pero Díaz de Toledo. He would have had access to the Archbishop's library too, where he very probably found other material that enabled him to build up his knowledge of biblical texts.

Analysing Manrique's verse as nearly as is possible in chronological order, it becomes apparent that he was able to adapt his style to suit the subject about which he was writing. His early love poetry shows an ability to use a wide range of rhetorical devices such as antithesis and anaphora, to name just two of these. His imagery in these poems is very conventional and typical of courtly love poetry, as he uses such well-worn metaphors as the flames of passion and the prison of love to express his feelings for the lady he addresses (who may well be imaginary). His elegy for Garcilaso is very different: composed in *arte mayor*, it contains elements that mirror the style of Senecan tragedy, while imparting a fusion of Stoic thought and Christian doctrine that will be found in later works such as the continuation of Mena's *Debate de la Razón contra la Voluntad* and the *Regimiento de príncipes*. In the elegy for Santillana he not only adopts an allegorical form, but develops an image from one of his mentor's own works, that of the temple as the dwelling-place of the muses.

This *planto* really heralds a turning point in Manrique's poetic trajectory. As he begins to use verse as a medium for declaring his views on the political ambience in which he is living, we find that he develops the range of his figurative language.

In this poem more than fifty similes are used to striking effect, not as a mere adornment, but to underpin the ideas he seeks to impart. The nautical image is one that recurs in various forms in his work, but especially in this second elegy, and in the poem addressed to Diego Arias. The sea voyage with its attendant storms is seen as man's journey through earthly life with its periods of confusion, struggles and perils. The image of the ship is also used to emphasize the necessity of social cohesion when it is compared to the state, with its oarsmen and captain required to work in harmony for the good of society. A state governed by a good leader is compared to a ship commanded by a good sea captain. This nautical image is also used in the *Esclamaçión e querella* in which, with its string of *ensienplos e sentençias*, Manrique conveys the intensity of his convictions and the frustration he feels regarding the current state of the Castilian nation. But it is perhaps in the poem addressed to Arias that we find Manrique at his most lyrical. Here he uses the nautical image to warn him of life's perils and the vagaries of fortune he may face, while reminding him that his ship may also be becalmed. Manrique finds a different set of images to warn Arias about the ephemeral nature of earthly life and its material possessions, a theme that pervades much of his mature work. Some of these images are more original than the nautical images: the transient nature of earthly pleasures is compared to the spray that follows the breaking of a wave at sea. Fame and honour are quickly lost in the same way that fire can be a destructive force, or flowers that wither with age or are destroyed by frost.

We end up with a sense of how, whether he was writing on the most important matters of state, debating ideas in quick exchanges, keeping his hand in as a producer of courtly love lyrics, advising princes, denouncing the contemporary problems of Castile, or consoling a family member by reflecting on the vagaries of fortune, verse composition was an activity that was an essential part of his existence, not an acquired adornment to it or an attempt to achieve literary fame. Nephew of Santillana, admirer of the great Mena, he must have been well aware of his limitations. I have made no claims for Gómez Manrique as a great poet; that is not the point. As the large body of his surviving work testifies, verse was a life-long practice that wove its way into nearly everything he did, or at least nearly everything we know of him. He was something quite different from his more illustrious poetic contemporaries: an assiduous and skilled writer of verse who thought that no vital aspect of the world that he found himself in was unworthy of poetic composition, and who for that reason kept writing until nearly the end of his life.

BIBLIOGRAPHY

ALVAR, MANUEL (ed.). 1965. *Libro de la infancia y muerte de Jesús (Libre dels tres reys d'orient)* (Madrid: Consejo Superior de Investigaciones Científicos)
ÁLVAREZ GATO, JUAN. 1928. *Obras completas*, ed. by Jenaro Artiles Rodríguez (Madrid: Compañía Ibero-Americana de Publicaciones)
ÁLVAREZ PELLITERO, ANA MARÍA (ed.). 1990. *Teatro medieval* (Madrid: Espasa Calpe)
ARCHER, ROBERT. 1985. *The Pervasive Image* (Amsterdam and Philadelphia: John Benjamins)
—— 1996. *Aproximació a Ausiàs March* (Barcelona: Editorial Empúries)
—— (ed.). 2001. *Misoginia y defensa de las mujeres: antología de textos medievales* (Madrid: Cátedra)
—— 2011A. *La cuestión odiosa: la mujer en la literatura hispánica tardomedieval* (Valencia: Institució Alfons el Magnànim)
—— 2011B. 'Un códice desconocido del *Doctrinal de los cavalleros* de Alfonso de Cartagena', *Tirant*, 14: 59–71
ATLEE, CARL W. 2007. 'A Reassessment of the Satirical Nature of Gómez Manrique's *Coplas para Diego Arias de Ávila*', *La corónica*, 35: 173–207
—— 2010. 'Political Protest in Gómez Manrique's *Defunzión del noble cauallero Garçía Laso de la Vega*', *Bulletin of Hispanic Studies*, 87: 169–85
AVERÇÓ, LUIS DE. 1956. *Torcimany*, ed. by José María Casas Homs (Barcelona: Consejo Superior de Investigaciones Científicas)
AZAUSTRE GALIANA, ANTONIO, and JUAN CASAS RIGALL. 1997. *Manual de retórica española* (Barcelona: Editorial Ariel)
BAENA, JUAN ALFONSO DE. 1966. *Cancionero*, ed. by José María Azáceta, 3 vols (Madrid: Consejo Superior de Investigaciones Científicas)
BATTESTI-PELEGRIN, JEANNE. 1990. 'Les Poètes convers et le pouvoir: le débat poétique entre Gómez Manrique et Juan de Valladolid', in *Ecrire à la fin du moyen-âge: le pouvoir et l'écriture en Espagne et en Italie (1450–1530)* (Aix-en-Provence: Publications Université de Provence), 241–51
BECEIRO PITA, ISABEL. 1985. 'La Biblioteca del conde de Benavente a mediados del siglo XV y su relación con las mentalidades y usos nobiliarios de la época', in *Estudios en memoria del Profesor D. Salvador de Moxó*, 1, ed. by M. A. Ladero Quesada (Madrid: Universidad Complutense), 135–45
BLÜHER, KARL. 1983. *Séneca en España: investigaciones sobre la recepción de Séneca en España desde el siglo XIII hasta el siglo XVII* (Madrid: Gredos)
BOASE, ROGER. 1978. *The Troubadour Revival* (London: Routledge and Keegan Paul)
BURRUS, VICTORIA A. 1998. 'Role Playing in the Amatory Poetry of the *Cancioneros*', in *Poetry at Court in Trastamaran Spain: From the Cancionero de Baena to the Cancionero General*, ed. by E. Michael Gerli and Julian Weiss (Tempe, AZ: Medieval Texts and Studies), 111–33
CAMACHO GUIZADO, EDUARDO. 1969. *La elegía funeral en la poesía española* (Madrid: Gredos)

CANTERA BURGOS, FRANCISCO. 1970. *El poeta Ruy Sánchez Cota y su familia de judíos conversos* (Madrid: Universidad de Madrid — Facultad de Filosofía y Letras)
CAPRA, DANIELA. 1992. 'La renovación del diálogo en las 'Preguntas y Respuestas' de Gómez Manrique', *Romance Quarterly*, 39.2: 185–98
CARRILLO DE HUETE, PEDRO. 1946. *Crónica del Halconero de Juan II*, ed. by Juan de Mata Carriazo (Madrid: Espasa-Calpe)
CARRIÓN, MANUEL (ed.). 1978. 'Gómez Manrique y el protonotario Lucena. Dos cartas con memoria de Jorge Manrique', *Revista de Archivos, Bibliotecas y Museos*, 81: 565–82
CARTAGENA, TERESA DE. 1967. *Arboleda de los enfermos. Admiraçión operum Dey*, ed. by Lewis G. Hutton (Madrid: Real Academia Española)
CASAS RIGALL, JUAN. 1995. *Agudeza y retórica en la poesía amorosa de cancionero* (Santiago de Compostela: Universidad de Santiago de Compostela)
CASTROJERIZ, JUAN DE. 1947. *Glosa castellana al Regimiento de príncipes*, ed. by Juan Beneyto Reyes, 3 vols (Madrid: Instituto de Estudios Políticos)
CÁTEDRA, PEDRO M. (ed.). 2001. *Tratados de amor en el entorno de Celestina* (Madrid: Sociedad Estatal España Nuevo Milenio)
—— 2005. *Liturgia, poesía y teatro en la Edad Media: estudios sobre prácticas culturales y literarias* (Madrid: Gredos)
CHAS AGUIÓN, ANTONIO. 2002. *Preguntas y respuestas en la poesía cancioneril castellana* (Madrid: Fundación Universitaria Española)
COLONNA, GUIDO DE. 1970. *La Corónica Troyana: A Medieval Spanish Translation of Guido de Colonna's Historia Destructionis Troiae*, ed. by Frank Pelletier Norris II (Chapel Hill: University of North Carolina Press)
CONDE SOLARES, CARLOS. 2009. *El Cancionero de Herberay y la corte literaria de Juan II de Navarra* (Newcastle upon Tyne: Arts and Social Sciences Academic Press)
CONTRERAS JIMÉNEZ, MARÍA EUGENIA. 1985. 'Diego Arias Dávila en la tradición y en la historia', *Anuario de estudios medievales*, 15: 475–95
COSTA, MARITHELMA. 2000. 'La contienda poética entre Juan de Valladolid, el comendador Román y Antón de Montoro', *Cahiers de Linguistique Hispanique Médiévale*, 23: 27–50
Crónica anónima de Enrique IV de Castilla. 1991. Ed. by María Pilar Sánchez-Parra, 2 vols (Madrid: Ediciones de la Torre)
CUMMINGS, JOHN G. 1973. 'Pero Guillén de Segovia y el Ms. 4114', *Hispanic Review*, 41: 6–32
CURTIUS, ERNST ROBERT. 1979. *European Literature and the Latin Middle Ages* (London and Henley: Routledge and Kegan Paul)
DÍAZ ROIG, MERCEDES (ed.). 1976. *El romancero viejo* (Madrid: Cátedra)
DEYERMOND, ALAN. 1987. 'La defunzión del noble cavallero Garcilaso de la Vega', *Dicenda*, 6: 93–112
—— 1992. 'Historia sagrada y técnica dramática en *La Representación del Nacimiento de Nuestro Señor*, de Gómez Manrique', in *Historias y ficciones: coloquio sobre la literatura del siglo XV* (Valencia: Universitat de València, Departament de Filologia Espanyola), 291–305
—— 1998. 'Women and Gómez Manrique', in *Cancionero Studies in Honour of Ian MacPherson* (London: Dept. of Hispanic Studies, Queen Mary and Westfield College), 69–87
DISNEY, A. R. 2009. *A History of Portugal and the Portuguese Empire*, 2 vols (New York: Cambridge University Press)
DOMÍNGUEZ, FRANK A. 1988. *Love and Remembrance: The Poetry of Jorge Manrique* (Lexington: The University Press of Kentucky)
DRAGONETTI, ROGER. 1960. *La Technique poétique des trouvères dans la chanson courtoise* (Bruges: De Templ)
DUFFELL, MARTIN J. 2007. *Syllable and Accent: Studies on Medieval Hispanic Metrics* (London: Department of Hispanic Studies, Queen Mary University of London)

DUTTON, BRIAN (ed.). 1990–91. *El cancionero del siglo XV, c. 1360–1520*, 7 vols (Salamanca: Universidad de Salamanca)
An Electronic Corpus, 2007: An Electronic Corpus of 15th Century Castilian Cancionero Manuscripts, ed. by Dorothy S. Severin, F. Maguire, M. Moreno, B. Bordalejo [and B. Dutton], <http://cancionerovirtual.liv.ac.uk>
ELLIOTT, J. H. 2002. *Imperial Spain, 1469–1716* (London: Penguin Books)
ENRÍQUEZ DEL CASTILLO, DIEGO. 1994. *Crónica de Enrique IV*, ed. by Aureliano Sánchez Martín (Valladolid: Universidad de Valladolid)
FERRER, FRANCESC. 1989. *Obra completa*, ed. by Jaume Auferil (Barcelona: Barcino)
GATIEN-ARNOULT, M. (ed.). 1841–43. *Las Flors de Gay Saber, estier dichas Las Leys d'amor*, 2 vols (Toulouse)
GAUME, JEAN JOSEPH. 1882. *Life of the Good Thief. Done into English by M. De Lisle* (London)
GERLI, E. MICHAEL. 1996. 'Performing Nobility: Mosén Diego de Valera and the Poetics of *Converso* Identity', *La corónica*, 25.1: 19–36
GIMENO CASALDUERO, JOAQUÍN. 1975. *Estructura y diseño en la literatura castellana medieval* (Madrid: Porrúa)
GITLITZ, DAVID. 1996. *Los Arias de Segovia: entre la sinagoga y la iglesia* (San Francisco: International Scholars' Publications)
GÓMEZ-BRAVO, ANA M. 2013. *Textual Agency: Writing Culture and Social Networks in Fifteenth-Century Spain* (Toronto: University of Toronto Press)
GÓMEZ MORENO, ÁNGEL. 1991. *El teatro medieval castellano en su marco románico* (Madrid: Taurus Ediciones)
GRIFFIN, CLIVE. 1991. *Los Cromberger: la historia de una imprenta del siglo XVI en Sevilla y México* (Madrid: Ediciones de Cultura Hispánica; Instituto de Cooperación Iberoamericano; Sociedad Estatal Quinto Centenario)
GUILLÉN DE SEGOVIA, PERO. 1989. *Obra poética*, ed. by Carlos Moreno Hernández (Madrid: Fundación Universitaria Española)
HUIZINGA, J. 1965. *The Waning of the Middle Ages* (London: Peregrine Books)
JOHNSTON, MARK D. 1998. 'Cultural Studies on the *Gaya Ciencia*', in *Poetry at Court in Trastamaran Spain: From the Cancionero de Baena to the Cancionero general*, ed. by E. Michael Gerli and Julian Weiss (Tempe, AZ: Medieval and Renaissance Texts and Studies), 235–53
KAMEN, HENRY. 1985. *Inquisition and Society in Spain in the Sixteenth and Seventeenth Centuries* (London: Weidenfeld and Nicolson)
KAPLAN, GREGORY B. 1996A. 'Rodrigo Cota's *Diálogo entre el Amor y un Viejo*: A Converso Lament', *Indiana Journal of Hispanic Literatures*, 8: 7–30
—— 1996B. 'Toward the Establishment of a Christian Identity: The *Conversos* and Early Christian Humanism', *La corónica*, 25: 53–68
LAPESA, RAFAEL. 1988. *De Ayala a Ayala: estudios literarios y estilísticos* (Madrid: Istmo)
LAWRANCE, JEREMY. 1985. 'The Spread of Lay Literacy in Late Medieval Castile', *Bulletin of Hispanic Studies*, 62: 1, 79–94
—— 2000. 'Santillana's Political Poetry', in *Santillana: A Symposium*, ed. by Alan Deyermond (London: Department of Hispanic Studies Queen Mary and Westfield College), 7–37
LIDA DE MALKIEL, MARÍA ROSA. 1984. *Juan de Mena, poeta del prerrenacimiento español* (Mexico City: El Colegio de México)
LISS, PEGGY K. 1992. *Isabel the Queen: Life and Times* (New York: Oxford University Press)
LÓPEZ DE AYALA, PERO. 2000. *Rimado de Palacio*, ed. by H. Salvador Martínez (Washington: Peter Lang)

López Estrada, Francisco. 1979. *Introducción a la literatura medieval española* (Madrid: Gredos)
—— 1984. 'La *Representación del nacimiento de Nuestro Señor* de Gómez Manrique. Estudio textual', *Segismundo*, 39–40: 9–30
McClure, George W. 1991. *Sorrow and Consolation in Italian Humanism* (Princeton: Princeton University Press)
MacKay, Angus 1977. *Spain in the Middle Ages: from Frontier to Empire, 1000–1500* (London: Macmillan)
—— 1981. *Money, Prices and Politics in Fifteenth-Century Castile* (London: Royal Historical Society)
Manrique, Gómez. 1885–86. *Cancionero*, ed. by Antonio Paz y Melia, 2 vols (Madrid: Imprenta A. Pérez Dubrull)
—— 1947. *Regimiento de príncipes*, ed. by Augusto Cortina (Buenos Aires: Espasa-Calpe)
—— 2003. *Cancionero*, ed. by Francisco Vidal González (Madrid: Cátedra)
Manrique, Jorge. 1997. *Cancionero*, ed. by Julio Rodríguez-Puértolas (Madrid: Akal)
March, Ausiàs. 1997. *Obra completa*, ed. by Robert Archer (Barcelona: Editorial Barcanova)
Marino, Nancy F. 2003. 'La Relación entre historia y poesía: el caso de La Esclamación e querella de la gouernación de Gómez Manrique', in *Propuestas teórico-metodológicas para el estudio de la literatura hispánica medieval*, ed. by Lillian von der Walde Moheno (Mexico City: Universidad Autónoma de México), 211–25
Márquez Villanueva, Francisco. 1960. *Investigaciones sobre Juan Álvarez Gato* (Madrid: Anejo del Boletín de la Real Academia Española)
—— 1982. '"Jewish Fools" of the Spanish Fifteenth Century', *Hispanic Review*, 50: 385–409
Martín de Córdoba. 1974. *Jardín de nobles doncellas*, ed. by Harriet Goldberg (Chapel Hill: University of North Carolina Press)
Mena, Juan de. 1505(?). *Coplas de los siete pecados mortales* (Sevilla: Jacobo Cromberger)
—— 1548. *Copilación de todas las obras del famosíssimo poeta Iuan de Mena* (Toledo: Fernando de Santa Catalina)
—— 1552. *Las trezientas d'el poeta Iuan de Mena, glosadas por F. Núñez. Tratado de vicios y virtudes (glosado y acabado por I. de Olivares). Todo corregido* (Anvers)
—— 1982. *Coplas de los siete pecados mortales and First Continuation*, ed. by Gladys M. Rivera (Madrid: Porrúa)
—— 1996. *La Ilíada de Homero: edición crítica de las "Sumas de la Yliada de Homero" y del original latino, reconstruido, acompañada de un glosario latino-romance*, ed. by Tomás Gonzalo Rolán, María F. Barrio Vega and A. López Fonseca (Madrid: Ediciones Clásicas)
—— 1997. *Laberinto de fortuna*, ed. by Maxim P. A. M. Kerkhof (Madrid: Castalia)
Mendoza, Fray Íñigo de. 1968. *Cancionero*, ed. by Julio Rodríguez Puértolas (Madrid: Espasa-Calpe)
Mendoza Negrillo, Juan de Dios. 1973. *Fortuna y providencia en la literatura castellana del siglo XV* (Madrid: Real Academia Española)
Montoro, Antón de. 1990. *Poesía completa*, ed. by Marithelma Costa (Cleveland, OH: Cleveland State University Press)
Moreno Hernández, Carlos. 1985. 'Pedro Guillén de Segovia y el círculo de Alfonso Carrillo', *Revista de Literatura*, 47.94: 17–45
Nader, Helen. 1979. *The Mendoza Family in the Spanish Renaissance, 1350–1550* (New Brunswick, NJ: Rutgers University Press)
Netanyahu, B. 2001. *The Origins of the Inquisition in Fifteenth Century Spain* (New York: New York Review of Books)

Nirenberg, David. 2006. 'Figures of Thought and Figures of Flesh: "Jews" and "Judaism" in Late-Medieval Spanish Poetry and Politics', *Speculum*, 81: 398–426

Oropesa, Alonso de. 1979. *Lumen ad revelationem gentium et gloria plebis Israel*, trans. by Luis A. Díaz y Díaz (Madrid: Universidad Pontífica de Salamanca)

Palencia, Alonso de. 1998–99. *Gesta Hispaniensia ex annalibus suorum dierum collecta*, ed. and trans. by Brian Tate and Jeremy Lawrance, 2 vols (Madrid: Real Academia de Historia)

—— 1998. *Guerra de Granada*, ed. and trans. by A. Paz y Melia (Granada: Universidad de Granada)

Parrilla García, Carmen. 1986. 'Dos cartas inéditas en la Biblioteca Colombina', *Epos*, 2: 341–50

Perea Rodríguez, Óscar. 2007. *Estudio biográfico sobre los poetas del Cancionero general* (Madrid: Consejo Superior de Investigaciones Científicos)

—— 2012. 'Night Moves: Nocturnality within Religious and Humanist Poetry in Hernando de Castillo's *Cancionero general*', *eHumanista*, 22: 289–329 <http://eHumanista.ucsb.edu.span>

Pérez de Guzmán, Fernán. 1965. *Generaçiones y semblanzas*, ed. by R. B. Tate (London: Tamesis Books)

Pérez López, José Luis. 1994. 'Un poeta de cancionero, sobrino del marqués de Santillana, Pedro de Mendoza, señor de Almazán', in *Actas del III congreso de la Asociación Hispánica de Literatura Medieval* (Salamanca: Universidad de Salamanca), 767–79

Pérez Priego, Miguel Ángel (ed.) 1990. *Poesía femenina en los cancioneros* (Madrid: Castalia & Instituto de la Mujer)

Pescador del Hoyo, María del Carmen. 1972–73. 'Aportaciones al estudio de Juan Álvarez Gato', *Anuario de estudios medievales*, 8: 305–47

Pontón, Gonzalo. 2014. 'Las cartas de Diego Valera', in *Mosén Diego de Valera entre las armas y las letras*, ed. by Cristina Moya García (Woodbridge: Támesis)

Pulgar, Fernando del. 1929. *Letras*, ed. by J. Domínguez Bordona (Madrid: Ediciones de "La Lectura")

—— 1943. *Crónica de los reyes católicos*, ed. by Juan de Mata Carriazo, 2 vols (Madrid: Espasa-Calpe)

—— 1971. *Claros varones de Castilla*, ed. by Robert Brian Tate (Oxford: Oxford University Press)

Rivera, Gladys M. (ed.). 1982. *Coplas de los siete pecados and First Continuation* (Madrid: Porrúa)

Rivera Garretas, María-Milagros. 2004. *Juana de Mendoza (ca. 1425–1493)* (Madrid: Ediciones del Orto)

—— 2007. 'Los testamentos de Juana de Mendoza, camarera mayor de Isabel la Católica, y de su marido el poeta Gómez Manrique, corregidor de Toledo (1493 y 1490)', *Anuario de Estudios Medievales*, 37.1: 139–80

Rodríguez García, José María. 2005. 'Poetry and Penal Practices in Late Fifteenth-Century Toledo', *Journal of Medieval and Early Modern Studies*, 35.2: 245–88

Rodríguez-Puértolas, Julio (ed). 1981. *Poesía crítica y satírica del siglo XV* (Madrid: Castalia)

Rodríguez Velasco, Jesús D. 1996. *El debate sobre la caballería en el siglo XV: la tratadística caballeresca en su marco* (Salamanca: Junta de Castilla y León)

Rojas, Fernando de. 1988. *La Celestina: tragicomedia de Calisto y Melibea*, ed. by Dorothy S. Severin (Madrid: Cátedra)

—— 2007. *La Celestina: Comedia o Tragicomedia de Calisto y Melibea*, ed. by Peter E. Russell (Madrid: Castalia)

—— 2017. *La Celestina*, ed. by Dorothy S. Severin (Madrid: Cátedra)

Round, Nicholas G. 1962. 'Renaissance Culture and its Opponents in Fifteenth-Century Castile', *Modern Language Review*, 57: 204–15
—— 2013. 'Gómez Manrique's *Exclamación e querella de la governación*: Poem and Commentary', in *Medieval Hispanic Studies in Memory of Alan Deyermond*, ed. by Andrew M. Beresford, Louise M. Haywood and Julian Weiss (Woodbridge: Tamesis), 149–74
Rubio González, Lorenzo. 1984. 'Juan de Valladolid: un poeta de juglaría en el siglo XV', *Castilla: Boletín del departamento de filología española*, 6–7: 101–12
Ruiz, Juan. 1988. *Libro de buen amor*, ed. by G. B. Gybbon-Monypenny (Madrid: Castalia)
Salinas, Pedro. 1947. *Jorge Manrique o tradición y originalidad* (Buenos Aires: Editorial Sudamérica)
Salvador Miguel, Nicasio. 2012. 'Gómez Manrique y la *Representación de Nuestro Señor*', *Revista de filología española*, XCII, 1: 135–80
Santillana, marqués de (Mendoza, Íñigo López de). 1984. *Prohemios y cartas literarias*, ed. by Miguel Garci-Gómez (Madrid: Editora Nacional)
—— 1988. *Obras completas* ed. by Ángel Gómez Moreno and Maximilian P. A. M. Kerkhof (Barcelona: Planeta)
—— 2003. *Poesías completas*, ed. by Maxim P. A. M. Kerkhof and Ángel Gómez Moreno (Madrid: Castalia)
Scholberg, Kenneth R. 1971. *Sátira e invectiva en la España medieval* (Madrid: Gredos)
—— 1984. *Introducción a la poesía de Gómez Manrique* (Madison, WI: Hispanic Seminary of Medieval Studies)
Seneca. 1969. *Letters from a Stoic*, trans. by Robin Campbell (Harmondsworth: Penguin Books)
—— 2006. *Moral Essays*, trans. by John W. Basore, 3 vols (Cambridge, MA: Harvard University Press)
Sieber, Harry. 1965. 'Dramatic Symmetry in Gómez Manrique's *La Representación del nacimiento de Nuestro Señor*', *Hispanic Review*, 33: 118–35
—— 1989. 'Narrative Elegiac Structure in Gómez Manrique's *Defunción del noble cavallero Garci Laso de la Vega*', in *Studies in Honor of Bruce Wardropper*, ed. by Dian Fox, Harry Sieber, Robert Horst (Newark, DE: Juan de la Cuesta), 279–90
—— 1993. 'Gómez Manrique's Last Poem', in *Letters and Society in Fifteenth-Century Spain*, ed. by Alan Deyermond and Jeremy Lawrance (Llangrannog: The Dolphin Book Company), 153–63
Sigüenza, José de. 1907–09. *Historia de la Orden de San Jerónimo*, 2 vols (Madrid: Bailly-Baillière)
Suárez Fernández, Luis, Ángel Canellas López and Jaime Vicens Vives. 1964. *Los Trastámaras de Castilla y Aragón en el siglo XV* (Madrid: Espasa-Calpe)
Surtz, Ronald E. 1983a. *Teatro medieval castellano* (Madrid: Taurus Ediciones)
—— 1983b. 'The "Franciscan Connection" in Early Castilian Theater', *Bulletin of the Comediantes*, 35.2: 141–52
—— 2004. 'In Search of Juana de Mendoza', in *Power and Gender in Renaissance Spain: Eight Women of the Mendoza Family*, ed. by Helen Nader (Champaign: University of Illinois Press), 48–70
Talavera, Hernando de. 1911. *De cómo se ha de ordenar el tiempo para que sea bien expendido*, in *Escritos místicos españoles*, ed. by Miguel Mir, Nueva Biblioteca de Autores Españoles, 16 (Madrid: Bailly-Baillière), 94–103
Torroella, Pere. 2004. *Obra completa*, ed. by Robert Archer (Soveria Mannelli: Fondazione Rubbettino)
Valera, Diego de. 1941. *Memorial de diversas hazañas: crónica de Enrique IV*, ed. by Juan de Mata Carriazo (Madrid: Espasa-Calpe)

———1959A. *Espejo de la verdadera nobleza*, in *Prosistas castellanos del siglo XV*, Biblioteca de Autores Españoles, 116 (Madrid: Atlas), 89–116

———1959B. *Epístolas* in *Prosistas castellanos del siglo XV*, ed. by Mario Penna, Biblioteca de Autores Españoles, 116 (Madrid: Atlas), 1–51

VIDAL GONZÁLEZ, FRANCISCO. 2000. 'Itinerario literario de Gómez Manrique: su primera etapa', in *Proceedings of the Ninth Colloquium* (London: Department of Hispanic Studies, Queen Mary and Westfield College), 201–10

VILLENA, ENRIQUE DE. 1993. *Arte de trovar*, ed. by F. J. Sánchez Cantón (Madrid: Visor Libros)

VIRGIL. 1967. *Georgics*, trans. by H. Rushton Fairclough (London: William Heinemann)

WEISS, JULIAN. 1990. *The Poet's Art: Literary Theory in Castile, c. 1400–60* (Oxford: The Society for the Study of Mediaeval Languages and Literature)

———2002. '¿Qué demandamos de las mugeres?', in *Gender in Debate from the Early Middle Ages to the Renaissance*, ed. by Thelma S. Fenster and Clare A. Lees (New York and Basingstoke: Palgrave), 237–81

WEISSBERGER, BARBARA F. 2004. *Isabel Rules: Constructing Queenship, Wielding Power* (Minneapolis: University of Minnesota Press)

ZIMIC, STANISLAV. 1977. 'El teatro religioso de Gómez Manrique (1412–1491)', *Boletín de la Real Academia Española*, 57: 353–400

INDEX

Afonso V, King of Portugal 3, 156
Alfonso, Infante of Castile 3, 30, 46, 98, 108, 155
Alfonso X, King of Castile (el Sabio) 41, 145
Alfonso V, King of Aragon 2, 136
Álvar, Manuel 57
Álvarez Gato, Juan 3, 8, 66, 69, 81–82
 Cualquier noble costunbre 82
 Dino de más memorado 70–71
 Porque vuestra discriçión 62
 Yo, señor, ya lo dexé 73–74
Álvarez Pellitero, Ana 145–46
Aragon, Infantes of 1, 9, 132
Arias Dávila, Diego 6, 7, 9, 55, 97–108, 159, 130
Arias Dávila, Pedro 70, 98
Archer, Robert 25, 27, 33, 43, 128
Aristotle 36, 41, 75, 115, 116, 128
Atlee, Carl 6, 38, 99, 102, 103, 104, 105, 107
Averçó, Luis de, *Torcimany* 1, 14
Ávila 46, 97, 98, 108
Azaustre Galiana, Antonio 43

Baena, Juan Alfonso de 11, 12, 61, 93, 94
Battesti Pelegrin, Jeanne 85, 94
Benavente, conde de, see Pimentel, Rodrigo
Blanca of Navarre 1, 8
Blüher, Karl 58
Boase, Roger 12, 78
Boccaccio 27, 75
Boethius 75, 141
Burrus, Victoria 13

Caesar 39, 76, 135
Calabazanos 10, 145, 151
Calatayud 136
Camacho Guizado, Eduardo 33
Canales, siege of 3, 5
Cantera Burgos, Francisco 79, 80
Capra, Daniela 61–62, 65
Carlos de Viana 83
Carrillo de Acuña, Alfonso, Archbishop of Toledo 2, 3, 8–9, 10, 65, 70, 81, 82, 89, 95, 98, 112, 113, 122, 155, 156
Carrillo de Huete, Pedro 1
Carrión, Manuel 10, 142
Cartagena, Alonso de 2, 42, 47, 71, 74, 94, 113
Cartagena, Pedro de 2, 64
Cartagena, Teresa de 2, 30, 40

Casas Rigall, Juan 16, 17, 43
Castañeda, Rodrigo de 151
Castillo, Diego de 62–63
Castrojeriz, Juan de 128
Cátedra, Pedro 10, 151
Catherine of Lancaster 2, 30
Charles of Burgundy 120
Chas Aguión, Antonio 61
Cicero 13
Colonna, Guido de 37
Conde Solares, Carlos 83
Contreras Jiménez, María Eugenia 98
conversos (New Christians) 8, 65–67, 76, 79, 81, 82, 86, 87, 88–90, 97, 105, 114, 115, 155–58
Coplas de la Panadera 7, 98
Coplas del Provincial 7, 98
Corominas, Joan 90
Cortina, Augusto 90
Costa, Marithelma 83, 90, 119
Cota, Alonso 79
Cota, Rodrigo 3, 6, 8, 66, 79, 115
 Al son del dulçe tañer 80–81
Crónica anónima de Enrique IV de Castilla 7, 71, 95, 97, 120
Cueva, Beltrán de la 3, 70, 109
Curtius, Ernst 74

Dante 39, 41, 49, 50, 75, 77, 85
Deyermond, Alan 6, 37–38, 148, 149
Díaz de Toledo, Pero 3, 9, 66, 112–17, 158
Dutton, Brian 3

Edward IV, King of England 95
Elliott, J. H. 122
Enrique II, King of Castile 2, 154
Enrique IV, King of Castile 1, 3, 6, 8, 9, 30, 46, 65, 71, 74, 79, 80, 81, 89, 95, 97, 98, 101, 108, 111, 114, 117, 120, 121, 135–36, 145, 155
Enrique, Infante of Aragon 1
Enríquez del Castillo, Diego 32, 38, 98
Espina, Alonso de 97

Fernández de Velasco, Pedro (conde de Haro) 98
Fernández de Madrigal, Alfonso (el Tostado) 40, 42
Fernando de Antequera, King of Aragon 30, 135
Fernando of Aragon, husband of Isabel, Queen of Castile 3, 9, 78, 96, 120–21, 122–25, 126, 130

Flors del Gay Saber 4, 14, 27

Garcilaso de la Vega 6, 8, 32–38, 47, 138, 155, 156, 158
Gatien-Arnoult, Adolphe-Félix 27
Gaume, Jean Joseph 57
Gerli, E. Michael 74
Gitlitz, David 105
Gómez-Bravo, Ana 157
Gueuara 62
Guillén de Segovia, Pero 3, 5, 6, 49, 66, 72, 80, 81, 87, 112, 120, 153
   Es enuidia mucho braua 117–19
   Más tenéys a mi entender 79
   Nauegando los estremos 67–68
   O soberano yntelecto 106–08
   Sy el comienço de la cosa 69
   Yo que siempre reproué 73
Guzmán, Teresa de 2

Homer 39, 41, 113
Huéscar 1
Huizinga, Johan 146

Imagery 17, 21, 24, 40, 42–45, 64, 67–68, 69, 72–74, 79, 80–81, 86, 87, 91, 92, 100, 104–05, 109–12, 127, 133, 135, 138, 140, 143, 159
Imperial, Francisco 50, 85
Inquisition 70, 79, 93, 94, 157
Isabel, Queen of Castile 3, 5, 30, 70, 96, 120, 122, 126–27, 128, 130, 131

Jeremiah 39, 114
Jews and anti-Semitism 3, 9, 66, 67, 76, 77, 80, 84–94, 97, 105, 115, 156–57
Joan I, King of Aragon
Job 22, 36, 72, 114–15, 137, 142
Joseph, husband of Virgin Mary 146, 150
Juan I, King of Castile 96
Juan II, King of Navarre and subsequently of Aragon 95, 120, 122
Juan II, King of Castile 1, 8, 9, 12, 13, 14, 69, 74, 79, 81, 83, 95, 101, 112, 114, 115, 132, 136
Juana de la Cruz, Sor 149
Juana, Infanta of Castile (La Beltraneja) 3, 125, 127

Kamen, Henry 81
Kaplan, Gregory 74

Lamentations 112
Lapesa, Rafael 133
Lawrance, Jeremy 7, 47
Leonor de Castilla 2, 145
Lida de Malkiel, María Rosa 49, 52
Liss, Peggy 130
Livy 39, 59, 138
López de Ayala, Pedro 2, 49–50, 72

López Estrada, Francisco 72
Louis XI, King of France 95, 120
Lucan 46
Lucena, Juan de 10, 142–43
Ludueña, Fernando de, *Dotrinal de gentileza* 12, 13, 29
Luna, Álvaro de, *condestable* of Castile 1, 74, 79, 83, 95, 101, 114, 132, 136

MacKay, Angus 102, 114
Manrique, Catalina 138
Manrique, Fadrique 32
Manrique, Gómez:
   life:
      birth and family 2
      career 1, 2–3, 4, 5
      education and upbringing 2
      library 5, 27n, 37, 59, 75, 139
   poems, consolatory and devotional:
      Coplas fechas para la semana santa 151–52
      La péñola tengo con tinta en la mano 54, 133–37
      La Representaçión del nasçimiento de Nuestro Señor 9, 145–51
      ¡O qué duda tan dudosa 152
      ¡O qué material tan dina 7, 10, 139–42
      ¡O tú reyna, que beata 30, 144–45
   dialogues:
      Con tormenta nin bonança 88–89
      De vos, varón adornado 70
      Eres para loco frío 84–85
      Es hazaña virtuosa 69
      Hizieron tan ynprisión 62
      La ynmensa turbaçión 1, 63
      Mal daragar nos podemos 68
      No teniendo del saber 77
      Poeta de la nobleza 85–86
      Pues no fallo quien se duela 62
      Pues vos vi sienpre maestro 72
      Que lengua memoria se pueda cobrar 63
      Quiérovos desengañar 92
      Señor Marqués de Villena 89–91
      Sy de vuestra detençión 86–88
      Syendo vos tanto priuado 92–93
      Tanto ha que no trobé 72–73
   elegies:
      A veynte e vn días del noueno mes (Defunsión del noble cauallero García Laso de la Vega) 8, 32–38
      Mys sospiros despertad (Planto por Yñigo López de Mendoça) 8, 39–48
   love poems:
      Amada tanto de mí 143
      Con la beldad me prendistes 17
      Con la belleza me prendés 17
      Conuiene que se castigue 8
      Dexadme mirar a quien 16
      Donzella desconoçida 18
      Donzella, diez mill enojos 19–20

El que arde en biua llama 15–16
Esperança de venir 16
Largos tienpos he gastado 21
¡O sy naçido no fuera 22
Quanto á que sé mirar 20–21
Quien el fuego mucho atiza 22–23
Señoras que muncho amo 17
Si los fines no mire 17
Si no me vençe pasión 18
Vuestros ojos me prendieron 17
moral and political poems:
   De los más el más perfecto 6, 48, 99–106
   Del Señor es fecho esto 9, 95–96
   Prínçipe de cuyo nonbre (*Regimiento de prínçipes*) 4, 6, 7, 9, 158
   Pues este negro morir 53–61
   Quando Roma prosperaua 6, 9, 48, 67, 108–12, 154
   Tales boluimos, señor 120–21
prose works:
   Carta de buena nota 10, 23–25
   epístola to Juana Manrique 133
   letter to Diego Arias Dávila 98–99
   letter to Juan de Lucena 143
   letter to Juana de Mendoza 18, 138–39
   letter to Pedro González de Mendoza 4, 38–39
   prohemio to the *Regimiento de prínçipes* 121–22
Manrique, Jorge 5, 106, 135
Manrique, Juana, condesa de Castro, sister of Gómez Manrique 113, 132–37, 154
Manrique, Luis 138
Manrique, María 145, 151
Manrique, Pedro 1
Manrique, Rodrigo, conde de Paredes 1, 2, 8, 32, 86
   Juan poeta en vos venir 93
   Si no lo quereys negar 93, 142
March, Ausiàs 4, 33
Margarit, Joan 78
María of Castile, wife of Alfonso V of Aragon 2
María of Aragon, first wife of Juan II of Castile 14, 136
Marino, Nancy 108–09, 112
Márquez Villanueva, Francisco 70, 94, 156–57
Martín de Córdoba, *Jardín de nobles donçellas* 7, 127–30
Martínez de Toledo, Alfonso 27
Mazuela, Juan de 8, 62, 66, 71
   Muncho más sé que no maestro 72
   No seáys vos la candela 62
Medina del Campo 138, 142
Mena, Juan de, *Canta tú, cristiana musa* 4, 8, 18, 37, 41, 49–52, 153, 155
Mendoza, Diego Hurtado de 2
Mendoza, Fray Íñigo 128
Mendoza, Íñigo López de, (see Santillana)
Mendoza, Juana de, wife of Gómez Manrique 2, 9, 18, 22, 30, 132, 138, 139, 142, 153, 157
Mendoza, Pedro González de (Cardinal) 2, 4, 38
Mendoza, Pedro de (poet) 9

Pues vos sobra la razón 63–65, 153
Meung, Jean de 52, 85
Mexía, Hernán 81, 82
Molinier, Guilhem de 14
Mondragón 81, 82
Montesino, Ambrosio 149
Montoro, Antón de 66, 67, 82, 89, 119, 157
   Juan, señor y grande amigo 91
   Noble reina de Castilla 92
Moreno Hernández, Carlos 8, 67
Muslims 1, 8, 32, 33 34, 88, 93, 97, 155–56

Netanyahu, B. 157
New Christians (see *conversos*)
Nirenberg, David 93
Noya, Francisco de 6, 8, 66, 69, 74, 77
   Vuestro entero mereçer 78–79, 80, 81

Olmedo, first battle of 1, 100, 114, 136
Olivares, Jerónimo de 8, 49, 59 n. 4
Oropesa, Alonso de 65, 66
Ovid 27, 37, 59, 139

Pacheco, María 133
Pacheco, Juan, marqués de Villena 70, 83, 89, 90, 94, 95
Palencia, Alonso de 7, 8, 32, 38, 95, 98, 102, 103, 108, 157
Parrilla, Carmen 24
Pascual, José Antonio 90
Paz y Melia, Antonio 5, 95
Pedro, *condestable* of Portugal 12
Pedro I, 'el cruel', King of Castile 123
Perea Rodríguez, Óscar 46, 69, 78
Pérez de Guzmán, Fernán 12, 30, 113
Pérez López, José Luis 63
Pérez Priego, Miguel Ángel
Pescador del Hoyo, María del Carmen 63
Pimentel, Rodrigo de (conde de Benavente) 2, 4, 62
Prudentius 49
Pulgar, Fernando del 1, 2, 32, 60, 157

Rhetoric 3–4, 13–15, 16–17
Ribera, Suero de 82
   O que nueuas de castilla 93
   Respuesta en defensión de las donas 29
Rivera, Gladys M. 49
Rivera Garretas, María-Milagros 142, 157
Rodríguez Puértolas, Julio 63, 97, 99, 105
Rodríguez Velasco, Jesús D. 74
Rojas, Diego de 62
Round, Nicholas 6, 108, 110, 111, 112, 156
Rubio González, Lorenzo 82–83, 86, 89
Ruiz, Juan 49

Saldaña, Diego de 62
Salinas, Pedro 37

Sallust 99, 116
Salvador Miguel, Nicasio 6, 150–51
Sandoval, Fernando de 132
Santillana, marqués de (Íñigo López de Mendoza) 2, 3, 32, 34, 38–48, 85, 94, 95, 112, 113, 132, 138, 153, 155
Sarmiento, Pedro 80
Sassoferrato, Bartolo da 75–76
Scholberg, Kenneth 5, 6, 37, 65, 99, 105, 106
Segovia 97, 102, 105, 111–12
Seneca 34, 35, 36, 50, 58, 60, 75, 82, 100, 102, 114, 116, 134, 137, 140, 153, 158
Sentencia-Estatuto of 1449: 80–81, 115
Seville 93, 157
Sieber, Harry 6, 32, 33, 38, 138, 141, 150
Sigüenza, Fray José de 65, 66
Soria, Antonio de 119–20
Speculum Humanae Salvationis 149
Stoicism 8, 36, 47, 52, 58, 71, 105, 114, 118, 124–26, 131, 137, 138, 140, 142, 152, 158
Surtz, Ronald E. 142, 145, 148, 149

Talavera, Hernando de 70, 133
Tate, R. Brian 32
Toledo 3, 5, 60, 65, 79, 80, 81, 93, 115, 138, 156–57, 158
Toros de Guisando 3, 127

Torroella, Pere, 7, 8, 10
  Quien bien amando persigue 25–29, 30, 31, 36, 61, 130, 154
Treviño, conde de 84
Trojan War 36–37, 41, 45, 135

Valencia 86, 93
Valera, Diego de, *Memorial de diversas hazañas* 7, 32, 38, 71, 74–77, 78, 95, 96, 97, 102, 105, 108, 120,
Valladolid 1, 3, 5
Valladolid, Juan de 61, 66, 67, 82–83, 105, 156–57
  En loaros syn mudança 88
  No veros mes osadía 83–84
  Podéis llamar menemigo 91
Velasco, Alonso de 81
Vidal González, Francisco 2, 5, 6, 10, 18, 22, 28, 72, 78, 95, 96, 99, 106
Villasandino, Alfonso Álvarez de 13, 61
Villena, Enrique de 14, 39, 40, 42
Virgil 39, 62–63, 77, 89, 113
Virgin Mary 128, 134, 144–45, 146–47, 149, 151

Weiss, Julian 13, 30, 61, 85, 113
Weissberger, Barbara 129–30

Zarco del Valle 5
Zimic, Stanislav 6, 150

www.ingramcontent.com/pod-product-compliance
Lightning Source LLC
LaVergne TN
LVHW061252060426
835507LV00017B/2032